DISCOVERING
THE COMIC

GEORGE
McFADDEN

DISCOVERING
THE COMIC

PRINCETON
UNIVERSITY
PRESS

201257

MARGARETAE CONIUGI

CONTENTS

PREFACE

THIS BOOK, as I hope the reader will find, is based upon a few simple but important principles. The first is that, in reading works of literary art, discovery is more important than interpretation. The second is that the competent reader will have some idea of what the enterprise of discovery is likely to find. The third is that the really good reader, or critic, will have an expectancy that is not so well defined as to close him or her off from a recognition that is coupled with astonishment. My object has been to present an idea of what it is that we essentially look for in comic writing, and a procedure of reading flexible enough so that we may find it (where it often is in recent writing) in unexpected places.

My work has been greatly assisted by a study leave and a grant of research funds from Temple University. I also want to thank my colleagues and students who join in the Critical Colloquium at Temple for many clarifications and good ideas during the last ten years. For helping with the present book by criticism and suggestions, I especially thank Robert D. Hume and Alexander Gelley. For their very valuable readings and advice generously offered, I am very much obliged to Stanley A. Corngold, Edith Kern, and James M. Holquist.

At Princeton University Press I have again enjoyed the advantages of working with Joanna Hitchcock, for whose help and encouragement I am very grateful indeed.

Glenside, Pennsylvania
December 12, 1980

DISCOVERING
THE COMIC

INTRODUCTION

LIKE MOST AUTHORS who have made the attempt, I have found that writing a book on the comic is no laughing matter. Looked at closely, Bergson's amusing little book *Laughter* is far more serious than it seems, even though it professes to be limited to vaudeville. Rather surprisingly, Freud refuses to venture within the boundaries of the comic itself, after conspicuous success in dealing with jokes and humor. And these two are our most productive inquirers. The topic is in fact notoriously difficult. I think it prudent, therefore, to say right off that I have no intention of explaining the comic. To explain would require me to establish laws—like the law of cause and effect, or of action and reaction, or of economy of forces—whereas in dealing with works of art I recognize the validity of Kant's insight that they are free in the sense that they give themselves their own laws. Works of art stand before us as examples of the working of principles we can make clear only by studying the works both as aesthetic and artistic objects—in the case of books, as joint products of the writer and of our reading, the writer free to write and the readers free to cocreate what is written. In the activity of a literary critic who accepts this double freedom, there is little to be gained by treating works as rule-governed members of a system that has already been established according to a stuctural model set up in advance.[1]

---

[1] Tzvetan Todorov, perhaps our most successful systematizer, admits as much: "As a rule, the literary masterpiece does not enter any genre save perhaps its own, but the masterpiece of popular literature is precisely the book which best fits its genre." See "The Typology of Detective Fiction," in *The Poetics of Prose*, translated by Richard Howard (Ithaca: Cornell University Press, 1977), p. 43. By genre Todorov means a system of linguistic production governed by rules derived from a model inspired by structural

This book is concerned with ways of discovering the comic quality not as a means of defining a genre but as offering a specific value feeling in widely different works of literary art. The term "quality" itself, of course, cannot pass without question. It can hardly be used in contemporary discourse in the old sense of separable property or attribute, as if it had a life of its own; I shall not be talking of "the comic spirit." I am content to follow Edmund Husserl in thinking of a quality as a "figural moment," associated in "moments of unity" with "sensuous intuitive wholes."[2] I say, then, that the comic is one of the figural moments of some literary works of art, when made concrete (or produced as a figural objectivity) by a reader of the text. To state my primary insight in general terms that the rest of the book will make more clear, the comic quality is a characteristic mode of aesthetic consciousness. Cocreative acts of author and reader attribute to the content of a literary work of art an objectivity of such a kind that we sense or interpret it as having the comic properties of continuance as itself and freedom in relation to a continued threat of alteration. This matter may be conveyed in various forms of literary art, whether the genre be comedy, satire, the novel, or some other form.

Husserl's conception of quality is peculiarly well adapted to the discussion of literary art and the protean nature of the comic, for we find him not only confirming the possibility of "combining any quality with any matter," but also defining

---

linguistics. Not only must popular literature fail to be "literary" by its conformity, but "literary" works, like angels in medieval theology, must each constitute a uniqueness that is somehow specific.

My own preference (already evident in this first paragraph) is for the literary theory of Roman Ingarden. See *The Literary Work of Art*, translated by George G. Grabowicz (Evanston, Ill.: Northwestern University Press, 1973), pp. lxvif.

[2] Edmund Husserl, *Logical Investigations*, translated by J. N. Findlay (New York: Humanities Press, 1970), I, 442. See section 4, original division. I have also been guided by Husserl's Fifth Investigation, sections 20–22, 30, 32, 38, and 41–43; see pp. 589f., 597–600, 617, 620, 641 and 648–651 in volume two of the translation.

"matter" as what is constituted in an objectifying act, whether posited (believed, affirmed) or not. Any matter, therefore, real or imaginary, may be handled in comic fashion, and the comic quality may be sought in the most extreme forms of black, absurd, or surrealist writing.

Simple as it is, this theory of a single quality may well be more effective as a discovery technique than one which tries to be exhaustively comprehensive. To take a recent example, Robert Bechtold Heilman's *The Ways of the World: Comedy and Society* proceeds by establishing three main characteristics as more or less shifting parameters of all that the playgoer and reader can find in comedy for the stage: elation, acceptance of the world and its fundamental disparateness, and liberating play.[3] Heilman's study is an unusually well-written book that obviously comes out of much experience and an excellent critical judgment. It aims, however, to include several rather incompatible criteria, each with ambiguities of its own, within a general statement that can be accommodated to the widest variety of comedies. This procedure, I believe, resembles the sort of stretching out and patching up process that Thomas S. Kuhn finds his "normal science" resorting to, at just those times of crisis when a breakthrough to a new, less composite theory is badly needed. Comic writing and criticism have been in such a crisis for some time; whatever else it may be, my theory is simple and direct enough to offer the basis for a breakthrough.

I have not tried to explain the comic as the cause of a certain result (e.g., laughter), or the result of a particular cause (e.g., an intersubjective relation of superiority and inferiority). Instead, I have treated it as an aspect of behavior. For any object that takes shape in a work of art, or in the literary works of art that we are concerned with, continuance-as-itself is an activity that necessarily takes on the character of spontaneousness, self-directed and self-governing behavior, or of what we might call self-determination. This is defi-

---

[3] Seattle: University of Washington Press, 1979, pp. 47f.

nitely the case when self-continuance is opposed and yet successfully maintains itself. In a work of art, the opposition is manifest as a threat directed at the self or kernel of the object (or objectivity as I prefer to call the fictive cocreation), rather than at some peripheral or nonessential aspect of it. There is then an overall reinforcing of the component self. What I shall go on to show is that a behavioral link has been created between a fictive self and freedom. These characters of self, self-maintenance and continuation, spontaneity, and independence have been attached to our ethical, social, and personal sense of freedom; and freedom has become the most important of all values during the present epoch, which can easily be recognized as having begun with the American and French Revolutions.

In committing myself to a modified historical approach, I am mindful that for any literary objectivity to manifest itself as such in fiction, there must be an ethos, that is, a mode of behavior convertible into human value terms, usually the terms of a "substantial" or "natural" concrete ethic, especially if the work is to have many readers. The concept of a concrete ethic (in Hegel's sense) is necessarily historical. Yet, though historical change constantly occurs, it only shows itself clearly over a span of many generations, so that at any one moment social behavior appears as if permanent and natural—except for the moments (again, in the Hegelian sense) when it undergoes revolutionary change. We may contrast two vast periods: the first, from Plato to the eighteenth century; the second, from the American and French Revolutions till now. Though this division is perhaps too gross to satisfy historians, is at least a useful critical limitation of a historical kind. It establishes a working diachronic base; with it one can see an emergent transformation of value feelings, including strictly aesthetic ones, belonging to comic perception and comic response.

The classic theory that the sense of the ridiculous depends on the laugher's feeling of superiority over some victim fails to account for several masterpieces of ancient comic writing. Nevertheless it became part of the ethos of theater comedy.

Specific class and social conventions were promoted to the status of universal laws of the dramatic genres and the decorum of the stage. During the eighteenth century, it is generally agreed, a revolutionary change occurred that altered ethos on the stage as well as off. Just as we can mark the moment of this change with the revolution in France, so we can mark the reversal of the former comic hegemony with the enormously successful *Marriage of Figaro* by Pierre-Augustin Caron, who named himself de Beaumarchais. In this comedy, instead of two plots maintained as separate, hierarchical structures, one conducted by upperclass and the other by lowerclass players, we have an acknowledged complicity among classes and actions. Instead of marking its upperclass figures with urbane wit and perfect manners, *The Marriage of Figaro* makes Count Almaviva a callous predator, humiliatingly dependent upon his valet. Figaro, on the contrary, is everything magnanimous and fine that the old comic ethos would have tied to nobility, but now the recognition-and-reversal scene prefers to show him to be by birth simply a good bourgeois. As for the count, he is to get back where he belongs, into bed with the countess, like any decent citizen with his wife.

Furthermore, it makes sense to see the emergence of humor against this moment of social and political revolution. English humor was recognized all over Europe as a strikingly novel development in a sphere where novelty is rare but immensely significant, the sphere of human feeling. *Humour* and *humanity*, whatever their background in the vernaculars of Europe, both became new terms, loaded with new and closely associated meanings derived from the new ethos. Friedrich von Schiller (another bourgeois who earned his "von") expressed the impact of the new idea of humor as a value quality in a remarkable comparison: "Thomas Jones," he observed, "pleases us much more than Grandison."[4] The reason? Fielding's Tom Jones is more natural

---

[4] *Kallias*, letter of 23 Feb. 1793; *Sämtliche Werke*, edited by Gerhard Fricke and Herbert G. Göpfert (Munich: Carl Hanser Verlag, 1962), V, 425f.

than Richardson's Sir Charles Grandison; and nothing con-
tributes so much to this difference as that Tom is treated
humorously, Grandison seriously.

I DEAL with changes in comic ethos at some length in the following chapters. On the development of comic theory, I go
back to a neglected text, Plato's *Philebus,* for my fresh start,
and show that Plato presented certain aspects of the comic
problem more clearly than anyone else during the next two
millennia. In his emphasis on the mixed pleasure-pain experience of laughter, however, Plato opened the door to the inadequate understanding of the comic as essentially limited
to the laughable and the ridiculous. Aristotle's writing pro-
mulgated this limited view much more specifically, in the
form of an opposition between tragedy as the genre of high
life and comedy as the dramatic form belonging to a lower
or mediocre life. One may adopt the deconstuctionists' tactic
and reverse the superiority relation implied in the opposition of these values, by preferring the comic over the tragic
and finding more worth in so-called ordinary life than in
high life. Here the critical procedure is in obvious accord
with developments in literary history.

It should be made clear at the start, however, that this
book is not intended as a contribution to European *Geistes-
geschichte.* My purpose is to be of service to literary critics, by
increasing their power to identify the comic quality in literary texts (especially in those borderline cases where it has
hitherto proved elusive), and by adding something to the
stock of concepts and terms for describing comic writing. I
would also wish to be of some small help to creative writers
who suffer from the present confusion about the comic. In
order not to compromise this dream of service to the art, I
have avoided all conscious effort to make jokes or be funny
myself.

Along with its theoretical and historical components, this
book offers a number of brief analyses of literary works. It
also includes some extended investigations whose length is
in keeping with the aim of disclosing in each work an essen-

tial structure, one that characterizes the work's comic quality as a whole. Since the book aims most of all to contribute to the practice of literary criticism, and draws on literary theory and its history mainly as a means to this end, I feel that it is essential to include in it at least a few full-scale critiques.

My accounts of individual works will not, I hope, strike readers simply as new interpretations. I offer, rather, disclosures of aesthetic structures that other readers can bring both to cognition and to sympathetic reenactment in a reading performance along the same lines as mine. I hope to make accessible aspects of a work that, though undeveloped in previous criticism, are there to be found if the work is read in a certain way. One could call this result a new interpretation, but that would suggest one had found a new and different meaning for the same known materials, whereas my intention is to discover new material by objectifying aspects and structures in the work that have not been selected and brought into focus so far.

Finally, when I recall the thoughts of Plato, or Schiller, or any other precursor, it is not with the Husserlian conviction that they are ideal objects, timelessly and necessarily true. Rather, I write as one who acknowledges and posits anew the guiding insights of others, while hoping to move a step or two further toward a more inclusive or more economical theory; one who feels the need to show that he is correcting and improving, or at least implicating in a new way, a particular historical act of thought, and not merely repeating it in redundant fashion. For this reason I have located my own theoretical enterprise in a period of time that I attempt to characterize as the still unfolding Romantic epoch of Western culture. I do not think that we have passed beyond that epoch yet, only that we now are in a position to understand some of its characteristic marks; and one of the most important of these is the greatly enhanced importance of the comic.

THE COMIC AS
A LITERARY QUALITY

1. PRELIMINARY INQUIRY:
THE ESSENCE OF THE COMIC

WHEN WE RETURN to a beginning and ask what is the comic, none of the familiar answers proves quite satisfactory. It is not that they are all wrong, but they are inadequate if we intend to form an idea of the comic that will reach its essence. The most natural reply, "the comic is that which causes laughter," was rejected by Aristotle long ago, and for good reasons. Anyone can see there is only a partial overlap in the appropriate use of the term "laughable" and the proper meaning of our term "comic." Still, if not laughter, then smiling, or at the very least a sparkling in the eyes or an enlivening of the expression on one's face, is a spontaneous accompaniment of the comic experience. Deadpan humor or dry wit is no exception to this rule, but is itself a branch of the comic that uses assumed insensitivity as a foil. In the presence of the comic, failure to respond to it is comic.

The comic appears to be neither a simple experience nor simply a response to a certain kind of experience. It is complex, at least in that it includes both an experience of something that can be called funny or amusing and some kind of gesture, expression, or formulation that marks if off and begins to make it communicable. Such communication, of course, need not be in writing, nor addressed to anyone besides oneself; all that is absolutely necessary is a seizure or comprehension of the amusing moment so as to make it in some degree noteworthy and memorable. One could be entertained for hours by the sight of children or young animals at play, but if one never had a particular momentary sense of certain of its aspects falling into a particularly characteristic structure, the experience would be pleasant or enjoyable but not ever comic.

The essence of the comic thus includes a positing and structuring moment when what-is-funny may be grasped with enough definiteness to be recalled or retold; it has acquired anecdotal permanence, if not continuance or duration. But the most important question still remains. It concerns the essence of that which is grasped as funny or amusing and which is made to continue. I shall be content to seek for an answer that will prove adequate to our sense of the comic as it has been perceived during the last two centuries. Modern people have found that the characteristic feeling of fun or joy that identifies the comic arises from their sense of the activity of a being that is notably engaged in being-itself, in self-activity, in self-assertion by utterly characteristic behavior; in self-maintenance, self-definition, and self-sustenance. This sense, of course, would be very weak or would vanish if the being *merely* maintained itself; such monotony would be boring or would simply pass without our notice. The comic prominently includes, therefore, an aspect of the changeable, actually posed as a threat of alteration to the self-continuing structure. It is essential that this threat be present, and also that it be successfully resisted by the self-governing process of the comic structure itself, rather than by factors exernal to it.

Within the romantic frame of mind which sees political independence as a necessary aspect of fully human existence, the term "self-governing" serves to disclose an actual, and perhaps universal, requirement for the comic: freedom. Since the mid-eighteenth century, self-government has been no mere metaphor for freedom but a necessary condition of it. The associations of the comic with spontaneity, liberation from inhibition and constraint, unblocking, vital movement, and ease and grace of behavior all point to freedom as an indispensable component.

The essence of the comic, therefore, is founded in a being that shows the power of continuing as itself, substantially unchanged, while overcoming a force or forces that would substantially alter it. Both continuance and change are necessary to the comic; but the impulse to change, as soon as it appears, becomes a movement of challenge or stimulus to the comic entity, a kind of test and proof of it. The comic itself, in its kernel, is so much itself, so characteristic, that it stands out, draws attention to itself, and invites or actually begets some counterforce—be it rivalry, mere conformity to the average, or sheer inertia. This force takes the form of a threat, or an opponent in some contest or game, either of which serves to accentuate the unchanging identity of the comic. What it overcomes is peculiarly visible in the light of the comic, so that the latter has a creative aspect to it: it seems to provide its own objects for fun-making. This active, independent, and productive power goes along with freedom and is always a mark of the genuinely comic.

2. The Question of Literary Genre

Before going further, however, we must face the problem of distinguishing the explicitly comic in literary works from the accompanying but universally aesthetic qualities of freedom, self-sustainedness, and spontaneity. Since we are trying to confront the question at a time when old, well-defined literary genres have ceased to retain much explanatory value except for historical purposes, we look for terms in the context of a modern literary theory. I choose Schiller's, believing that it emerged along with explicitly romantic writing and also helped give the lead to its development. The basis of his theory is Kant's opposition of the human mind to nature, and Schiller's analysis of the alienated stance of the modern writer is indispensable if we are to bring the problem of the comic to a contemporary focus.

Schiller realized that once the writer saw nature as something other than himself he became free of nature as a universally determining source or model but at the same time

lost his feeling for nature as the human home. His resultant
sense of loss provoked the most powerful of all romantic
feelings. Its name, *Heimweh*, only dates from Schiller's youth
as a word in German, and it was soon converted into the
learned term familiar to the world, "nostalgia," by a back-
formation using the Greek *nóstos* (journey back to one's
home) and *álgos* (pain, distress). The term is highly appropriate, recalling the *nóstoi*, or sad wanderings, of the Greek
heroes after their victory at Troy, when they sought home-
comings that most of them never achieved. In an irresistible
movement, loss by human beings of their natural home was
converted into a sense of loss of innocence and of their simple happiness in childhood. We should call this dominant
feeling, I am convinced, "nostalgia for the naive." Provided
we think of nostalgia as having its positive, re-creative side
as well as its distressful one, nostalgia for the naive is the
most persistent identifying mark of literature written during
the last two hundred years.

Schiller used this development of alienation from nature
and of nostalgia to uncover a new structure of the literary
genres. He also described two different kinds of writer, with
opposing temperaments and sensibilities to match. The new
situation appears most clearly in Schiller's description of the
opposing genres of elegy and satire. In elegy, we have the
artistic overcoming of alienation in the form of a beautiful
lament for a once-existing harmony of the human in nature,
especially in the setting of classical Greece; or we have the
idyll, which in easy disregard of actuality treats that harmony of human and natural as if it were existing "now." For
the latter treatment, however, we need a new kind of writer,
the idealist. He seeks to re-unite mind and nature in the
ideal rather than in the historical past.

Similarly he identifies two kinds of satire: the sublime and
the mocking or playful. The basis for the distinction is the
kind of feeling involved. Sublime satire employs tempes-
tuous, even tragic, passions. It is serious, punitive, or pathetic in its demands. It works powerfully upon the will,
driving to put an end to the disjunction between what is and

what ought to be. On the other hand, playful satire (which Schiller clearly prefers) often treats a morally neutral subject; yet it avoids the trivial because the beautiful soul (*schöne Seele, Bel âme*) of the poet redeems and supports his material.[1]

At this point in his account of the specifically new genres Schiller enters into a digression amounting only to two paragraphs wherein he discusses tragedy and comedy. Like sublime satire, tragedy arouses strong passions and hence it limits freedom, if only temporarily. Comedy, on the other hand, never suspends freedom but perpetually asserts it, not least because the comic writer need admit no dependency at all upon substantial, fateful ties to state, society, and history. He is free to move at will in his imagination, free to *play* with these "substantialities" and to call his readers to an equal freedom. What he must do, however, is to remain himself, to be always at home in his own beautiful soul (or sensibility, or vision, as we should say), preserving a lively vigor that pervades and sustains his themes with inner resources of his own. He must beware of pathos and oracular meanings, and "look serenely about and within himself to find everywhere more coincidence than fate, and rather to laugh at absurdity than to rage or weep at malice."[2]

Making the most of this account, we can conclude that the comic is in a special relation to freedom. Other genres of art cannot do without freedom; but comedy is the only genre continually to assert it. Furthermore, though no genre may be adequately defined by a simple quality, comedy is the only one wherein freedom predominantly gives the tone to the complex quality that emerges from the work as a whole. This statement can be made while admitting that one should not attempt to base rules upon it, but only point to freedom among a set of exemplary conditions, as Kant proposed. The kind of freedom that is exemplary for art, according to

[1] Friedrich von Schiller, *Naive and Sentimental Poetry*, translated by Julius A. Elias (New York: Ungar, 1966), p. 119. Elias gives cross-references to the text edited by Oskar Walzel in the *Sämtliche Werke*, Säkular-Ausgabe, 16 vols. (Stuttgart and Berlin: Cotta, 1904–1905), XII; see p. 195f.

[2] P. 122; ed. Walzel, p. 199, with *Bosheit* for "malice."

Schiller, differs in the naive writer and the reflective one, and, in the latter, between the idealist and the realist. Likewise, among the genres—which in modern times tend to be satire, comedy, elegy, and idyll—there are differences in the kinds and extent of freedom.

Finally, Schiller would seem to be the first writer on art to introduce the notion of a Fall, in the manner of Roland Barthes's division between "works of our modernity," which are "writable," and the bygone "classic" works, which are only "readable." There is an important difference, of course: Schiller's Fall is an historical one in the main, although he does insist that "reflective" geniuses have written in the age of the "naive," and "naive" writers can still exist in a world that has lost its naiveté. Barthes's "modernity" is more like an ever-shifting present, a rather arbitrary canon including Sade, Flaubert's *Bouvard et Pécouchet,* and Mallarmé, because they still have something new to offer to the reading and writing community of which Barthes found himself a member. Schiller, on the other hand, was Professor of History at Jena at the time of his aesthetic inquiries, and he wrote in direct response to the events of the revolution in France—in all of European history, surely, the most plausible septennium (1789–95) for an actual fall. Schiller's Fall, nevertheless, like that of Adam and Barthes, involved human freedom above all. When human beings fell out of nature and began to look at all the rest of the world as "other," they became free and responsible in essential ways, unsuspected before the *novus ordo seclorum* we celebrate on our paper money.

My thesis is that the concepts and terms with which Schiller described the new order of writing are still valid. They account both for the systemic state and the ongoing transformations within literary work and literary studies today. This means, I believe, that we are still in the cultural epoch widely known as the romantic period. The extraordinary turbulencies of the last thirty years may well prove to be threshold phenomena of a breakthrough in our progress to an entirely new epoch; still similar disturbances have already occurred (around 1830 and 1910) without putting a closing bracket to the stage of Western consciousness that Schiller described in two critical masterpieces, *Letters on the Aesthetic Education of Man* and *Naive and Sentimental Poetry*. (Lest this last claim seem forced, it should be pointed out that the Hegelian dialectic, Marxist alienation, the all-importance of artistic culture, and other essential components of our continuing world view were already present seminally in Schiller's texts.)[3]

3. THE COMIC IN MODERN LITERATURE

Let us proceed, then, with an inquiry into the conditions that are exemplary for the comic in modern literature, trying first to explore the content of Schiller's concepts and to determine (not too aggressively) the applicability of his terms to works that are of interest to us now. A convenient text will be the material from Kant and Schiller collected and commented upon by R. D. Miller in his *Schiller and the Ideal of Freedom* (Oxford, 1970). First, let us reaffirm Kant's insistence upon exemplary rather than rule-governed or constrained generation either of art or the experience of works of art. Kant, as Miller says,

> is concerned to safeguard the principle of freedom in aesthetic experience . . . from the restricting influence of all "interests," all concepts, and all purposes, so [that] the necessity which is a feature of aesthetic experience is not imposed by a rule or a law. Kant calls this aesthetic necessity "exemplary," because we notice a certain regularity, certain effects which appear to be *examples* of the working of a rule, without being able to state what the rule actually is.[4]

---

[3] See the comments of Thomas Mann in "On Schiller," *Last Essays*, translated by Richard and Clara Winston (London: Secker and Warburg, 1959), pp. 15ff. Elsewhere, according to Elias (p. 1), Mann referred to "Naive and Sentimental Poetry" as "the greatest of all German essays."

[4] Miller, pp. 73f. (my emphasis). Miller refers to the *Kritik der Urteilskraft*, edited by Georg Reimer in volume five of the collected works published for the Royal Prussian Academy of Sciences; see p. 236. Miller's valuable

We can ask, "What is the rule of Falstaff's character?" meaning its secret, its idea or principle, its essence; but we cannot hope to supplant the insights of Dryden, Morgann, or Bradley into Falstaff with any final formula.

In an essay of 1793, "Grace and Dignity," Schiller developed in a highly significant way the need, as Miller puts it, to "reconcile the freedom of man, as an independent rational being, with the freedom of nature."[5] On the one hand, grace is restricted to human beings, but on the other hand, for their own sake human beings are led by grace in themselves to go further and set nature free. Here Schiller very clearly puts forward the principle of preserving the natural and liberating it from inhibitions, one of the most important clues for us in our grasp of the comic.

4. AESTHETIC FREEDOM
AND THE COMIC REDEMPTION OF POWER

In his essay "Of Grace and Dignity" Schiller established a metaphoric union between the aesthetic and the political that was at the heart of his whole response to the demands of his time. Miller sums it up: "Just as a liberal government refrains from treating individuals as a means to an end, but respects their individual freedom, so man with his aesthetic sense is concerned not to interfere with the freedom of nature."[6] Schiller sees the aesthetic as a way of redeeming power: it becomes a freely flowing energy within a community governed by mutual respect, instead of being mere violence against aggressive enemies, passive subjects, and inert nature.

---

study was first published in a limited edition in 1959 and then republished by the Clarendon Press with a foreword by Sir Isaiah Berlin, praising it as "by far the clearest, most accurate, and intelligent account of the intellectual relationship between Kant and Schiller" (p. v), particularly in their treatment of freedom.

[5] Miller, p. 102.

[6] Miller, p. 103; cf. "Über Anmut und Würde," edited by Fricke and Göpfert, V, 460.

Schiller described his own age as one torn between the perversity and artificiality of the refined classes, with their moral rootlessness, and the rawness, coarseness, and mere nature of the lower classes, with their superstitions. Schiller also talked of ancient Greece as a naive state of ideal harmony between nature and reason, which too soon declined. After the Greeks, an artificial political structure of lifeless mechanical parts replaced an organic community, and the human was neglected in the specialized pursuits of each man.[7] In Schiller's protest, we have seeds that fell on fertile ground not in Matthew Arnold alone, but in Marx, Nietzsche, Bergson, and Freud. Schiller's way of meeting the needs of his chaotic era was through totality of personal character, where principles and feelings united, and where the victorious forms of art served as examples (but not as programs or manifestoes) and helped individual human beings to solve the problem, posed so sharply by the Terror in France, of a disintegrating modern community ripe for an intellectual tyranny. This urge toward freedom from compulsion and violence was bound to promote the comic, as Schiller saw, and to undercut the tragic except as an historical mode, a genre fit for revivals rather than premieres.

Schiller identifies, as the beautiful task of comedy, the promotion of what he calls *Freiheit des Gemüts*, a concept that may be said to include freedom of mind, soul, and natural disposition. But he says it cannot be identified with moral freedom, the particular quality tragedy is concerned with. Comedy can only be identified with aesthetic freedom. Tragedy is concerned with death; in it the life formed by art is cut off and terminated in order for greatness to be achieved in a final, catastrophic manner. But in his comic writing, where the poet remains himself, at home in a world of his own, the forms to which he gives life are made free, without effort and always.[8] What Schiller gives us as the aim of comedy is almost a definition of aesthetic freedom: "Its

[7] Miller, p. 109. The references are to *On the Aesthetic Education of Man*, fifth and sixth letters; see Fricke and Göpfert, V 580f. and 582.

[8] Miller, p. 126; translation by Elias, p. 121; ed. Walzel, pp. 197f.

purpose is uniform with the highest after which man has to
struggle: to be free of passion, always clear, to look serenely
about and within himself, to find everywhere more coincidence than fate, and rather to laugh at absurdity than to rage
or weep at malice."[9]

In comic writing the two opposed kinds of mentalities that
Schiller sees as marking the reflective epoch, the realist and
the idealist, can find agreement, for the disproportion between real and ideal can be dissolved in what we call a sense
of humor. Overcoming victoriously what otherwise might
crush them, both kinds of person are then found laughing
rather than raging or weeping.

THE THEORETICAL STRUCTURE of the comic quality, as
sketched out so far by way of introduction, can be illustrated
in a simple and direct fashion with a short passage from
Book Two of *Gulliver's Travels*. Gulliver, a voyager of considerable self-sufficiency and aplomb, has been taken up as a
pet by the giant Brobdingnagians. He entertains them with
tricks of skill that include building a small boat, and handling it in the equivalent of a bathtub. In one of the many
adventures brought on by his smallness, he has to deal with
a giant frog:

> Another time, one of the servants, whose office it was to
> fill my trough every third day with fresh water, was so
> careless to let a huge frog (not perceiving it) slip out of
> his pail. The frog lay concealed till I was put into my
> boat, but then seeing a resting place, climbed up, and
> made it lean so much on one side that I was forced to
> balance it with all my weight on the other, to prevent
> overturning. When the frog was got in, it hopped at
> once half the length of the boat, and then over my head,
> backwards and forwards, daubing my face and clothes
> with its odious slime. The largeness of its features made
> it appear the most deformed animal that can be con-
> ceived. However, I desired Glumdalclitch to let me deal

---

[9] Miller, p. 122; ed. Walzel, p. 198f.

with it alone. I banged it a good while with one
of my sculls, and at last forced it to leap out of the
boat.   (Chapter V)

In accordance with the theory, we may say that Gulliver
himself is a comic figure. He steadfastly remains himself, a
sober, cleanly, self-reliant seafaring man, coping with an extraordinary set of threats arising out of his size, itself a characteristic feature of his ordinary humanity. On the other
hand, the frog is very much a frog, behaving exactly as we
know a frog would do. The appalling effect of "the largeness
of its features" upon Gulliver can readily be imagined, but
the whole scene is made into pure fun by the slapstick, yet
soberly efficient, self-assurance of the hero. "I banged it a
good while with one of my sculls" strikes, in its combination
of exaggeration and understatement, the great chord of
English underplayed humor. All we have to do, as cocrea-
tors, is to imagine the scene vividly and it is unforgettably
comic. One might apply the theory further and suggest that
Book Two of the *Travels* is comic throughout, because both
self-maintenance and the threats against it are kept up. This
is somewhat less true of Book Three. In Book Four, the theory leads us to decide that Gulliver, as a character, ceases to
be a comic figure in himself, and becomes merely ridiculous;
degraded by the experience with Houyhnhnms and Yahoos,
he loses not only his self-assurance and self-reliance, but his
sense of belonging to the human race. Nevertheless, this sacrifice of his character helps Book Four itself to function in a
sublimely comic way. It enables *Gulliver's Travels* as a whole
to show us how human nature remains itself while it freely
resists distortion to the extremes of big and little, strong and
weak, clever and stupid, immortal and mortal, master and
servant, mental and bodily, superman and beast. We are
creatures of the middle state in life.

   As the following chapters of this book will show, the closest approaches to my theory of the comic quality in literature appear in Hegel, with the notion of a character rising
superior to its own contradiction, and in Freud, who linked

our enjoyment of children with our response to great criminals and humorists in literature. They all "compel our interest by the narcissistic consistency with which they manage to keep away from their ego anything that would diminish it. It is as if we envied them for maintaining a blissful state of mind—an unassailable libidinal position which we ourselves have since abandoned."[10] I shall develop such partial insights in order to incorporate them into a more general concept that applies to the comic as it appears in all the features of literary works.

[10] Sigmund Freud, "On Narcissism: An Introduction" (1914), *Works*, standard edition (London: Hogarth Press, 1957), XIV, 89.

⌐2⌐

DESCRIPTION OF THE COMIC
AS A GENERAL FEATURE
IN LITERATURE

1. EXAMPLES OF THE COMIC IN GENERAL

THE COMIC is an aesthetic value quality of a marked kind: like the sublime, the tragic, the awesome, and the ironic, it is the keynote of many successful works of art. In the theater we call such works comedies, but comic works are to be found in a variety of different art forms.[1] Any effort to describe the comic will bring us face to face with the problems involved in making the transition from an aesthetic quality ("the comic") to the literary genres (comedy, farce, fabliau, humorous novel) that incorporate it.

To be comic, something must be seen as itself, but also as impelled to become other than itself, to change into some alternate and permanent form that is actively constituted as a threat to its self-maintenance. The comic is something that would never exist in art or in life without the imaginative impulse of the viewer or reader, alone or in cooperation with an exhibitor or writer; as we say, "one must see the joke." Picturing the situation indicated in a comic cartoon is the necessary objectifying activity that makes the caption

---

[1] I have been convinced by the studies of Robert D. Hume that we must not look for the essence of the comic expecting to find it in any single art form; see his "Some Problems in the Theory of Comedy," *Journal of Aesthetics and Art Criticism,* 31 (1972), 87–100.

amusing. One of the most characteristically comic of *New Yorker* cartoons shows a crowd gathered around an open manhole, helplessly watching an octopus drag a Con Ed man into the sewer. Across the street two familiar New York types, unable to see anything but the ring of spectators, exchange supercilious looks while one comments, "Doesn't take much to draw a crowd around here." The objectivity we cocreate is a fairly complex structuring of the notorious *sang-froid* of people in New York: the crowd watching but doing nothing, the two blasé walkers lacking the curiosity to take a closer look. The threat of the octopus nevertheless emerges from the bowels of the city itself, sensationally illustrating but not altering the nature of the continuing urban situation.

Moreover, verbal structures of comic threat, unlike the oppositional relations of linguistics, are not arbitrary and merely virtual. In order to work they must already be strongly coded and highly recognizable entities. In what may seem merely to be a piece of Shakespeare's verbal wit, "Bless thee, Bottom, thou art translated," we can uncover a very complex play of visual structures, of which the malapropism is only one component, and recognize a perfect caption for the picture of Bottom suddenly revealed wearing an ass's head. The comic arises from Bottom's genuine force of personality in surviving as himself the treacherous passage from Bumpkin to ass, from catachrestic to fictive asininity. The comic objectivity would not exist without the extraordinary, ingenuous force of Bottom's character as Shakespeare so rapidly develops it against the whole courtly structure of *A Midsummer Night's Dream*. Moreover, if the exclamation of Peter Quince did not share in the unsophisticated naiveté of the whole group of rustic players and their behavior, the line would not be so exquisitely comic. Literally the line states that Bottom's features have been put into a different language but without appreciable change of meaning—the essence of Bottom is still being expressed ("thou art"). In correct speech about persons, however, only an important author or the body of a saint is ever "trans-

lated"; so the comment is honorific where it might have been
boorish. The delicate essence of comic pleasure in Shakespeare's play is to see how even the clownish behavior of the
rustics is lifted up by the courtesy that prevails on the happy
occasion of Theseus' wedding to Hippolyta.

Granted the need for several levels in comic structure,
complexity as such is not a specific means of producing the
comic. Any great comic performer will convince us that
Northrop Frye was off the track when he asserted that there
is something inherently comic in complications. The purest
comic turn of Chaplin's career is the simple little dance he
performed in *The Gold Rush* with forks and rolls in the guise
of legs and feet. The basic comic structure here is the dance
movements, making as if to turn the rolls into feet, yet always leaving them rolls as before. "The Dance of the Two
Rolls" is a good caption for what is involved. But the core
situation is Charlie's reliance on his imagination and his
purely personal clown's skills to entertain his girl at a meal,
and thus to maintain the event as a proper feast. It is the
continued hospitality and sustained good will and cleverness
of Charlie, despite the threat of privation, that creates the
comic. It is also instructive to reflect that if he had dressed
up the rolls with something like shoes or booties the effect
would have been spoiled. Change of nature is the threat of
the comic dynamism, and it is not to be evaded by mere disguise.

2. Inadequacy of Formalist
and Structuralist approaches

These varied examples help to make clear the nature of the
comic. They also make it evident that one cannot talk about
the comic as a merely verbal structure. Whatever difficulties
we now see in the way of the concept of representation, it
will prove impossible to discuss the comic by going to the
opposite extreme of postulating a purely virtual interref-
erentiality of signifiers as the only reality in the text of a literary work of art. We shall not attempt to catalogue various

modes and techniques of comic writing within a stucture of "literary specificity."[2] Nor shall we map out an enclosed totality of the literary genres for the express purpose of giving a set of frontiers to the land of the comic, as if it were a sovereign state that could only come into existence behind securely defended borders dividing it from other genres, subgenres, and even transitional genres. Our model is neither the Mendeleev table of periodic elements, nor a Victorian world map marked off in imperial colors, nor a purely virtual, interrelationary, and arbitrary *combinatoire*. Our model is the principle we have stated for the comic: a characteristic maintenance-as-itself, despite the implicit threat of alteration.

I shall now attempt to give this principle some necessary behavioral content by discussing a few acknowledged instances of the comic in all literature, without particular regard for their time of composition. I am mindful, as I imagine the reader is also, of the fact that my own overview is made in the present, which I shall characterize as a moment of the still-operative romantic phase in our culture. But first I must clarify my rejection of what seems to some critics the inevitable scientific approach, and I will begin with a brief historical summary.

3. FRENCH STRUCTURALISM

In the human sciences, "scientificity" has come to mean "systematicity," especially in France. Those who put together the *Course in General Linguistics* made it clear that Saussure himself felt the invention of the static phonemic system he called *langue* was his revolutionary contribution to linguistics. He thought that it freed his own work on language from a lifetime of servitude to historical philology. Instead of tying him down to the minutiae of how each indi-

---

[2] In my contribution to the volume edited by Paul Hernadi, *What Is Literature* (Bloomington: Indiana University Press, 1978), pp. 49–61, I use arguments derived from Ingarden to defend the position taken throughout this chapter.

vidual speech development occurred, the concept of *langue* as a simultaneous system enabled him to work "generally"—i.e., systematically (or scientifically)—with universal principles of an abstract rather than an anthropological kind, so that the new discipline would have its own field and method, separate from those of history and philology. Saussure himself said that his model for this move was the scientific foundation of political economy upon the systematic relationship of commodity value and labor value.[3] At about the same time as Saussure, Sigmund Freud made the same move in deriving his value system for the energy of the unconscious. The "labor" of the dreamwork, along with "cathexis" or expenditure and the saving of it, form an "economics."[4]

In the years while general linguistics was indeed developing into a new scientific discipline with its own field and methodology, Marcel Mauss and Claude Lévi-Strauss sought to bring a similar scientificity to the rather composite field of anthropology. Mauss's central principle was the exchange of gifts, as the equivalent, for anthropology, of Adam Smith's labor value, Freud's cathexis, and Saussure's equation for signification, the opposition signifier/signified and the linguistic sign. Lévi-Strauss then improved on Mauss's principle by specifying family relationships as the most meaningful "commodity" of exchange for use as the model

[3] *Course in General Linguistics,* edited by Charles Bally and Albert Sechechaye; translated by Wade Baskin (New York: McGraw-Hill, 1966), pp. xiii, 79.

[4] *A General Introduction to Psychoanalysis,* translated by Joan Riviere (New York: Washington Square Press, 1960), p. 365: "Pleasure is *in some way* connected with lessening, lowering, or extinguishing the amount of stimulation present in the mental apparatus; and . . . pain involves a heightening of the latter. Consideration of the most intense pleasure of which man is capable, the pleasure in the performance of the sexual act, leaves little doubt upon this point. Since pleasurable processes of this kind are bound up with the distribution of quantities of mental excitation and energy, we term considerations of this kind *economic* ones. . . . We can say that the mental apparatus serves the purpose of mastering and discharging the masses of supervening stimuli, the quantities of energy." (Emphasis in the original.)

of "structural anthropology." He also called eloquently for
the adoption of Saussure's proposal for a master science of
semiology, and the elaboration of myth studies in the direction of Saussure's *langue*, toward a primary system of signification, motifs, and themes with its own stucture. Between Saussure and Lévi-Strauss, French structuralism was
born. Soon Maurice Merleau-Ponty recognized the influence of Saussurian systematization in a very important essay
and tied it in to the phenomenology, or scientific philosophy, of Edmund Husserl.[5]

Merleau-Ponty's link-up was entirely legitimate, for
structuralism had been recognized by Husserl from 1900,
and by Husserl's disciples in the twenties. The outstanding
feature of structuralism, considered as an international
movement in the behavioral and life sciences, is its concept
of the living process as an open, changing, but continuing
state organized in several levels with some kind of hierarchical arrangement. The philosophical elaboration of this concept owed a great deal to Husserl.

The most problematic aspect of phenomenology has been
the ontological issue that appeared in Husserl's early work
and divided him from most of his early coworkers and
eventually from his best students, including Roman Ingarden and above all Martin Heidegger. In Husserl's *Formal and
Transcendental Logic* (1929), and especially in the two texts
that were most influential in France, the *Cartesian Meditations*
(1931) and *The Crisis of European Sciences and Transcendental
Phenomenology* (1939), he emphasized the ideal, rational, abstract nature of philosophical truth in its approach to scientific certainty. At the same time, though always as a kind of
hors d'oeuvre, Husserl passionately insisted upon the genu-
ineness of everyday reality as we all experience it. Considering that his own first step was the "bracketing" of our en-

---

[5] "On the Phenomenology of Language" (1951), included in *The Essential
Writings of Merleau-Ponty*, edited by Alden L. Fisher (New York: Harcourt,
Brace and World, 1969), pp. 214–229. See also Jacques Derrida, *Speech and
Phenomena*, translated by David B. Allison (Evanston, Ill.: Northwestern
University Press, 1973), pp. 46ff. and note 5.

tire "natural attitude," Husserl was in a highly ambiguous
position. He himself accentuated it by his revulsion against
Heidegger, whose *Sein und Zeit* and later works seemed to
Husserl a betrayal of his teaching and a lapse into the
unreason and anti-science that was bedeviling Europe.[6]

This Husserlian, Saussurian "scientificity" was the spirit
behind French structuralism as it organized linguistics and
anthropology. Jacques Lacan took the combination into the
field of Freudian psychology. Where Freud habitually used
the imagery of hydrostatics, Lacan used the abstract terminology of linguistics. He thus avoided simplistic metaphors
that smacked of outmoded positivism. His rethinking of the
signifier/signified relationship for the purpose of psychoanalysis has perhaps had more influence on literary critics
than Saussure's original version, limited to rudimentary
phonetic relations, ever had.

The aspect of scientificity that directly bears upon my
own investigation is a certain structuralist view of literary
genre, as well as a general rejection of qualities in the sense
of continuing properties that make an entity identifiably
what it is in a permanent way. In order to justify my presentation of the comic as a quality of the literary work of art not
by Aristotelian but by phenomenological arguments, I must
argue against the necessity of what these structuralists demand, namely a *combinatoire* or a simultaneously organized
totality of literary features and devices wherein a set of particular networks of relations is constituted, according to a
strictly mental model, as a literary genre. In this view, such a
systematized totality would be necessary before the comic
could become apparent not as a quality by itself, nor as a
quality of our experience in real life, but specifically as a
merely literary network of features generated according to
certain rules in a particular textual ambience.

What is remarkable about this demand (well satisfied by

[6] See Roman Ingarden's reminiscences in his collection of the letters he
received from Husserl and Frau Husserl: *Briefe an Roman Ingarden: Mit
Erläuterungen und Erinnerungen an Husserl,* Phaenomenologica, vol. XXV (The
Hague, 1968).

Tzvetan Todorov's *The Fantastic: A Structural Approach to a Literary Genre*[7]) is that it clings so faithfully to the ambiguous, even contradictory, elements that produced French structuralism itself, as I have just suggested. The movement in France is marked by a more-than-Husserlian rejection not only of "the natural attitude" but of nature itself as a compulsive mind-set inherited from an outmoded imperialist and ethnocentric Western culture. It insists on the rejection of poetic mimesis and representation of nature. More radically, it also does away with genre in the sense of a kind of being identifiable by an essential structure proper to itself alone. It substitutes for this sense of "belonging-together" (accepted not only by Aristotle but by Husserl, his coworkers, and his students) a mere associational network. This emphasis on systematicity is everywhere in Todorov, even when it leads to obvious contradictions. Having dismissed Frye and stated his own theory of the work, of literature, and of genre, he faces up to the anomaly that he is requiring genres of literary works of art to conform to his theory. He is stuck in the old pretense of adequation of the thing to the mental model. Yet for Todorov there can be no commmunication between non-literature and literature, because they are two different languages; not historically or philologically different, but systematically cut off from each other by the almighty bar. On the one hand, literature is defined by transgressive violence upon *langue* and its prescribed linguistic rules. On the other hand, there is the "violence wrought upon literature" by the critics' need to "use ordinary language in order to speak of literature."[8] It is clear to see, however, that this hopeless opposition arises from the attempt to restrict one's idea of the literary work to its linguistic features only. A deficient theory of the work creates a false need for a completely separate literary language (or rather *langue*), one constituted as a different system from the ordinary *langue* and in which, alone, works of literature can

[7] Ithaca: Cornell University Press, 1975
[8] P. 22

be written. To get out of this impasse, critics need simply to recognize both the imagination and the freedom of the artist and the reader, the first to create and the second to cocreate. In the making of fiction this imagination and this freedom become concrete. Fictive making on both sides is an indispensable differentiating factor that enables us to distinguish between two works, both in the same language, and to find one to be a work of art and the other a work of non-art.

Todorov himself, with remarkable candor, exposes the weakest point of his genre theory: "Every theory of literary themes, for example (up till now, in any case), tends to reduce these themes to a complex of categories borrowed from psychology or philosophy or sociology. . . . Were these categories to be borrowed from linguistics, the situation would not be qualitatively different."[9] The fact is that Todorov's own thematic system is organized around a purely psychological and linguistic opposition of "self" and "thou"; he must, therefore, mean to point here to a defect in his own theory, "one of the limits we cannot transcend." He goes on, with attractive humility, to state the problem in a picturesque, though plainly fallacious, example: "The goal of knowledge is an approximate truth, not an absolute one. If descriptive science claimed to speak *the* truth, it would contradict its reason for being. (Indeed, a certain form of physical geography no longer exists since all the continents have been correctly described.) Imperfection is, parodoxically, a guarantee of survival."[10] Reading this, one would think that writing was a lost art, and that the critics would work themselves out of their jobs if they were to do them "correctly" for any length of time.

One should not exploit such a good-natured obiter dictum. It is manifest, however, that the structuralism of Todorov cannot be correctly called descriptive. By his own admission it is impossible to convict a theoretical model of error by citing any number of empirical facts, for a fact is a

[9] Ibid.
[10] P. 23.

fact in the first place only by virtue of the theoretical structure (arbitrary, mental, nonreferential) that provides it with the system wherein it can be discerned as factual and without which it could not be located at all. This kind of thinking is perhaps productive in the area of epistemology of science. It is hard to see it as anything but illusory when applied to one of the practical arts. Its basic idea of a totalized system will infallibly be breached by the next artist who transgresses it. Todorov concedes this fact, but rather blindly clings to the theory and practice of systematicity while admitting, and even building into the future of his enterprise, necessary breakdowns in coherence. Perhaps this is a way to establish science of criticism as a university discipline. I think, on the contrary, it will prove to be an ephemeral set of rules for writers to transgress rather than the basis for an activity capable of nourishing the minds of scholars or students. To take just one instance, Todorov continually stresses the insubstantial, arbitrary, diacritical, inessential nature of those marks that nevertheless are said to characterize literary works of art. He wants a definition that will "further emphasize the differential character of the fantastic (as a dividing line between the uncanny and the marvelous), instead of making it a substance. . . . As a rule, moreover, a genre is always defined in relation to the genres adjacent to it."[11] One wonders how such definitions, continuously regressive as they are, can describe anything, or ever constitute a descriptive science. This result becomes even more doubtful when, in a later obiter dictum, Todorov declares "all definitions are, as we know, arbitrary."[12] His homology—nuclear physics and the evanescent, laboratory-produced elements in the addenda to the Mendeleev table— seems hopelessly far-fetched for the critic who works on the fantastic in its actual range between Matt Lewis's *Monk* and Shakespeare's *Macbeth*.

Returning to the issue of quality, Todorov, to do him jus-

[11] P. 27.
[12] P. 62.

tice, seems to be more open to literary qualities than many
structuralist critics, especially in obiter dicta. Still, his workaday attitude toward the job of literary description, even the
clarity of his prose, leads him to the enunciation of formulas
that a literary critic cannot live with—this, for example: "not
to confuse the problem of truth with that of representation:
only poetry rejects representation, but *all* literature escapes
the category of the true and the false."[13] The one sense in
which this statement is correct is so banal that it insults the
intelligence. Todorov has already conceded that some poetry does represent, and has just finished saying that "literature does admit a requirement of validity or internal coherence"—in other words, truth to itself. If the work of fiction
can be identified as self-representative, or, as we say, true to
its world, it is certainly the case that some fictional worlds
are outstandingly more true to the world—or the Pelopon-
nesian War, or the modern burgeois world, or our world—
than others. The critic whose formulation of literature shuts
out these categories of the true and the false dooms himself
to frivolity.

The preceding argument rejects a structural genre theory
that is limited to linguistic features and aims at setting up
first "a structure, a configuration of literary properties, an
inventory of oppositions," and secondly "a certain rule by
which the work in question—and many others as well—are
governed."[14] Instead, I employ a genre theory which does
not use the concept of *langue* or that of a *combinatoire* or inventory of devices, and which avoids the application of
rule-governance to works of art, except as a work may be
said to generate its own rules in an exemplary way. My theory of the comic does not set up rules and immediately ne-
gate them by making a positive virtue of transgression, but
rather builds a threat of transgression into the concept of the
comic itself. My most important concern, however, is not so
much to restore a historical consciousness to literary theory,

[13] P. 83.
[14] P. 141.

but to strengthen the sense of the diachronic and of temporality in current criticism. I cannot accept Todorov's sharp breach between the universally systematic, externally descriptive "poetics" of abstract literary genres and the totally individualistic "interpretation" of each work that is all he is willing to allow. Far from defining each work as the linguistic site of a meaning that exists nowhere else, I believe first that works are defined very inadequately by their meanings (especially by their verbal meanings only), and secondly that these meanings can be determined to the satisfaction of the majority of scholars by reference to the period of composition, more successfully perhaps than by any nondiachronic method. I realize that this claim has been made before and has been difficult to prove; that fact, however, only confirms my belief that exclusive concern for meaning makes little sense in literary studies. It is difficult to transpose meaning from one period to another or from one culture and one language to another, and for that reason scholars specialize in particular languages and periods. Structuralists specialize in the timeless and the placeless.

4. The Comic Quality in Literary Art

In my initial attempt at establishing the comic as a quality of literary works, I shall deal only with those masterpieces that we cannot omit if the argument is to carry conviction. The terms of my examination are largely familiar, and I hope this persistence in applying Aristotle's "qualitative parts" to comic works will not be taken amiss. Since I wish to justify a constant reference to freedom as one of the parameters of my theory, I shall be especially careful to stay alert to the dangers of authorial imperialism in concepts like plot and character and situation which may be thought to cut back the free play of the texts and the freedom of the reader's response. I shall try to convey a sense of the pervasive fictionality of all these literary features, as well as of their actual location in particular texts. Nevertheless, I propose substantial rather than merely differential relations between genres,

holding that true genres possess dominant qualities such as
the tragic, the satiric, the idyllic, the epic, the lyric, even if
some genres and qualities are scarcely achieved any more in
new writing. In the second place, I maintain that in a literary
genre the characteristic quality has to be produced by means
of particular, contingent art forms such as the epic, lyric, and
dramatic verse meters of the Greeks, the Latin satire, Ara-
bian fairy tales, the English humorous novel, the French *conte*
and realistic novel, and the Gothic romance. Once a dominant generic quality has been successfully manifested
through an appropriate art form, it can endure recognizably
in reading and in other kinds of performance for long periods of time and through great cultural changes, despite the
fact that the contingencies of the art form may prevent the
successful use of it in writing new works. If the quality is to
take on new historical manifestations, however, it must
reappear in a new practical art form, as happened in Virgil-
ian epic. There is a literary quality which, mutatis mu-
tandis, is the same in Homer and in Virgil's *Aeneid;* we call it
epic in both.

This distinction between a dominant (i.e., generic) quality
and a practical art form specifically capable of manifesting
that quality is not one that makes art merely the expression
of pre-existent qualities. Some of these generic qualities
(perhaps all) would not have appeared without the art forms
that focused and manifested them. The proof is in the fact
that none of the qualities is universal in the forms it takes in
practice, and some of them, in all their forms, are limited to
Western writing. Others, like the tragic, have traveled to
alien cultures, but largely as the result of practical art forms,
like opera and film, originating in the West. Surprisingly
few have been adopted by the West from other cultures.
Whereas the tragic has proved the most ethnocentripetal of
generic qualities (above all in its consumate Athenian form),
the comic, on the contrary, now seems most open of all in its
nature and its appeal. True, the close affinity of the comic to
everyday social behavior leads also to the development of
socially limited practical art forms like Renaissance court

comedy and the drawing room comedy of British high society. Still, for all their allegiance to a limited practical form,
the comedies of Shakespeare or Bernard Shaw display
enough fundamental comic power to appeal to worldwide
audiences, though in the process (usually that of being made
into a film) their purely verbal texture is much modified.

5. Guiding Principle: The Discussion and Its Means

Practically any literary device or feature can be employed to
comic effect. The principal feature I have chosen as an index
of development was celebrated by Bernard Shaw under the
name of "the discussion." By a ruse, Shaw attributed the discovery of his own playwriting theory to Ibsen, and praised
him for revolutionizing European drama with the discussion. Nietzsche employed the same ruse when he credited
Euripides with discovering his own critical theory, that
Sophoclean tragedy might be transformed by means of
Socratic talk, debate, and reflection. Both "discoveries,"
Euripides' and Ibsen's, actually mark moments of the as-
cendancy of the comic discussion—first over Attic tragedy
and then over the sentimental *drame*. The essence of the discussion is that it tests and sorts things out but changes nothing radically; it shows up situations and characters for what
they are. In examples taken from the theater, it appears that
comedy favors free discussion, while tragedy does not.

One might object at this point that discussion suspends
action, that it is undramatic in the theater and uneventful,
and thus eventually uninteresting even in prose fiction.
There is a good answer: the successful comic art form is the
one that overcomes these problems of inaction and unevent-
fulness—not by a preferred means, but by one means or another. The means need not include a closed plot. Whereas
tragedy normally can have only one end, in the disastrous
fall of the hero, comedy may end with any completed instance of self-assertiveness in the comic objectivity (hero,
heroine, situation, instance of assertion of style, etc.). The

so-called rejection of Falstaff is a truly comic ending because it leaves his character unchanged. He is still the same
imperturbable, infinitely witty rascal, as his final quip to
Justice Shallow proves. The usual endings of comedies—
marriages, dances, feasts, processions, discoveries of trea-
sures, of inheritances, or of long-lost parents—are essentially wish-fulfillments rather than terminations or closures.
As we know, wishes have no limit and no end. Melodramas,
not comedies, end in terminations: the villain is killed or
jailed, the case is solved, the disruptive factor is removed.

Likewise, the structure of a tragic plot consisting of beginning, middle, and end is of little importance in comic
writing. Even if a tightly knit intrigue is used as plot, it can
be treated quite illogically so long as the comic rhythm of
substantiation and challenge is maintained. Again, one main
function of an intrigue will be to give the audience a sense
that the comedy will end sometime (at this performance, or
within the covers of this book). The other function will be to
set the comic pace, anywhere between a leisurely andante
and a hilarious presto, but firmly.

For an understanding of what is peculiar to comic plot-
ting, we may restate our original definition as follows: the
comic resides in an hypostasis that is constantly asserted,
frequently threatened with alteration, but always maintained. It may be said, then, that the development of a comic
plot is one that is accomplished with the greatest threat to,
but the least possible loss of form in, its hypostatized figures
and situations. What happens in tragedy is the destruction
of the humanly good, marking a moment of loss in the historical order by which we are enabled to take the measure of
human nature at one of its greatest moments. What happens
in comedy is the conservation of a state of affairs (not necessarily a character) that is aesthetically satisfying but not insistently good, bad, or great, so as to affirm its continued opportunity for existence and action.

IN ADDITION to plot, three very important means of writing
the comic discussion are through situations, characters, and
diction or style. Greek Old Comedy is famous for its cele-

bration of the political situation of the Athenian city state, where each citizen was free to assert his ideas in the institutional discussions of the agora and where comic satire functioned as part of a divinely sanctioned chastening process aimed, like tragedy, against hubris. In Aristophanes' comedies, it has been pointed out that the protagonist always has some bright idea that is intended to make things better. In the course of the action, the trying out of the idea draws into play a series of impostors, who betray the evils of things as they actually are in Athens. The most distinctive feature of the art form is the parabasis or elaborate poetic address of the chorus to the audience, making fun of its shortcomings and exhorting its members to be more true to the ideals of their Athenian citizenship. This political discussion was so successfully incorporated into Aristophanes' comedies that Plato recommended them to foreigners who wished to understand Athens. It is to be seen even in *Lysistrata*, though the protagonist, being a woman, is not a citizen and the normal political conditions of life in the city are turned upside down. The situation that emerges is more fundamental and human than the political mode of existence of any single city. It serves to display the human male and female as they are, driven more by sex than by imperial concerns. There is a discussion along these lines between Lysistrata and her women helpers, and the climax of the play comes in a highly interesting exposition—not entirely a discussion, but certainly not an agon—over an essentially sexual model of desire that resembles political conquest and might be a welcome surrogate for it.

We can cite Chaucer's *Canterbury Tales* as a revival, in some essential aspects, of Aristophanes' communal situation. Like Plato recommending Aristophanes, Dryden recommended Chaucer to his contemporaries for a true and varied picture of their medieval forebears. The religious, Dionysian force is perhaps even more recoverable for us in Chaucer's pilgrims than in the Greek polis. The fellowship of thirty quite different individuals, all with a common goal, is a social equivalent for the bond of Athenian citizenship. The pilgrims find each other at an inn and gather together.

This gathering is as essential as anything can be to the comic, for it is bound up with our notions of sameness and difference, continuance as a whole and division into parts. Nothing shows up differences better than proximity; gathering both accentautes identities and sharply displays idiosyncrasies. It allows threats to develop: of assimilation to something else, of alteration to what one is not, of the destruction of one by the other. Chaucer's situation begins in natural and religious harmony. The pilgrims are drawn along together by the prick of spring as well as by the miracle-working saint, by wanderlust as well as devotion. The ineffable security and desirability of their initial situation characterizes the greatest comic writing. Thus it would be a mistake, I think, to make a general axiom of Northrop Frye's observation that blocking or usurping forces are in control at the beginnings of stage comedies. The freedom of the Athenian constitution is in force in the overtly comic, whether the place be Corinth or London, Prospero's island or Louis XIV's Paris. The beginning of *The Tempest* and the ending of *Tartuffe* show Shakespeare and Molière using the strongest means, the roughest narrative magic, to avoid what would otherwise distort the comic in the direction of melodrama. In the prologue to *The Canterbury Tales*, Chaucer takes care to add to this initial sense of security by cultivating the fellowship of the pilgrims himself, and much more by adding to their company the excellent Host of the Tabard Inn, Harry Bailey—the first of many genial Harrys in English comedy. The Host organizes everything for the tale-telling sport, and later serves to keep the group in harmony whenever the highly individualistic figures threaten to fall out in their discussions with each other.

6. Comic Character: Falstaff

Discussions require gathering and inclusiveness; this, and their requisite condition of initial and continuing security, fosters an essential comic tendency. Both discussion and security create occasions for the most strongly marked feature in the whole sphere of the comic: the great character, the great clown. The two richest comic figures are Falstaff and Don Quixote, unlike one another as they can be, and each without a rival in the comic writing of the world, unless it be the other. Both derive their being in a special way from the security of their worlds.

Falstaff, the most personal of comic heroes, is fully himself only in the *Henry IV* plays. The reason is that the structure of his character consists of an hypostasis centered in the witty mind's extralegal freedom from care and responsibility, and its accompanying threat of creating a state of affairs where irresponsibility is sanctioned and protected by authority itself. This structure takes fuller comic shape in a plot where care and responsibility are real and pressing, and where the facts of unruliness and misrule are presented in due proportion to their destructive effects in actual life. Likewise, Falstaff's vigor and freedom of mind, as Dryden saw, become fully comic in his fat body, given over as it is to the corruptions of gout, old age, and the pox. Yet his selfish ambition to exploit others with impunity would perhaps be repulsive rather than comic, were it not for two prominent features of the plot: the internecine selfishness of the rebel leaders, who are so much more shrewdly self-interested than Falstaff, and the impenetrable calculating hardness of Prince Hal, the son of his father, already a politician not to be trifled with and a judge of men whom we never really expect to connive at Falstaff's ambitions. Outside a plot including something like a civil war and such politicians as King Henry IV and his sons Hal and John, the true Falstaff character would not appear with such force.

The tendency away from the hypostatic character in Falstaff and his propensity toward something he is not is universal within comic characters and normally involves an element of self-deception. In disreputable Falstaff the tendency is revealed in his wish to enjoy a privileged, respected status by exploiting his imagined influence over the prince. When we first meet him Falstaff wants to be assured that when Hal becomes king he may play the rogue by royal commission. The real danger to the comic character of Falstaff is that Hal will give in to him, thus turning him into a

privileged criminal and a kept buffoon, as partly happens in
The Merry Wives of Windsor. The rejection of Falstaff is profoundly right, for it leaves him intact and unchanged. We
have only to recall by contrast the cruel fate of Mr. Doolittle
in *Pygmalion* when his hypostatic underservingness was recognized as merit and rewarded by an American millionaire.

The relationship of peace and security with the comic depends upon the provision of a special sort of ambience
wherein the comic characters can be themselves to the fullest degree in what we have called, after Shaw, "the discussion." In the *Henry IV* plays Shakespeare somehow keeps a
sanctuary free for comedy either in the classical Boar's Head
Tavern in Eastcheap, in the darkness on Gadshill or in that
sort of *tabernaculum* or privileged space that invisibly accompanies the royal person and his entourage. "The royal presence" was an original "great good place" in the strongest
possible sense, for it was the place whence every benefit
proceeded. All the courtesy books agreed that it was the
place par excellence for urbane wit, and hence a place of
privilege for the likes of Falstaff, witty in himself and the
cause of wit in other men. This ambience accompanies the
prince even onto the field of battle, and extends to its
protégé Falstaff a kind of lucky inviolability. Prince Hal does
not hear Falstaff's soliloquy on honor, but he makes it possible, and he tolerates Falstaff's satirical abuse of noble pride
in the dead Hotspur. When we compare Hal's indulgence of
Falstaff with Odysseus's beating of Thersites we sense the
vast increase in the substance of the comic between Shakespeare and Homer. The richness may be noted in several
scenes in the royal presence of Shakespeare's Cleopatra.
The wit of her ladies-in-waiting requires a special place and
a special kind of security where everyone, commoner and
imperial divinity alike, may speak freely so long as they do
it wittily.[15]

---

[15] The tragic death of Shakespeare's Cleopatra does not tell against this
analysis. The peril that concerns her is the destruction or defamation of her
relationship with Antony, and their comic scenes support the security of

The exceptional instances just cited from the entourages of Prince Hal and Cleopatra suggest that comedy normally goes with peace, not warfare or real peril. Its proper scene is the Forest of Arden, or Athens when Theseus and his one-time enemy Hippolyta are to be married, or Olivia's house in *Twelfth Night* and Portia's in *The Merchant of Venice* or—most charmingly comic of all, perhaps—Shallow's garden, where he and Falstaff recall hearing the "chimes at midnight" in their youth. The reason for this peaceable preference, I think, is in order that the substantiality of the comic self or situation may be mainly self-induced and not forced into being by external conditions, as in gallows humor. Spontaneity has nothing to do with stimulus-response. For that reason, there cannot be much real peril or toilsome adventure in great comedy. Even *The Odyssey* is only occasionally comic, and perhaps never greatly so. For a similar reason, if the comic is too eventful the emphasis will shift away from maintenance of selves to the imbroglio or contretemps, the merely ridiculous mixture of things. This is one of the main differences between the comic and the farcical.

Perhaps the most important reason for the connection between the comic and peace is the need for security of character, not strong character as in serious drama or fiction where great risks are run, but strongly marked, always inviting some kind of entropy or nullificaton but always evading it. The great fools are perfectly secure, even respectable, in their characters; take Bottom the Weaver for example. The same is true of the great scamps: Uriah Heep, Flaubert's Homais, Faulkner's Flem Snopes. They seem able to take hold of their authors first and then of the reader, who is likely to recall them more favorably than they deserve. This security is also important as a guarantee of the discussion. The character to be put on display and the place to expatiate in are two essential requirements of the best comic writing, and between them they produce the discussion.

---

that strongly sexual relationship by subjecting it to a variety of sexual threats (teasing, exposure, degradation and so on).

7. The Comic Discussion in *Don Quixote*

The kind of security achieved by Shakespeare in positing theatrical characters was fundamental to the classic English novel from its beginnings. In addition, novelists writing in the prose normally reserved for records, documents, and argument, lacking the action, costumes, and rudimentary scenery of the theater, found it necessary to assume a boldly fictional approach, even though the setting itself was real. In the first and one of the greatest of all comic novels, *Don Quixote*, the setting, the Campo de Montiel, in its crude and bare reality maintains an essential function in the comic unfolding of the novel. The text of Cervantes accents this function at the outset, when Quixote is beginning his first sally. One of the earliest interior monologues in the history of the novel ends with these words, in which the hero anticipates the opening and style of the book of chivalry that will celebrate himself: "The famous knight, Don Quixote de la Mancha, forsaking his own downy bed and mounting his famous steed, Rocinante, fared forth and began riding over the ancient and famous Campo de Montiel." Cervantes then makes the following comment: "And this was the truth, for he was indeed riding over that stretch of plain."[16] The flamboyant mania of Quixote will continue to play itself out against the barrenness of the scene and the irony of his creator.

The stroke by which Cervantes keeps the antics of his hero in touch with reality and the Campo de Montiel is that of making him quite insane. His insanity is repeatedly and strongly emphasized, and furthermore it has a function directly connected to the security of the comic character. As long as Don Quixote is immediately recognizable to others as a madman, no harm will be done to him, at least on the Campo de Montiel. People there wish to leave crazy people

[16] I use the translation of Samuel Putnam, conveniently found in *The Portable Cervantes* (New York: Viking, 1951). Page references to this and other standard translations of very familiar works are only footnoted in cases where there are problems with the original text.

alone. Their scruple is all the more acceptable to us today because of what we know of primitives and their respect for the insane. So the mad knight gets the kind of respect we have spoken of as belonging to the great comic figures.

As for the even more important step of establishing the comic character itself, Cervantes does it in the classic manner of a full dress introductory portrait, after which the rest of the novel unfolds as an enrichment by showing Don Quixote in actions that grow from and extend the original picture. Far from being satisfied with Aristotle's advice to find a typical name for a typical and rather mediocre person, Cervantes posits his hero as a real person whose actual name he insists upon, despite scribal disputes over its exact spelling and form. The name Quixote is indeed made up, but the knight makes it up for himself. All this, however, the author blandly tells us, "means very little so far as our story is concerned, providing that in the telling of it we do not depart one iota from the truth."

In other respects the character of Quixote is both highly marked and self-generated. There is demonic passion in his curiosity about chivalry, but no self-interest (i.e., normal selfish ambition), for "he even sold many acres of tillable land in order to be able to buy and read the books that he loved." When finally "his brain dried up and he went completely out of his mind," there is a kind of immolation or fall that seals, in a certain individual form, the fictional figure and evokes the kind of events that such a being brings upon itself, almost regardless of plot in the usual sense. All that can be said of the particular plot of *Joseph Andrews* or *Tom Jones* is secondary compared to the massive importance of its dependence upon these comic structures founded by Cervantes. The latter include, most of all, the interplay between the naive hero and the ironic narrator, and also the use of a reciprocal as doubling figure, one of the most valuable resources of the comic whose unrivaled exemplar is still Sancho Panza and of whom Partridge is a weak, and Parson Adams a great and very original, homologue.

Joseph Andrews, Tom Jones, and Don Quixote are what

might be called curably comic figures. Age and experience will cure Joseph and Tom of the naively human impulsiveness that makes them amusing, and though Quixote is a far more difficult case, he is at least subject to a deathbed recovery. But Adams, Partridge, and Sancho Panza have something in them that corresponds to the naive immersion in daily existence that we find in the primitive. Closely linked to their more temperamental masters, these three middle-aged and intensely stable figures bring out, by their deficiencies as much as by their positive qualities, genuine, substantial traits that we could never find in mere youth or madness. All three heroes begin as generous and idealistic; none of the followers shows these qualities at first (one is a poor cleric, one a pedant, the third a peasant). In their discussions, when the generous, self-expanding energy of the hero calls forth a supportive response from the less susceptible follower, we have a kind of underlining or echo that grounds our enjoyment and laughter on a positive quality without any hint of didactic pretensions. The events as narrated are funny in a good-natured way, without depending upon satiric ridicule of the hero or his double. An independent system of mutual exchanges is set in operation with each adventure the couple undergoes. The continued presence of the real Spanish or English scene prevents us from taking the account as mere frivolity; the irony of the narrator spares us altogether from the moralistic role of judge; we are left free to cocreate and to enjoy the manner in which each of the two helps the other to be himself. On a higher level, the narrative voice of Fielding, like that of Cervantes, doubles the unfolding of events in the text; it, too, involves the reader in a continuous discussion.

This mutuality is rendered explicitly in discussions within the text. Much of the first part (1604) of *Don Quixote* consists of reported conversations between Quixote and Sancho, some quite lengthy and always capable of a remarkably high level. One of these is the very amusing Chapter XV (echoed by Sterne near the start of *Tristram Shandy*) wherein Rocinante is almost killed following the lusts of the flesh, as are

Quixote and Sancho while Sancho's ass escapes scot free. A long post-mortem discussion finally brings the master and servant, who by now are close friends, to the most serious of questions, leading Sancho to ask, "What greater misfortune could there be than that of having to wait on time and death?" With indomitable cheerfulness, Don Quixote then declares he will let himself be slung helplessly across the back of the ass and travel thus to "some castle" where his wounds may be healed:

> "And I may add that I do not look upon it as a disgrace to go mounted like that, for I recall having read that good old Silenus, the tutor and instuctor of the merry god of laughter, when he entered the city of the hundred gates, was pleased to do so mounted upon a very handsome ass." "That may very well be," said Sancho, "but there is a big difference between going mounted and being slung across the animal's flanks like a bag of refuse."

Don Quixote, far from taking umbrage, argues quite learnedly against this view of Sancho's. By the end of Chapter XIX he is laughing at Sancho's wit and adopting the new name his friend had thought up, The Knight of the Mournful Countenance. And in Chapter XX, to me the most delightful in the whole novel, Don Quixote and Sancho get through a whole frightening night simply by talking to each other, until finally the Don orders his servant to keep his distance and talk much less—a command that has no effect at all on their conversation then or later. Both of them laugh heartily when they realize that the dreadful noises they have heard all night come from a nearby fulling mill. Don Quixote and Sancho, then, are the kind of comic figures that Plato praised Aristophanes for inventing—the ones who themselves know that they are funny, like Falstaff and unlike Bottom. Neither master nor servant, however, possess this self-knowledge beyond a certain point, and Chapter XX allows the one to show up the other in a delightful way.

For one thing, the peasant common sense of Sancho opens

up all those sides of Don Quixote on which his monomania has not clamped down. His intelligent good nature and well-read humanity are always forces to be conjured with and thus form an important part of the threat that produces the comic when they are taken in conjunction with his madness. When at the end of the whole book he becomes sane again, the threat takes effect: a sweet, decent old man, he ceases to be comic and can only die. (Shakespeare did better by Falstaff, carrying him off to a heaven of his own without a change in his comic self.)

Finally, before leaving *Don Quixote* I would like to point out that it is the first great novel that could not exist if it were not supported by the consciousness imparted to the invented figure (or character, or personage—whatever term one wishes to use) of Don Quixote. This all-pervasive function of what is called characterization goes much further than mere point of view; we cannot ostracize it by tabooing the subject, and in genuine works of art it cannot be adequately dealt with by analysis according to codes of a so-called naturalizing process. No matter how committed one may be to verbal theories of the text, there is no getting around the implication of world and person in such great works of art. We shall return to this argument; for now, it is impossible to ignore the extent to which the creation of Don Quixote and his world contribute to the past, present, and future values of Cervantes' novel.

8. Self and Character in the Comic

Nowhere is the creation of character more essential to the success of writing than in the comic. It is a direct judgment on the fiction of the new wave in France that it found the comic to be out of its reach. One might suggest, of course, that French criticism has reacted against centuries of overexposure to character-criticism in the hands of the English. Nevertheless, from Jonson, with his humours types, through Dryden, who clearly established the high road of character study in his brief but inspired sketches of Caliban and Falstaff, to Morgann, Coleridge, and Hazlitt, there is no better practical criticism of the comic anywhere than there is in England.

One point is particularly worth anticipating here: the relation this criticism brought to light among freedom, play, and the disinterested element in that English discovery, humour. Kant's "purposefulness without purpose," given as the essence of art, along with Schiller's coupling of freedom with the play instinct, perhaps helped Coleridge to the insight that the groundwork of a comic character of the genuinely humorous sort is the absence of effective self-interest. In line with the motive of self-deception, which Plato made the basis of the ridiculous, it seems to me that this humorous negation of self-interest presents a vision of the hollowness of mere selfishness, of calculating motives, and of their disproportion to "the godlike within us," or the Dionysian, if that is a more acceptable term. The fact of self-deception allows us the amused pardoning of its attendant follies, rather than burdening us with their stern condemnation, so long as they have not proved to be self-serving to the eye of true understanding.

This ethos is present in difficult comedy, that is, comedy such as *The Cherry Orchard* that has been continually mistaken for serious drama by bourgeois producers and audiences moved by self-pity. Madame Ranevsky and her entourage are utterly selfish but at the same time have no sense of where their real interests lie. Therefore we willingly forgive them, and thus we are ready to laugh at them painlessly, without sentimental pity. Likewise, at the other end of the scale, the success of Homais in *Madame Bovary* proves the hollowness of all such success. When we see that such artful scamps can become rich and even receive civic honors, we feel that we have been freed from the danger of imitating or admiring that kind of ambition, and so we can laugh at them without bitterness. The appeal to "the godlike in us" is no mere idealistic flourish, but takes on a practical meaning, for we are able to posit ourselves over against society and see its judgments as frequently absurd. Once again, the outcome is an enhanced sense of the self and its freedom, especially when Homais is posited against a self-contradictory character like Emma Bovary, whose exploitative insecurity might be expected to extinguish the comic rather than help to generate it.

Coleridge's insight also applies to Horner in *The Country Wife*. His motives are conscious and apparently self-interested; in the development of the plot, however, he puts himself in the position of the man in the Gospel who gave up everything he had for the pearl of great price, which in Horner's case is the silly boon of coition with hypocritical city prudes and a naive country idiot. By the cool judgment of his own world of the town (including all its fine women), and by our judgment too when we think carefully about it, Horner is an enthusiast, a humorous type, a fanatic devotee of sex. His scheme therefore lacks reasonable self-interest, and we can be amused by him without any sense of reservation.

The same is true of Sir Fopling Flutter in Etherege's *The Man of Mode*. His concern for dress has passed the point where it does him any material good. He is therefore less selfish than the hero Dorimant and is treated more kindly as a figure for positive comic satisfaction rather than a butt of satire. Dorimant is not a comic figure in himself until Harriet comes along and begins to put this proud, stiff, callous libertine to the self-denying service of a true lover: the combination of the witty, strong-willed man and the wittier, stronger-willed woman is gratifyingly comic. In addition to these figural creations, Etherege's play puts on the stage for all time the most successful of "great good places" for the politely comic, Lady Townley's house—that is, the prototypical setting of all drawing room comedy. Add to this the Mall Scene in St. James's Park, and we have in *The Man of Mode* the essential ambience of English comedy of manners. Most of all, we have its great product, the free and witty discussion of life and society.

3

COMIC ETHOS:
THE CLASSICAL VIEW

THE TERM ETHOS ($\mathring{\eta}\theta$os) is used by Aristotle in the *Poetics* to indicate human behavior. It was properly translated for many years by the English word "manners," then mistranslated by the anachronism "character." Aristotle, of course, had no concept of modern notions of individual personality. At present, when writers have begun to repudiate the portrayal of closed characters in their fictional texts, the original less determinate Greek form in its modern equivalent "behavior" may well be restored. For the comic, what is needed is a word indicating a mode of behavior common to a group of people, including habits of using language and typical ways of thinking.

A history of comic ethos can be sketched in two epochs, based on the classical and romantic mentalities. Both incorporate concepts of substance and freedom and exhibit the comic dynamism of substantial continuity maintained against threatened alteration. The romantic, however, always tends to be critical of the ethos that underlies customary response, at least in the sense of reflecting upon it, whereas the classic tends to accept that ethos implicitly. Our present purpose is to inquire into the kinds of behavior that have been marked as comic in literature; we are not seeking a moral ethos or ethics that determines the good, but a bias or an emphasis that creates the ridiculous, the humorous, and the comic.

The nucleus of classical rhetoric for comic speech and

comic writing first appears in Plato and Aristotle. Later, Cicero and Quintilian upheld the view that a well-rounded
speaker would be able to make his audience laugh as well as
weep; between them, these two have more to say in their
rhetorical writings about devices and techniques of the
comic than is to be found anywhere else until we come to
the rhetorics and courtesy books of the Renaissance. Even
then, the social assumptions still remained the same. The
court of a Renaissance prince was supposed to be on a level
with the Roman senate both for the dignity of its members
and the urbane quality of their discourse. As to their everyday converse, the prince was by definition a magnanimous
man, and he and his circle of companions would (ideally at
least) maintain a level of conversational activity like that described in Book 8 of the *Nicomachean Ethics*, including the
fine-souled wit Aristotle prized. Manuals for the instruction
of courtiers therefore provided a section on repartee and on
how to tell entertaining stories. The ideal and the practice
are illustrated with incomparable richness by Shakespeare's
plays. It has been pointed out by F. M. Cornford, Northrop
Frye, and Charles Mauron that the motifs, rhetoric, and dramaturgy of New Comedy, developed by the Greek theater
and passed on by the Romans, still determine much popular
comic writing today. Its theoretical basis was very well understood in antiquity, beginning with Aristotle. He lays
down two sets of rules for the comic ethos. The first is in the
Poetics, where he suggests (only in passing, since his main interest is tragedy) that the field of comedy is confined to ordinary social activities without life-or-death seriousness and
restricted to unhistorical figures (neither heroes nor gods)
whose stage behavior is "worse than ours" only in that it is
ridiculous, not in any other respect. Further, in his historical
account of drama Aristotle traces the development of comic
performances from their beginnings in village custom
scarely a hundred years before his time. Bands of young
male revelers once had license to taunt respectable seniors at
the very doors of their houses with the most indecent and
scurrilous language and songs. Later on, in Sicily and in various mainland cities including Athens innovators had taken

the essential step of unifying this practice around particular stories and at the same time generalizing both story and characters, thus transforming lampoon into comedy and fitting it for public performance at the city Dionysia.

In the *Ethics*, on the other hand, Aristotle leads his whole argument toward a final picture of the great spirited or magnanimous man whose most characteristic activity is conversation among his equals in a free play of mind that is both active and godlike and also the most delightful state possible to humans. Wit and amusement belong to this conversation, but ridicule and laughter are only accidental, if not rudely out of keeping with it. The magnanimous man is good company, to be sure; he is witty and will often make others laugh, but he himself is content to smile. Aristotle, in fact, condemns *to geloíon*, the term translated by Cicero as *ridiculum* (or "the laughable") and the origin of *le ridicule* in French as well as of the English "ridiculous." He points out that the Athenian Old Comedy was banned because it provoked laughter by ridiculing individuals, even using their real names; this throwback to its origins in village lampoons was false to the urbane institution of comedy as a public ritual. The New Comedy, as he explains in the *Poetics*, avoids proper names and personalities, as we should say, and merely designates an imagined complex of social and individual traits by an appropriate proper name.

In his *Rhetoric*, also, Aristotle discusses the characteristic behavior of the main types encountered in Athenian society. When he explains how the orator should envisage a typical young man or a typical old one, he lists traits that would hold good for thousands of stock characters in neoclassic comedy. He left the more laughable types, however, to his student Theophrastus, whose *Characters* are almost all examples of potentially ridiculous obsessions rather than of either criminal or commendable behavior. This kind of stereotyping seems inseparable from the dramaturgy of New Comedy, where a dozen or so standard masks were enough to include the entire range of types open to the dramatist.

Scholars used to think that Aristotle's *Poetics* once con-

20/257

tained a lost second book dealing at greater length with
comedy. Even as we have it, however, Aristotle's theory of
comedy, so briefly stated, is strongly dovetailed with his ethics and his whole concept of human society. We might speculate that Aristotle was never prepared to say much more
about the problems posed by the comic. In contrast to the
situation with regard to tragedy, where he was able to draw
upon an abundance of texts, Aristotle says that the development of comedy has had no records because "from the beginning it was not treated seriously" (1449^b). When he defines the laughable by saying it is "a sort of defect or
ugliness which is not painful or destructive" (1449^a), all he
offers by way of explanation is the example of the comic
mask, which "is ugly and distorted, but does not give pain."[1]

What was certainly available to Aristotle, of course, was
the Platonic corpus, including the figure of Socrates in the
context of the Platonic dialogues. Both the figure of Socrates
and the atmosphere of the dialogues are perceptibly
comic—not excepting the potentially tragic *Crito*. Parallels
have been found, even in their deaths, between Socrates and
Falstaff. The discussions of Socrates and his companions on
the banks of the Ilyssus, in *The Symposium*, or before his
death when he pictures his future life as continued conversation with the best of men in the fields of the blessed are all
models for the highest activity of Aristotle's great-souled
man. The same is true of Cicero's philosophical dialogues in
the form of imaginary conversations, recalling great men he
knew as well as those who died before his time. Nothing like
this atmosphere appears on the stage before Shakespeare,
though we find it at times in Dante and Chaucer. Yet as an
ideal this tradition surely helped to guard readers of the *Poetics* from thinking of the comic as the mere concentration
upon ugly, deformed, and trivial objects calculated to raise a
superior laugh.

Through some strange oversight—for the text is well

[1] *Poetics*, 1449^{a-b}. Greek text and translation in S. H. Butcher, *Aristotle's
Theory of Poetry and Fine Art* (London: Macmillan, 1902), pp. 20f. I have
modified Butcher's translation where it is anachronistic.

known—the source from which Aristotle drew his very inadequate remarks on the ridiculous is almost never examined in our present context. It is Plato's *Philebus*, where Socrates acknowledges that comedy is a very serious subject of
study, and one so difficult that developing a procedure for
understanding it will make other problems easy to work
with.[2] In comedy the mind is swayed simultaneously by opposing feelings of pain and pleasure. Socrates wished to set
this feeling apart from other mental feelings just mentioned
by him: anger, fear, desire, sorrow, love, all "pains of the
soul," not of the body, and "also full of the most wonderful
pleasures," such as the anger

> Which stirs even a wise man to violence,
> And is sweeter than honey and the honeycomb.

These mental feelings, all of them (except the ridiculous)
then associated with tragedy, are very much like the ones
Ingarden refers to when he discusses metaphysical qualities,
and they remind us of Edmund Burke's description of the
sublime. The specific feelings Socrates associates with comedy, however, are envy, a malicious satisfaction we feel at
the sight of some deformity or mishap when it happens to a
person who is not an enemy of ours and not able to harm us
in return, and the sense of superior immunity that causes us
to laugh. This envy Socrates thinks of as a form of pain that
becomes a pleasure when our own feeling of security enables us to laugh. If, however, the ugly, deformed, or unhappy victim were powerful enough and vindictive enough
to make us fear him, we should find the whole episode de-
testable from the beginning.

Socrates seems rather primitive and Homeric in defining
envy, and yet he anticipates the best-known maxim of the
polished cynic La Rochefoucauld, one that was a favorite of

---

[2] *Philebus*, 47–49. I use *The Dialogues of Plato*, translated by Benjamin
Jowett (New York: Random House, 1937), II, 343–403. The discussion in
Plato: Philebus, translated with notes and commentary by J.C.B. Gosling
(Oxford: Clarendon Press, 1975), p. 120, is of some help on φθόνος, the
term translated as "malice" in English and French, *Bosheit* in German.

Swift's. The elements he invokes are in fact quite profound, and take us all the way to Freudian ideas of laughter as economizing on feelings of guilt, inferiority, and inhibition. His analysis also enables us to distinguish, as both Plato and Aristotle did, between the objects of comic ridicule, on one hand, and of satiric attack on the other. Unlike the butts of comedy, the victims of early classical satire were enemies and as such were to be attacked (if one dared) with all possible venom, as in the satires of Archilochus. In the case of the magnanimous man such venom would never be required, for his life of peace and freedom was unthreatened by enemies.

Plato gives us an example of how Socrates would treat a comic butt in the dialogue with Ion. Socrates entices this acquaintance of his, who is an elocutionist and performer of poetry in public, to make a fool of himself over his assumed knowledge of every art that his set pieces happen to mention. According to the *Philebus*, there are three general ways people make themselves ridiculous, always by forms of self-delusion: by extravagance, by personal vanity, or by thinking they are more knowledgeable than is actually the case. Poor Ion qualifies as a fool in the third department. Just because he has memorized Homer, he thinks he is equal to Agamemnon in the ability to lead troops, and equal to each of the other heroes in their special fields of excellence. He also, of course, thinks he is perfectly aware of the virtuous and the good. He exits as self-deluded as ever, unpunished except by our laughter (or, more likely, by an ironic smile). Whether or not he is chastised is of no importance; he is not one of our enemies. Ion has been shown up as a weak person who is vulnerably ignorant about himself; that is, he is ridiculous. He is a part of that combination of pleasures and pains, as Socrates explains,[3] that exists off the stage in human life as a whole and that only needs to be detected and brought out in order to be laughed at.

Cicero caught this Socratic attitude when he gave comedy

---

[3] *Philebus*, 50.

its most famous definition: *imitatio vitae, speculum consuetu-*
dinis, imago veritatis ("imitation of life, mirror of manners,
image of truth"). The quotation survives only in Donatus'
preface to his commentary on Terence. As an admirer of
Terence, Cicero was undoubtedly aware that creative handling of human behavior carries the best comedy far beyond
mere exploitation of malicious but pleasurable envy. In his
own discussion, would-be orators are told that there is no
personal merit in getting a laugh by mimicking ordinary
foolish mannerisms, for these are already ridiculous without
our wit, and they exist all around us. Mimics only need to
notice them and present them in lively fashion, mugging as
actors do in pantomimes. Cicero repudiates mimicry as a
technique for the orator, though he admits such buffoonery
is the most common source of laughter. The manners of a
buffoon are to be exposed by the orator, not copied. Thus
Cicero preserves Aristotle's important distinction between
the witty person and the buffoon, pointing out that everything that is ridiculous is not witty. Wit is not a matter of
mimicry so much as of thought and language: "Whatever is
expressed wittily consists sometimes in a thought, sometimes in the mere language, but men are most delighted with
a joke when the laugh is raised by the thought and the language in conjunction."[4]

With the caution that one needs to have a natural talent of
invention and delivery to use the methods successfully, Cicero proceeds to identify types of facetious speaking. First is
the famous *contra expectatum*, which Kant was to make the
basis of the comic itself. He also mentions, along with
mockery of others, laughter at our own mistakes—an insight
of peculiar validity today. His "comparing a thing with
something worse" works along the same lines as Freud's
"degradation." What he calls dissembling probably includes

---

[4] *De Oratore*, II, lviii–lxxi. For this and other texts cited I shall use where
possible the well-edited and extremely convenient anthology of Paul
Lauter, *Theories of Comedy* (Garden City, N.Y.: Doubleday, 1964); see pp.
24–26. See also G.M.A. Grube, *The Greek and Roman Critics* (London: Me-
thuen, 1965), pp. 187–191.

double-entendre (of which he earlier gives an excellent example) and also what we call dry or deadpan humor. Finally he refers in the phrase "apparent absurdities" to what we still find witty in the paradoxes of Wilde or Chesterton.

Cicero, as well as most of the other great men and great speakers he sets talking in his dialogues, had a high regard for the facetious and was famous for his ability to amuse. Thus he wittily defines the ridiculous as "the presentation of something offensive in an inoffensive manner" (II, lviii, 236), the definition of Socrates rephrased as a paradox. Wit itself he perceives as aptness of thought and language to one another. The most valuable aspect of his insight into oratorical humor, however, is that he included, along with the ridiculous and wit, the element of delight. The delightful, he suggests, though it often includes laughter, goes beyond it and can exist without it.

Another notable aspect of Cicero's analysis is his explanation why great vice (the kind that goes with serious crime) or great misery are ineffective as subjects for laughter and ridicule. "People will have those guilty of enormous crimes attacked with more formidable weapons than ridicule," he has his spokesman say, "and do not like the miserable to be derided, unless perhaps when they are insolent. And you must be considerate, too, of the feelings of mankind, lest you rashly speak against those who are greatly beloved." In these "feelings of mankind" we have the first clear emergence of the concept of "humanity" as a sentimental source of value and judgment peculiarly important to the comic. Cicero also, when he cautions against bad taste in mocking deformity and bodily defects, suggests as a guideline that jests are most readily made on what is "neither provocative of violent aversion nor of extreme compassion."

Cicero, of course, was writing about oratory. We know, however, that after the lapse of centuries when dramatic genres were again discussed, the functions of the dramatists and in many cases of the speaking characters themselves were still considered in a purely rhetorical light. Cicero's remarks on comic speech and joking had a remarkable currency, especially in conjunction with Terence, and with the rhetoric-based preface and commentary by Donatus that accompanied the text of Terence's plays as handed down in manuscripts for a thousand years. Donatus also refers to public games of four types, in honor of Father Liber and other gods, particularly Apollo, and says that "acts are assigned to diverse games."[5] Such comic "acts," or plays, still survived as part of the academic midsummer exercises at Oxford as late as Dryden's time and evoked his best critical prologues and epilogues.

Donatus lists eleven types of comic personae and gives their stock costuming: old men (old-fashioned white clothes), young men (multi-colored costumes), slaves (lightly clothed, to show their poor origins and to permit agility in their stage business), parasites (no special dress), the joyful man (bright colors), the troubled man (worn-out clothing), the rich man (purple), the pauper (rusty purple), the soldier (a purple mantle), the girl (foreign clothing), the procurer (a cloak of many colors), the courtesan (golden-yellow, denoting greed). He clearly refers to private as well as public comedies, farces, and mimes. He makes music an identifying accompaniment of comedy; a "light prick" on a certain kind of flute was used, he says, to underline the point of a joke, and interpolated songs were customary.

These matters are worth including here because the comic theater was revived during the Renaissance with astonishing fidelity to these few hints of what it had been like in Roman times. The stereotyped cast, in particular, severely limited the form of comedy accepted as classic, and it is a standing wonder that the romantic comedies of the Italians, Shakespeare, and the Spaniards were able to exploit this pattern so freely. Nevertheless, there is a vast augmentation of comic possibility when we pass from the *Comedy of Errors* to *A Midsummer Night's Dream*. The range if barely hinted at by the difference between Plautus' *Menaechmi* and his *Amphytrion*. Yet the latter is the only extant comedy of antiquity

[5] As translated by George Miltz in Lauter, pp. 27–32.

that violates the law limiting comic personages to local common life and contemporary times. Almost all the humanists of the sixteenth century who commented upon the *Poetics* or who dealt with classical literary theory were agreed upon the domestic and mean status of the comic milieu, as if the distinction between dramatic genres were equivalent to a distinction between social classes. The principal influence at work was no doubt the precedent of the still extant Latin comedies and the fact that their stock roles helped to stereotype the personnel of players' companies; but there was also the statement by Aristotle near the beginning of the *Poetics* that persons in comedy were worse than us (1449a). Somehow this term was always stressed, while its important qualification, that this "worse" was only by reference to what is ridiculous, was ignored. Instead, it became the frequent practice to give the double plots of the Roman plays—made up out of two Greek comedies—an upperclass and a lowerclass set of characters, acting at times in two quite different social worlds. In thousands of European plays meant for production by stock companies, the result was all too often a mongrel combination of gentlefolk's graces and their servants' low comic mugging. The inclusiveness natural to theater from its institution as ritual was thus perverted into a reinforcement of class privilege.[6] Even the language suffered a division when verse was retained for the speeches of the ladies and gentlemen and prose was considered good enough for the business of the under plot. Yet both Plautus and Terence had left extraordinary models of dramatic verse style behind them: Plautus, a rollocking long line full of sound play and clever expressions, Terence a classical utterance that Cicero himself praised beyond all others for the formation of style.

---

[6] This is a perfect instance of an "opposition" that is in reality a "complicity," as Jacques Derrida would say, giving superior status to one of the opposed members in anything but an innocent fashion. It seems quite legitimate to deconstruct and reverse the terms of this opposition in describing the movement of comic ethos from its classic to its modern epoch.

The divisive tendency of split-plot drama could be rationalized somewhat (in *Upstairs, Downstairs* fashion) by saying that the two classes were integrated in a hierarchical community wherein "knowing one's place" made up for the subordination of most citizens to a small group of superiors. Low comic players in low comic parts, in fact, were often more successful with all classes of theatergoers than colleagues who specialized in playing the fine gentlemen and ladies. In a strange way, though, the ancient theater had managed things better, even while representing actual social conditions of slavery. A clever servant, when successful, would be given his freedom; a pretty girl, unmarriageable to a young Roman because she was a foreigner (often the property of a pimp), would be discovered to be the daughter of a citizen. There was a great gift of freedom in the bestowal of the comic action, whereas in the European split-plot comedy of 1600–1900 a lordly gratuity and permission to marry a fellow servant had to do for the happy ending.[7] Technically at least, the "under plot" was necessarily dependent upon the "upper plot," just as the persons of the "under walk" were subordinate to those of the "upper walk," even when (as was often the case) the main plot was rather dull and the subplot provided the real reason for the audience's coming to the theater. What is important here is the visible action: the servant (or dependent, in the case of a clever parasite), instead of being powerless, is shown actively controlling the situation; or a persuasively attractive slave girl is discovered to be eligible for the socially including rite of marriage; or an extraneous and misfitting person is discovered to be someone else who is really quite in place within the social community. Eventually inferiority and superiority come to be defined comically not by fixed social position but by ability to use power (such as beauty) and solve problems. Freedom comes to be defined as full membership in the society, with

---

[7] This is the situation that Beaumarchais' *Marriage of Figaro* treated in a revolutionary reversal of the conventional hegemony.

rights to all of its important functions such as marriage and owning property.

As THE BASIS of comic ethos, a strongly humane flavor is already to be found in Greek and Roman comedy. Nothing could be more inclusively human than Aristophanes' disgust at Athenian imperialism, or less ethnocentric than Terence's "homo sum, nihil humanum a me alienum puto." These comedies reject honorable warfare in favor of the harmless strife and enjoyments of leisure and curiosity. Their tone has manifestly little to do with tribal or universal rites of purgation and fertility; it is more in keeping with the philosophical tradition running back through Cicero to Terence, Plautus, and Menander, and through these writers to the ideas of Aristotle and Plato.

Over two millennia, however, the literary texts become more and more scarce. Aristophanes is put beyond the pale by Aristotle and then his plays are lost. The work of the most influential and perhaps best-loved writer of the ancient world, Menander, is allowed to disappear almost completely. Even Terence, so highly appreciated, is absorbed into rhetoric and ethics. Very great comic works come into being and are allowed to pass almost without investigation: *The Satyricon, The Canterbury Tales, The Praise of Folly, Gargantua and Pantagruel.* The Italians, led by Dante and Boccaccio, are perhaps an exception; but even their theoretical discourse on comedy seemed determined to pour itself into the same old rhetorical bottles.

In the earlier Renaissance scholars were mainly engaged in duplicating for comedy Aristotle's analysis of tragedy. As theatrical practice far outran criticism, it was left to the comic authors to feel the need for a fresh critical start and to provide it themselves: Guarini, Jonson, and Dryden set the enterprise on its feet. A small but valuable series of texts became available: Guarini's *Compendium of Tragicomic Poetry,* Jonson's prefatory dialogue in *Poetaster* and *Cynthia's Revels,* and several pieces by John Dryden. Dryden's *Essay of Dramatic Poesy* broke new ground in England, as did the prefaces, prologues, and epilogues inspired by his own efforts as comic writing but even more by the greater successes of Shakespeare, Jonson, Molière, Etherege, Wycherley, and Congreve. Dryden was followed by his disciples in criticism, Congreve, Dennis, and Addison, who provided valuable insights of their own. The effect was to establish an original movement of English comic writing and thinking in readiness for the great development of "humour" by Swift, Fielding, and Sterne that was to inspire the romantics all over Europe.

Guarini and Dryden, in their own ways, were arguing for breaking out of the classic pattern that had been outlined by Donatus and incorporated, with the peculiar class degradation we have analyzed, into much seventeenth-century stage comedy. They wanted to establish play-structures that contravened generic conventions still maintained in *The Comedy of Errors* or *Twelfth Night* but without taking the romantic license of *Love's Labor's Lost* or *The Tempest*. The latter plays are not mirrors of custom in the classical sense of New Comedy, and they move freely beyond its prescribed social milieu. John Dryden, in *Marriage à la Mode,* avoided dealing with the objects Aristotle specified—people more ridiculous than we are—and made them much more clever and witty than us. He especially wished to abandon the social inferiority foisted upon comedy by the Renaissance critics. He wrote a split-plot tragicomedy, therefore, in which the comic persons in a romantic subplot are on a high social level, although their speech is in prose instead of the heroic couplets still used by the "upper walk" of persons involved in the political upper plot.

While not exactly a revolutionary, Dryden was at least structuring his play according to new and artistic rather than old and routine conventions. Dryden is on record, moreover, with a remarkable claim based on broadly social rather than class grounds. He states that the court of Charles II was more free in giving access to the people of the nation than any of its predecessors. He argues that the intercourse among royalty, courtiers, and populace that marked Charles's regime should be reflected in a leveling up of the ethos and language of stage comedy in order to keep pace with the widespread improvement in manners. Whether the court of Charles II was, in actual fact, more cultivated or freer of access than its predecessors is not our concern. What still strikes us today is Dryden's awareness of certain fixed social attitudes regarding stage comedy and his own opposing consciousness that theatrical practice ought to be changed so as to share in the broadened intercourse of a changing society.

Dryden was a competent classicist; he had read widely and had a good memory. Besides Plautus and Terence, Aristotle and Cicero, he knew Plato, and he knew the truth of Socrates' doctrine in the *Philebus* that the ridiculous is a pleasure we feel maliciously. Many times during his career Dryden accused himself of "malice"—as a critic who naturally enjoyed finding faults in what others wrote, or as a natural-born satirist who tried to hold himself back from poetic overkill. He consistently expressed a distaste for the comic genre as he had inherited it from Ben Jonson because it was based upon envious or malicious observation of lower-class human beings whom we had not reason to fear or to hate because they were powerless.

As we have seen, however, there was another tradition leading back through Aristotle and Plato and far beyond to the banquets and royal entertainments presented in Homer. Shakespeare had certainly invoked this nobler tradition with complete success. Dryden preferred Shakespeare to Jonson for just this reason. He is disinclined to snoop about the sleazier quarters of London, noting down the silly and depraved antics of cheats and fools in order to regale the coarse-minded portion of his audience with a vulgar entertainment—a role to which he represents himself as doomed if he were to attempt Jonson's kind of comedy. On the contrary, if not quite the magnanimous man described by Aristotle, Dryden tried to be at least a candid observer (to use a favorite word of his) instead of an envious or malicious one.

By the eighth book of the *Nicomachean Ethics* Aristotle's earlier emphasis on social and political obligations and needs gives way to the presentation of an ideal style of living, where the human is most godlike. It is deeply social without being inclusively so, based as it is on the elite communion of peers in perfect friendship, and it is political in its celebration of the highest degree of freedom. Its most essential activity is speculative play of mind brought out in good talk. In accordance with Aristotle's favorite principle of entelechy, this is the truest fulfillment of human nature, the activity wherein it is closest to the divine. It would have been arrogant of Dryden to claim this ideal as part of his personal experience, though his daily sessions at Will's Coffee House were an approach to it. The good manners of the time, however, allowed him to imagine such ideal activity as taking place in the courtly milieu. Since he was more free than Jonson had been to mingle with members of the court and even to speak in friendly fashion to the king himself, he felt entitled to disregard the old, superior/inferior idea of the comic and to substitute a higher conception. He soon perceived that he himself would not be the comic writer to take full advantage of the more open society. But as others moved onto the new ground he watched them with satisfaction and outspoken admiration.

The specific disability Dryden found in himself was an incapacity for the graces of light conversation. The generic leap forward, the positive mutation in comedy that left him behind, was what Shaw later discerned as the discovery of the discussion. As a better synthesis for the action of plays than the intrigue plot, the discussion was a better organizing center for comic drama. It was less contrived than the combats of wit of couples and rivals, and less mechanical and far more free than ancient theatrical devices of entanglement, suspense, and discovery. It brought the theater into a new leading relationship with society, encouraging actors and actresses to develop a more human and natural range and eventually to break away from the fixed posturing, declamation, and farcical mugging of their traditional art. Great actors had always been able to act kings better than kings themselves could, and to act gentlemen better than gentlemen. The players of more ordinary talents now had the opportunity to exercise them with greater wit and restraint in more varied and genuine roles. All of them now had the chance to live up to the social function sketched out by Prince Hamlet seventy-five years earlier than Dryden: "To give back the age its very form and pressure."

WE HAVE NOW REACHED in our inquiry one of those occasions when changing social institutions impinge upon more permanent structures of human behavior and feeling. Our investigation is limited to the comic, and our question now concerns the structure of the comic quality present in the new discussion plays compared with the traditional intrigue plots involving stock personae. The latter, we have shown, were based on a concept of the ridiculous involving deformity, powerlessness, exposure to laughter—and, in the audience, envy (i.e., malice not involving an enemy). In the tradition going back to Greek New Comedy, the play ended well (as Plato perceived) when the audience's malicious satisfaction at discovering the faults of others had been thoroughly dissolved in unresenting laughter as the discovery was made general.

The better/worse formulation of Aristotle's *Poetics*, moreover, should never have been applied socially; it needed only to relate to immediate theatrical situtations that degrade some characters by exposing their universally human foibles to derision by the spectators. The *Poetics* certainly does not decree the hard-and-fast social compartmentalization of the dramatic genres that marked Renaissance theater. In fact Dryden's whole project, aimed at restructuring comedy in relation to a new freedom and inclusiveness in society, is sanctioned by explicit comments in a few chapters of the *Poetics*. Aristotle lays down that the pleasure "proper to comedy" is found when "those who, in the piece, are the deadliest enemies—like Orestes and Aegisthus—quit the stage as friends at the close, and no one slays or is slain" (xiii). First one is struck by a formula that makes reconcilia-

tion of enemies a proper part of the comic action and sets
the comic goal as positive friendship. Then one notes that
the two characters cited are of the highest social station. The
text seems to suggest an action in which the son is reconciled
with the man reputed to have cuckolded and killed his father. There might have been such a play; but even if Aristotle chose the two names merely because they stand for a pair
of seemingly irreconcilable enemies, he certainly is not suggesting a burlesque or travesty.

The same chapter of the *Poetics* brings into view another
possibility of the classic comic genre in what it says about
the audience: "The poet is guided in what he writes by the
wishes of his audience." Later it states a principle very congenial to the Renaissance, and especially so to an inquiring
artist such as Dryden: "The more refined art is the higher,
and the more refined in every case is that which appeals to
the better sort of audience" (xxvi). "In every case" would of
course include comedy, and there is a strong suggestion that
if a poet can manage to write for a better audience, he can
match their wishes with a higher and more refined ethos and
set of objects. Furthermore, Chapter XXV of the *Poetics*, concerned with "critical difficulties and their solutions," positively encourages a writer to seek "the higher thing" even
when it leads him to present the actually impossible—"for
the ideal type must surpass the reality." Dryden recognized
that Shakespeare had done this in comedy with his "fairy
way of writing." He himself tried to achieve the ideal type
both in tragedy and comedy by refining his language as well
as by aiming at a "better sort of audience." In comedy he
was among the most successful (after Shakespeare) at putting witty, intelligent, good-humored, and well-written
speeches on the lips of well-bred comic characters. Unfortunately, his situations were too schematic or implausible to
be taken to heart entirely by an audience of the better sort
or, indeed, by Dryden himself; something essential was
lacking, such as the human quality and fictional substance
that might have been developed by emphasizing the discussion.

The classical model for the discussion, as we have pointed

out, was the free exchange among friends on a footing of equality: eating, drinking, and talking at their leisure, actively thinking and entertaining each other with wit and imagination. Shakespeare provided such splendid examples that he might have institutionalized the discussion, having exploited it through an extraordinary range of stage applications. Such milieus as the Boar's Head Tavern, the Forest of Arden, Portia's and Olivia's houses, Theseus' court, and Prospero's cave are exactly the kind of poetic objectivities that are essential to the higher type of comedy along classical lines. The more familiar comic techniques of complicated intrigue, clever tricks, and stock roles still find their place in this higher type: they often lead up to it in fact, as in the intrigue between Falstaff and Justice Swallow that brings on the latter's marvelous reminiscences of "chimes at midnight" in a discussion of their youth.

In the comic drama of less titanic genius, however, one of the first really clear instances of the discussion in the standard English repertory is in *The Country Wife,* when the "virtuous gang" of women let their hair down and drink and talk with Horner in his lodgings. Their conversation is not exactly edifying or without malice, but it is certainly free, easy, innovative, and entertaining. The sense of equal communion is very strong indeed, and the women show no sign of inferiority to the man whose presence provides a convenient stimulus. A year later Etherege's *The Man of Mode* successfully institutionalized the discussion in the new setting he created, Lady Townley's house in London. "London: Lady Townley's drawing room" henceforward could serve as the archetypal milieu for the comedy of manners. In the same comedy Etherege created another important comic objectivity in the course of his Mall scene in St. James's Park. Both settings were places where the best society assembled and put its behavior on exhibition, mainly through speech, but also in action, dress, dance, and even song. The importance of these milieus was that they set up substantial conversations that played freely with the topics of a comic ethos in situations that threatened to undermine that ethos by other means than moral or physical compulsion. Keeping in mind Kant's distinction between moral and artistic purposefulness and the necessity for freedom in art, we can see that some place, in the real world or not, needs to be marked off where people can talk freely about their behavior in the assurance that they have found the secure, right place to do just that. An almost total physical safety is required, where issues of personal conduct and prestige are subject to the closest scrutiny and fixed ideas as well as reputations are in jeopardy at every moment. All of Shakespeare's comedies, for example, occur in situations of complete security. *The Tempest* is the exception that proves the rule, for the opening shipwreck only establishes the island as a miraculous refuge where the disorder of life can be examined speculatively and enemies may be reconciled.

The ideal comic ethos that Shakespeare achieved over and over again in his "great good places" remained out of reach for lesser talents. Dryden was sensitive to it in Shakespeare and in Chaucer as well, but perhaps only with respect to characterization. As a critic he gave us splendid insights into Falstaff and Caliban, but when he tried to imitate them as a playwright, he failed to recapture the essence of either character, though he produced two of his biggest comic hits. One reason is the absence from his *Spanish Friar* and *Tempest* of the discussion passages that abound in Shakespeare's plays, where the characters have the opportunity to develop themselves in talk. When opportunity was granted to Sir Fopling Flutter in Etherege's *Man of Mode* (1676), Dryden immediately recognized the result in his epilogue to that play. His verses are almost a compendium of classic doctrine on the ridiculous in comedy, but at the same time Dryden suggested something quite new: that there is a point at which a comic character ceases to be a mere composite of the exaggerated and out of place and comes to possess an ideal and original individuality in his own nature:

> Most modern wits such monstrous fools have shown,
> They seemed not of heaven's making but their own.

Those nauseous harlequins in farce may pass,
But there goes more to a substantial ass.
Something of man must be exposed to view,
That, gallants, they may more resemble you.
Sir Fopling is a fool so nicely writ,
The ladies would mistake him for a wit.
And when he sings, talks loud, and cocks, would cry,
I vow methinks he's pretty company;
So brisk, so gay, so travelled, so refined,
As he took pains to graff upon his kind.
True fops help nature's work, and go to school,
To file and finish God a'mighty's fool.
Yet none Sir Fopling him, or him can call;
He's knight o' the shire, and represents ye all.
From each he meets he culls what e'er he can,
Legion's his name, a people in a man.
. . . .
Yet every man is safe from what he feared,
For no one fool is hunted from the herd.

By invoking the notion of substance (already rather dated in philosophy) Dryden is pointing up the judgment that Sir Fopling is at the same time very human and very much a fool; more originally, he suggests that there is an added perfection of selfhood in him, the work both of nature and of art, of personal choice as well as self-expression. Not only does Sir Fopling enjoy an imperviousness to ridicule, but he and his folly have been so perfectly fused that he may be simply enjoyed by everyone in the audience, regardless of behavioral inhibitions or ulterior didactic considerations.

About twenty years later, William Congreve, in a published letter to John Dennis "Concerning Humour in Comedy," briefly outlined the development of comic characterization, in which he claimed English dramatists led the world. He begins with a rhetorical refusal to define humor, suppressing the very familiar lines of Ben Jonson from which, in fact, he is taking his point of departure. Congreve's suppression is explained when, after expounding what humor is

not, he does offer his own notion of what it is: "A singular
and unavoidable manner of doing, or saying any thing, peculiar and natural to one man only; by which his speech and
actions are distinguished from those of other men." Congreve, perhaps knowingly, has made humor equivalent to
character in one of its modern senses. Congreve in fact substitutes a new comic ethos of individuals for Jonson's ethos,
which was based on major types and subtypes in a manner
much more reminiscent of the classic conception of general-
ized characters. Congreve's comic ethos marks off individuals, not social categories. No matter if a person is an eccentric, so long as he is centered in his own nature.

Congreve nevertheless insists, like Dryden, on the necessity that these characters also remain human, singular
though they may be. In the late seventeenth century, the
spirit of humanity was beginning to prevail and nowhere
more visibly than in dissatisfaction with superiority and ill
nature as causes of the legitimate pleasure people take in
comedy. Theories based on these attitudes had been exclusive and condemnatory. Now the concept of humanity, an
all-inclusive and natural recognition rather than a mere social category, was beginning to determine a judgment of delight instead, comprehending the liveliness and variety of
human possibilities. Shirley Kenny's name for this new tone
in comic writing, "humane comedy," is well chosen.

Congreve displays a new zeal in rejecting ridicule by
means of buffoonery and simian mimicry as unworthy of
the godlike in human nature:

> Is any thing more common, than to have a pretended
> comedy, stuffed with such grotesques, figures, and farce
> fools? Things that either are not in nature, or if they are,
> are monsters and births of mischance; and conse-
> quently as such should be stifled and huddled out of the
> way, like sooterkins, that mankind may not be shocked
> with an appearing possibility of the degeneration of a
> godlike species. For my part, I am as willing to laugh as
> anybody, and as easily diverted with an object truly ri-

diculous: but at the same time, I can never care for seeing things that force me to entertain low thoughts of my
nature. . . . As I do not think humor exclusive of wit,
neither do I think it inconsistent with folly; but I think
the follies should be only such, as men's humors may
incline 'em to, and not follies entirely abstracted from
both humor and nature.[8]

Congreve goes on to develop what in Cicero was only prudent counsel on avoiding offense into what we can now recognize as a rather shallow humanitarian sentiment, rejecting
the insight of the *Philebus* in favor of Ciceronian good taste:

sometimes characters are barbarously exposed on the
stage, ridiculing natural deformities, casual defects in
the senses, and infirmities of age. Sure the poet must
both be very ill-natured himself, and think his audience
so, when he proposes by showing a man deformed, or
deaf, or blind, to give them an agreeable entertainment,
and hopes to raise their mirth by what is truly an object
of compassion.

The lesson of Lucretius and Augustine, which Congreve
forgot, we have relearned in Freud, and we know poets and
audiences are ill-natured in ways that laughter can sometimes alleviate. The young Congreve, however, developed a
new superiority theory, that of nascent sentimentalism,
which makes humanity a little too godlike, especially in its
feelings of compassion.

After rejecting definitions of humor that would attach it to
mere wittiness, folly, or personal defects, to ethnic, class, or
métier types, or, finally, to affectation, Congreve launches
into an account that comes remarkably close to a modern
understanding of personality in the fullest sense of the
word:

Humor I take either to be born with us, and so of a natural growth; or else to be grafted into us, by some acci-

[8] Lauter, pp. 207–208 (I have normalized spelling, etc.)

dental change in the constitution, or revolution of the internal habit of body; by which it becomes, if I may so call it, naturalized.

Humor is from nature, habit from custom, and affection from industry.

Humor shows us as we are.

Habit shows us as we appear under a forcible impression.

Affectation shows what we would be, under a voluntary disguise.

Though here I would observe by the way that a continued affectation may in time become a habit.[9]

After a few examples, he continues in a rising vein, first remarking (like Cicero and Socrates) that ethnic and class characters "may be painted without much art or labor, since they require little more than a good memory and superficial observation. But true humor cannot be shown without a dissection of nature and a narrow search to discover the first seeds from whence it has its root and growth."[10] On this subject, which he declares is "entirely new, and was never touched upon before," he launches into bold speculation:

Our humor has relation to us, and to what proceeds from us, as the accidents have to a substance; it is a color, taste, and smell, diffused through all; though our actions are never so many and different in form, they are all splinters of the same wood, and have naturally one complexion; which though it may be disguised by art, yet cannot be wholly changed; we may paint it with other colors, but we cannot change the grain. So the natural sound of an instrument will be distinguished, though the notes expressed by it are never so various, and the divisions never so many. Dissimulation may by degrees become more easy to our practice; but

[9] Lauter, p. 209.
[10] Lauter, p. 211.

it can never absolutely transubstantiate us into what we
would seem: it will always be in some proportion a violence upon nature.[11]

It is amusing to see how at this early stage Congreve's term
"transubstantiate" introduces the ontotheological dimension
into the discussion of character, for it is this element, detected in the relationship between author-creator and fictional creature, that many writers and some critics have been
rejecting for some time now.

Finally, it is very striking to find that Congreve points to a
direct link between freedom and the emergence of humor in
comedy. In unusual language for the year 1695, he even appears to invoke the democratic spirit, on political, social, and
physiological grounds:

> I look upon humor to be almost of English growth; at
> least, it does not seem to have found such increase on
> any other soil. And what appears to me to be the reason
> of it is the great freedom, privilege, and liberty which
> the common people of England enjoy. Any man that
> has a humor, is under no restraint or fear of giving it
> vent. They have a proverb among them, which maybe
> will show the bent and genius of the people as well as a
> longer discourse: "he that will have a may-pole, shall
> have a may-pole." This is a maxim with them, and their
> practice is agreeable to it. I believe something consider-
> able too may be ascribed to their feeding so much on
> flesh, and the grossness of their diet in general.[12]

Congreve's dietary observation is probably jocular, in keeping with the format of the letter to a friend so frequently
used in those days to account for the publication of a private
person's ideas on a matter of public concern. The compli-
mentary close is nevertheless significant: "Your real friend,
and humble servant." Congreve is writing out of one of
those rings of friends, like the one Gaston Boissier described

[11] Lauter, pp. 211–212.
[12] Lauter, p. 214.

as surrounding Cicero, that form proof wherever they exist of the lasting force of Aristotle's vision in the *Nicomachean Ethics.* Congreve and Dennis, along with many others, belonged to the company of Dryden, and met at Will's Coffee House in London for food, drink, and conversation. We can assume they shared the sentiments that Dryden had expressed on freedom:

> Freedom, which in no other land will thrive,
> Freedom, an English subject's sole prerogative,
> Without whose charms ev'n peace would be
> But a dull quiet slavery.
> > *Threnodia Augustalis* (lines 300–303)

Though Congreve at twenty-five already surpassed Dryden in comic consciousness and in composition too, his debts to the older poet are everywhere to be seen. One important example is his dramatic principle, identical to what Dryden had set forth earlier, of bringing out a principal character's individuality by careful management of the ethos of the play as a whole:

> ... though we allow every man something of his own, and a peculiar humor; yet every man has it not in quantity to become remarkable by it. Or, if many do become remarkable by their humors, yet all those humors may not be diverting. Nor is it only requisite to distinguish what humor will be diverting, but also how much of it, what part of it to show in light, and what to cast in shades; how to set it off by preparatory scenes, and by opposing other humors to it in the same scene.[13]

Congreve established a form of comedy in which each character exists so as to set off and augment the others, achieving thereby the maximum of variety in a unified whole while maintaining individuality in the parts. His Millamant and Mirabell are not just a pair of witty lovers, as Dryden's had been, but two distinct individuals who set one another off to

[13] Lauter, p. 213.

perfection. Even in his pairing-off of fops one sees mutuality and reciprocation without rancor or rivalry and, much more important artistically, without mere duplication. Each character is given his own track and a clear right of way. They find no cause in each other for what Socrates called envy, and give none to the audience, for each of them rides a hobby-horse he or she is happy with. They are thus admirably adapted to the purposes of the comic discussion. To serve the necessary function of intrigue, however, Congreve allows envy to appear in crass forms that hardly seem to impinge on the area of comic discussion except to heighten the latter's interest in freedom by injecting a concern for certain niceties of the law concerning marriage. The concern is alas necessary to protect wealth, which itself is required for the leisure and freedom of the people Congreve portrayed.

It will not be premature to introduce at this point in the general investigation of comic ethos an inquiry into the nature of the discussion itself, especially as it relates to characterization, individual personality, self-consciousness, and freedom. These issues are deeply involved in the transition (perhaps the revolution) from classic to modern ethos that has profoundly affected the nature and significance of the comic. We have seen the classical ideal as exemplified by Plato in the behavior of Socrates among his companions and as presented with analytic thoroughness by Aristotle. This ideal was provided with a new literary form in the dialogues of Plato and a somewhat different one in those of Cicero, a subgenre that served Dryden for his *Essay of Dramatic Poesy* in 1668. The ideal is still marked by its Athenian origin as civic and political; freedom is established in the security of the city defended by the association of good men. Those who participate in the leisurely banquets and conversations strengthen their mutural esteem, which is based on considerations of family and rank, wealth and education, by the added bond of their common experience in managing the city and defending it against its enemies. As Aristotle explains, they have enough in common to make them appropriate as friends to each other, and sufficient leisure to make it possible for them to enjoy the delight of companionship in conversation. Such conversation is itself the goal, and as final end or entelechy it is also the founding motive of all their work and strife as citizens, indeed as human beings.

For ethos in general, or for comic ethos, this classic ideal had three great deficiencies: it was exclusively masculine, it was aristocratic, and it was public—or, at least, never intimately private. It had a further defect as theater in lacking business for actors. Such conversation was better adapted to the discussion of facetiousness than it was to merrymaking itself. It nevertheless figured in the minds of playwrights and audiences as an ideal, a tone, a limit situation. During the eighteenth century, however, it developed most rapidly in two new literary forms, the familiar essay and the novel, where these limitations of scope, tone, and intimacy were overcome; the comic discussion was then ready for a new career as the chief source of fictional personalities.

Nobody has thought more effectively on the subject of literary conversation and personality than Roman Ingarden. Because it is inadequately known, I shall quote a rather long passage from *The Literary Work of Art* (pages 390–392, added in an appendix in 1959); it will form the basis for a great portion of what I have to say about the importance of the new comic ethos in modern writing. It begins with a recognition of language as gesture or speech act, and then of intersubjective behavior:

> where a psychic state is expressed verbally or mimetically, its function in social intercourse is not so much that of an objectivity to which we are attuned in an expressly cognitive way; rather, it is something noticed in passing which stimulates us to further action. The act of answering (including the verbal one) also evokes an analogous reaction on the part of the first interlocutor, so that in the course of the (active) conversation there occurs a psychophysical joining of the two speakers and an interplay of answering reactions and of the experiences, thoughts, feelings, desires, etc., manifested in

them. Hence there is *one* conversation process of argument, conflict, or collaboration between speakers. These speakers and the psychic changes occurring in them constitute only a relatively dependent factor in this process.

From this analysis we see that the discussion is a form of behavior or action with a unity of its own, that of *"one* process" which may be given a unifying synthesis or plot like the *synthesis praxeōn* linking the actions in a drama or fiction. Thus there can be no necessary reason that a discussion play should lack plot or action. We see also that the interaction of speakers is more important than the personality or changing psychic state of characters taken singly. This accords with Aristotle's contention that character is subordinate to plot, but it is expressed in a modern formulation that does full justice to our deepened idea of personality:

> . . . there are also indirect consequences of the conversation, or of the spoken words, which occur only a certain time after the conversation. These later consequences can also be intended by the represented person's speech. . . . The existing "dramatic" literature, with its extraordinary wealth of different forms of human intercourse in speech acts, can best inform us of the manifold functions of speech in human life. . . . It will be necessary, however, to add one more observation, which points in a perhaps unexpected direction.
> There is a special consequence of the fact that men speak to each other and, in doing so, manifest their own thoughts and experiences; this is the self-influencing of the speaker by his "expression" of himself. First of all, our thoughts, and frequently our decisions as well, ripen in the speaking. They unfold in the words that are uttered and take on developed form in them. To be sure, this can also occur in "silent" thought; nonetheless, speaking with another is a kind of thinking "out loud" which we ourselves hear and of which we can be much more conscious than when we merely think

something to ourselves without having to externalize it in verbal form. Second, we feel much more at ease when our speech and the thought developing in it can be effective—if it is understood by the other person and if it can incline him toward a certain action or conviction. For it to be effective, however, it must be perfected in verbal form; it must unfold in individual parts, clarify itself, justify itself, and in this way attain persuasive power and impact. In speech we become clearly conscious of matters which frequently slip away from us in the "silent" life and which, like uncompleted acts, burden our intellectual and moral conscience. This is therefore the first form of *self-influencing* by speaking with another person: our thoughts, and we ourselves, ripen. This becoming-conscious that is achieved in speaking often has the effect of suddenly making one sensitive and awake to one's own errors, thus inducing one to make the first step toward an internal transformation which, without this self-expression, would perhaps not as easily be attained. Expressing ourselves before another person frequently liberates us: the heretofore unexpressed, which lay heavily on the soul, now falls away; after a long and dogged silence something that was concealed from us enters, through conversation, into the bright light of day and is cast aside like wornout clothes without any particular exertion. By speaking with another person, we not only reveal ourselves to him—be he friend or foe—but to ourselves as well. And this frequently unties our hands and warms our hearts.

At this point, even though Ingarden does not mention it, we can see that several concepts formulated long ago in thinking about drama are prominent: development, discovery and transformation or reversal, freedom, purgation, reconciliation. We are conscious also that in this process enough self-recognition and fellow feeling is bound to develop so that our attitude as audience for comedy can hardly be the classic one of malicious or envious ridicule. Ingarden's description restates what we can now see as having occurred historically, that the new emphasis upon character as personality rather than as type goes along with the substitution of humor for the ridiculous in comedy. At the same time, however, it creates very serious problems for the identification of the comic, as Ingarden's continuation shows:

> Basically this concerns all our feelings and attitudes: whether friendship or enmity, admiration or contempt, they want to be expressed, and only in this expression do they attain their ultimate fulfillment. In their fulfillment, however, the definitive formation of the given person is also effected; he, too, is ultimately formed, or he matures into a good or bad figure. In a play we are fundamentally witnesses to this sort of maturation of a person, though it need not necessarily be understood as positive growth or improvement. If, for example, we follow Peer Gynt's fate, we see how, in the various situations and discussions, he slowly ripens in his peculiar empty soul until at the end, in his last form, he is revealed to be barren. In a life of silence, without the frequent verbal encounters with other people, without the consequences of every discussion and the action effected in each discussion, he would not have been able to discover himself and to arrive at his tragic truth.[14]

The words in which Ingarden identifies *Peer Gynt* as a tragedy actually suffice to mark it as a comedy, according to the ideas presented in this book, for the principal figure remains the same through a series of tests or developments (the discussion Ingarden mentions), any one of which might have been expected to bring about an alteration of his barrenness. Recognition of the comic, it would seem, is an unavoidable problem of modern writing, one posed sharply in the work of Chekhov; but it was already apparent to Congreve in the

---

[14] This passage from Ingarden makes an illuminating contrast to Derrida's exposition and critique of Husserl on "expression." See *Speech and Phenomena*, pp. 35ff.

letter from which I quoted earlier. Without fully grasping the problem as one of literary theory, Congreve shows how impossible it is to solve either on psychological grounds or merely by asking about the laughable when he remarks: "A man may change his opinion, but I believe he will find it a difficulty to part with his humor. . . . Some weep, and others laugh at one and the same time."[15]

In the hundred years between Congreve's little essay and Friedrich Schiller's revolutionary reorganization of the literary genres there were of course many insights into the comic in its modern form, some much deeper, perhaps, than any in Congreve's letter. Yet we find enough in that letter to go straight from the one playwright to the other. Schiller was in his early thirties when he made his contributions to literary theory, profiting from his fascinated study of Immanuel Kant. Kant put Congreve's comic/tragic paradox into the metaphysical terms of ideally necessary freedom and naturally necessary law. As we have already seen, Schiller was able to demonstrate that the comic has a greater capacity than the tragic to deal with this paradoxical human situation.

[15] Lauter, p. 212.

4

THE ROMANTIC THEORY
OF THE COMIC

1. THE IMPORTANCE OF CHARACTER

WE HAVE CONSIDERED the importance of the discussion in bringing out dramatic characters to the full, especially in providing scope for the expression of their freedom, spontaneity, and self-maintenance as part of a comic action. It now remains for us to show that the literary personality, while never real in fiction—being only an intentional objectivity like any other in a play or a novel—is capable of manifesting more power as a literary device than almost any other kind of objectivity. After being highly privileged for a hundred years or more, this power is in abeyance today—at least for new writing, as Barthes maintained, though not for our appreciation of former writing. There are many reasons for the falling off of character, including the phenomenon of overexposure, or the simple fact that there comes a point with every good thing when we have had enough of it. This point was visible to Ortega when he wrote *The Dehumanization of Art* (1925). From the time of the lectures on Shakespeare given by Coleridge and Hazlitt, however, character had had a glorious run not only in the writing of new fiction but also in the criticism of drama. Both psychologists and ordinary readers found literary works to be an unsurpassed source of enrichment for their interest in human personality. The individualist quality of interplay between literature and personal life continued to find its focus in the personalities of fiction.

We have already noted the mistranslation involved in the use of our modern term "character" for Aristotle's "ethos." It was during the nineteenth century that it became prevalent. Essentially "ethos" means a mode of behavior, either individual or (more frequently) common to a group or type. "Character," on the other hand, derives from the Greek term for a particular letter in the alphabet and includes the notion of something individually, even arbitrarily, fixed and marked—a schematic outline capable of being correctly perceived, however differently it may appear in accidentals. The letter *e* is recognizable, for example, in any of a thousand different styles of printers' type, and in numberless uniquely personal signatures. The term "character" was appropriate enough for Theophrastus' collection of stereotyped human profiles. We cannot, however, speak in the same sense of "the character of Socrates in Plato's *Dialogues*," or "the character of Trimalchio in Petronius' *Satyricon*," because these two are anything but arbitrary schemata or stereotypes. They are only recognizable as themselves. Obviously, our word "character" has changed its meaning. The same is true, and in a peculiarly striking way, of the word "person." As is well known, *persona* originally meant one of a dozen or so type-masks an actor wore when he played a role in the Roman theater. The word "person" now has as profound and sacred a meaning among us generally as it is possible to have today. With both words, the process of enrichment was one of substantiation or individualization of the self, and it involved every manner of human agency over two and a half millennia: religious, political, social, intellectual, and artistic institutions collaborated with individuals of outstanding gifts in bringing about the change.

To refer to characterization as a privileged device is perhaps useful just now, but no one can deny the centrality of this device in literature as a whole. We need, in fact, a much clearer understanding of the ways in which it stands out among the other objectivities produced in literary composition. Perhaps we need simply to recognize the important sense in which characters are only, as Ingarden calls them, "formal structures" and "subjects of attributes" in all fiction, and hence not essentially privileged but members of a class of the most necessary fictive (rather than "fictional") entities that includes narrative itself. For literary discussion, Husserl's word "objectivity" may be defined as "a fictive subject of attributes." As Ingarden says, "We impute to the given qualities, so to speak, the formal structure of a subject of attributes, which is materially determined in its nature in a way suggested to us by the apprehended quality."[1] Our "imputation" is part of a constitutive activity in reading or listening whereby we put together a succession of frameworks for the whole experience we are engaged in cocreating. We continuously modify the nature of this structure-of-the-whole so as to follow and include the suggestions that come to us as we gradually perceive the new qualities our reading presents. Suggestions received are not simply apprehended as givens, but rather as taking shape to a greater or lesser degree in accordance with what the reader reads into them. Depending on the work and also on his or her own knowledge, literary culture, and alertness, the reader's imputations will be in need of revision or rejection as the reading process goes on. Obviously, this activity on the reader's part is a kind of re-presentational process; but what is being presented by the work, as well as what is being represented by the active reader, is never a fully determined portrait, neither in a work of painting nor a fortiori in a work of literature. Even when a realistic portrait is the purpose of the painter or novelist, undue persistence in their filling in of descriptive detail would only prevent the work from being a work of art at all, as Balzac shows in his philosophical tale, *The Unfinished Masterpiece*.

The process of cognition in reading a novel is therefore better understood as cocreation rather than as representation. Ingarden describes it clearly and convincingly, and as we read his description we see that our cognition of characters is not essentially different from the process whereby we

[1] *The Cognition of the Literary Work of Art*, §26, p. 202.

come to know any other part of a work of fiction; all that can
be said is that a memorable character is a subject of attributes par excellence in fiction, but never *hors de concours* with
other kinds of objectivities. The generality of Ingarden's
language makes for some difficulty, but it shows that what is
said about the subject of attributes applies also to an institution, a scene, a phase of plot, an atmosphere, and indeed
anything that offers the reader a basis for cocreative, constitutive activity, for each of these objectivities will have a
character in the general sense of that word:

> . . . as soon as it is created by us in imagination, this
> new subject of attributes begins to appear even in the
> concrete qualities apprehended by us; it assumes the
> character of a particular object which is present to us.
> And correlatively: upon the phase of
> [1] categorial forming of the object which is por-
> trayed in the work of art, [there] follows . . .
> [2] the phase of perceiving (of receiving) the object by
> the aesthetically experiencing subject [i.e., the reader],
> as well as
> [3] the phases of [the reader's] varied emotional reac-
> tion to the imagined quasi-existing object.[2]

These three phases, "categorial forming of the object which
is portrayed," perceiving aesthetically by the reader, and the
"varied emotional reaction," are separated here for the sake
of analysis, although in the most enjoyable reading they
would seem to be simultaneous. What helps to unify and (in
the more particular sense of the word) to characterize this
threefold process is the phenomenon of empathy, which Ingarden accepts from Theodor Lipps, though only in one restricted sense: "This is especially evident when we impute a
psychological or psychophysical subject to the qualities
given us. We then 'empathize' into those qualities not only
this subject, but also his definite psychological states and

---

[2] For this and the other references in the next three paragraphs, see ibid.,
pp. 202–218, where the argument may be found in full.

acts, . . . whose 'external expression' . . . appears among the qualities we are given."

Although Ingarden's favorite in fiction seems to have been Thomas Mann, and *Buddenbrooks* his exemplary novel, his predilection for realistic writing does not prevent his description from applying adequately to other kinds of narrative, even the most abstract. Like Aristotle, who had a predilection for *Oedipus the King*, Ingarden nevertheless achieves the degree of generality that valid theory requires. Thus when he describes what Lipps called "aesthetic reality" he takes care to qualify it as not quite real, and his differentiation of phases enables us to recognize that the experience of empathizing with a literary character as if he were a real person is only a phase, and a dispensable one, of the total experience of reading; it is a phase limited to a certain kind of literary experience, associated with a particular group of works of art. What sets it apart (or perhaps gives it privilege) is the fact, not necessary in every literary work of art, that the objectivity we are cocreating or constituting is a person we place in his or her own imagined world, not in the institution of literature or the history of culture. In this sense it is an experience of intersubjectivity that every reader has had, and Ingarden's continuation is therefore valid:

> We are struck by the phenomenon of this expression; when it is apprehended in emotional sympathy, it leads to "empathizing" [the feeling] of the person we have imagined into the perceived phenomenon, and transforms it thoroughly. But as soon as the act of empathy is performed, there takes place that strange direct intercourse or companionship with the imagined person and his condition. Feelings arise. . . . Everything is almost as if this imagined person and his life existed in reality.
>
> These acts of emotional coexperiencing are the first form of the emotional response of the aesthetically experiencing subject to the constituted aesthetic object.

The acceptance of this kind of literary (or aesthetic) experience is now under heavy attack. Ingarden himself would be the first to admit that the phrase "that strange intercourse or companionship with the imagined person and his condition" is entirely metaphorical. It has a certain solidity, however, with the thinking on art of Kant, Schiller, and Hegel and with the thought of the whole romantic tradition on the function of the imagination not only in art, but in the free, moral, and human existence of the person. In the mode of thinking that produced the modern idea of the person, such imagined intercourse is a necessity if any one of us is to complete the dialectic that alone results in our seeing ourselves as individual persons, capable of intersubjective activity with other individual persons. The old name for direct intercourse or companionship was conversation, meaning those persons with whom one associated and had frequent exchanges of familiar talk. The profound notion of concrete thought in Hegel is an activity like mental conversation with an imagined interlocutor, as Plato too had defined it. The notion of freedom and of moral judgment in Kant is bound up with a similar ability to imagine things other than they actually are, so that possibilities of responsible action may be weighed in the form of alternatives actually present to the mind. The relation to real human life thus established for the imagination has lost its authority for many critics today, but it has proved very difficult if not impossible for them to do without it.

As a matter of fact, we need just such a description as Ingarden's to understand why the device of characterization has fallen into disfavor along with realism in general. One of the most obvious marks of modern bourgeois culture is its self-critical attitude, particularly among the intelligentsia. Once it was discovered that realism and its stylistic techniques, emphasizing exact, socially determined features, had a pervasive reinforcing effect—even when the author's conscious purpose was a reforming one—realism was discredited. From Ingarden's description just quoted, it is easy to see that the most direct lines for the conduct of empathy are those that have been predetermined by the reader's social sympathies and experiences. A responsible critical writer will seek to baffle such routine predeterminations either by challenging them directly, undercutting then ironically, or giving them as little as possible to take hold of.

Indeed Ingarden soon goes on to emphasize that the experience of "direct intercourse or companionship" with a portrayed character results from only one of many possible formings of "the structure of the qualitative harmony in the content of the aesthetic object." A comic forming tends to qualify the reader's response. To take a literary example congenial with Ingarden, one might cite Hanno Buddenbrook in the realistic passage that presents his last day at school (the best thing, it seems to me, in the whole novel). The details are real enough to bind us to a sentimental, reinforcing empathy; but the comic situation frees us from it. Hanno is a genuine, though still incomplete, artist; he should really be in a conservatory instead of the (admittedly very good) *Hochschule* of his native city. All the classical and scientific learning that is being forced upon him is the product and the means of self-maintenance of the bourgeous society; but Hanno himself, the musician, is transcendently the product that might redeem that society from the verdict of its own best conscience. The way Mann presents the case, the ordinary self-maintaining operation of the social institution seems to destroy the only kind of result that might justify the institution and the society. Hanno is the last of the Buddenbrooks, and with him the greatness of the bourgeois phase of human history seems to die out. In full accord with its own best ideals, it was an artistic greatness with standards too high for the society that made it possible. If we compare Hanno, however, with that other suffering boy who dies of meningitis in *Doctor Faustus*, the comparison helps us to realize that Hanno is a comic not a pathetic figure. His death is not meant to glorify, tragically, the closing of an era. This critical meaning, I am sure, belongs to Mann's understanding of bourgeois decadence as a comic rather than a tragic phenomenon.

Yet, to return to our proper subject, no one could mistake the comic quality of that last day when Hanno was truly himself: a potential genius, but still only a boy, compelled to do his homework and recite in class, inefficient, irresponsible, frustrated, caring and not caring. He is about as happy as most schoolboys; certainly he is not tragically unhappy. It helps much that Mann gives him a rather ordinary school-boy companion with whom the young genius is perfectly on a par. Their conversation helps in the comic forming, and this comic aspect is the central and richest formation of the objectivity grounded in *Buddenbrooks* and given the name Hanno. Furthermore, the impact of this objectivity (or characterization) is sufficient to tip the balance and to make *Buddenbrooks* a comic rather than a tragic work of art. A good case can be made for arguing that at the end of the nineteenth century the young Thomas Mann saw with confidence and optimism the end of the bourgeois epoch (in its most limited and purest character) and the immanent necessity of its transcending itself into something less limited and less pure. Yet the reader with a different social interpretation may still agree that Mann succeeds brilliantly in the comic portrayal of that objectivity I have called "Hanno's last day at school." And I believe most readers will recognize the artistic power of this kind of fictional objectivity, even if some reject its use today as "imperialist," unwritable, and bygone.

Let us proceed, then, in the knowledge that the characters of fiction or drama are portrayed objectivities. Like other representations of natural realilty, they are "subjects of qualities," set up in the text and then coconstituted by the reader. The bringing into being of such an objectivity is, as we said in the first chapter, *a sine qua non* of the comic. Without it there can be no self, no self-maintenance, no threat of alteration, and no continuity despite threat of alteration. It seems evident in fact that a certain robustness, purity, or even simplicity, on one side, or a highly stable intricacy on the other, when found in the objectivity as such, is even more important to comic success than the variety and ingenuity of the threats applied against it.

2. The Romantic View Of Comic Ethos

The preceding argument establishes a theoretical basis for considering fictional characters on the same footing as other intentional objectivities. In its absence we should have to think of romantic theory as lacking in the reflectiveness that would make it modern, for in fact it is often marked by a naive insistence on treating fictional characters as if they were real invididuals. This is particularly true of English criticism—and not surprisingly, for the greatness of English literature is often thought to reside in the force of its unforgettable characters. Our discussion in the previous chapter, centered on ethos, showed that emphasis on individual behavior shattered the classical basis of comedy in the ridiculous. It also suggested a development toward humor that would hardly have been possible without the peculiarly English contributions of humane sentiment and eccentric individualism. This development, which was far enough under way in the seventeenth century for Congreve to build upon it, became very prominent in the literature of the following two hundred years. It tended, however, to inhibit the critical understanding of the comic. By placing more emphasis on character, it encouraged the reader to identify with and sentimentalize individual comic objectivities. When prominent critics can regard the rejection of Falstaff as high tragedy or at least Sophoclean irony, distortion of this kind is obvious. The same is true of "enskyed and sainted" Isabella in *Measure for Measure,* as I hope to show later. Even so, the romantic criticism of comedy and the comic is probably the best we have. Certainly some of it has more than a merely historical value today, especially if we avoid its psychologizing tendencies and examine what it tells us of the ethos of the comic.

First, we ought to revert briefly to Shaftesbury's view of urbane wit and raillery in his *Characteristics* (1711). The third earl was a leader in recommending humane sentiment to the world, and the most important European voice in re-evaluating ridicule as a nonviolent weapon to be used in the social reform of political injustice and oppression. Shaftesbury, not surprisingly, failed to acknowledge the success of Dryden's *Absalom and Achitophel* in undermining his grandfather's Whig maneuvers. He preferred to compliment a fellow peer, the Duke of Buckingham, for introducing in *The Rehearsal* a new style of comically oversimplified and allusive raillery in place of the exaggerated and scabrous ridicule that marked the old political satire. The new style was a social advance, since it operated without violence in the serene atmosphere that makes for the most civilized and humane political state and thereby helped make possible a free marketplace of ideas. As Shaftesbury argued, raillery is more compatible than scurrility with the free discussion of actions and opinions, for it keeps the discussion good-natured. What Buckingham had done (and he deserves great credit for it) was to provide a language, format, and tone for the comic criticism of government, using devices that still serve political humorists like Art Buchwald today. The method consists in singling out a trait in a public figure and then not so much exaggerating as oversimplifying it while transforming the simplified figure into a naive spokesman for obnoxious public policy. Shaftesbury, in connecting the ethos of freedom with the comic treatment of the relationship between governors and governed, stated an ideal that has come to be identified with democratic behavior.

Proceeding to the era of full-blown romantic thought on the comic, we find Hazlitt, in his remarkably absorbent way, already turning one part of Schiller's thesis on the naive and the reflective against the other in "On Modern Comedy." He states a problem that shows his dedication to the old-fashioned forms of classic comedy: Why are there so few good modern comedies? His answer is that men and women have become too reflective. Hazlitt criticizes the people of his own time because, he says, he and they "exist, not in ourselves, but in books—all men become alike mere readers—spectators, not actors in the scene, and lose all proper personal identity." According to this almost Nietzschean insight, Hazlitt's contemporaries prevented others' ridicule by laughing at themselves first; their characters were too shallow, too "unselved." They are no less foolish than their ancestors, only clever enough to avoid commitment to any characteristic mode of folly. Hazlitt is clearly looking back

to the ridiculing comedy of the classic time with nostalgia—
that is, reflectively and romantically. In particular, he shows
that pervasive nostalgia for the naive that is still the mark of
the romantic today: "There is a period in the progress of
manners . . . in which the foibles and follies of individuals
are of nature's planting, not the growth of art or study; in
which they are therefore unconscious of them themselves,
or care not who knows them, if they can have their whim
out. . . . This may be called the comedy of nature, and it is
the comedy which we generally find in Shakespeare."[3]

Hazlitt fortunately forgot his nostalgia long enough to
supply us with an excellent name for the important comic
phenomenon he points to but does not quite uncover in the
passage above: he used the word "keeping" to describe the
quality in a character of always being himself or herself, despite dislocations of situation and behavior.[4] This integrity
and substantiality of self, which is threatened on many sides
during the cultural period we still share with Hazlitt, was
thinning out in drama but triumphantly increasing in fiction.
Dickens' comic characters seem the direct answer to Hazlitt's nostalgic longing; Jane Austen's, indeed, should have
silenced his complaint.

This very important phenomenon of "keeping" in comic
characters becomes clear in Hegel's lectures on aesthetics,
dating from about 1820. Hegel's ideas on comedy are perhaps not so original as his theory of tragedy, but they pull
things together in his powerful way. He makes distinctions:
the comic is different from and profounder than the ridiculous. As for laughter, it is "little more than an expression of
self-satisfied shrewdness."[5] Envious scorn of others and

---

[3] See "On Modern Comedy," *The Round Table,* Everyman ed. (New York:
Dutton, 1957), pp. 10–14; the quotation is from p. 12.

[4] "On Wit and Humour," in *Lectures on the Comic Writers,* I; Lauter, p. 270.

[5] Hegel's phrase is "eine Aeusserung der wohlgefälligen Klugheit,"
Sämtliche Werke, Jubiläumsausgabe (Stuttgart: Frommann, 1954), XIV, 534;
translation in Lauter, p. 351. Lauter's selections (pp. 350–354), though adequate for my citations here, are from the superseded Osmaston translation
(four vols., London, 1920). Where differences from Hegel's German are

pleasure in their misfortunes, an important part of the ridiculous, are not comic at all according to Hegel. On the contrary, the comic is marked by infinite geniality and confidence. It rises superior to its own contradiction without
bitterness—that is, it transcends its antithesis, or overcomes
defeat by an antagonist, while maintaining good humor. The
comic frame of mind is happy, fully aware of itself. It can
suffer the dissolution of its aims. The truly comic character
is most the master of itself when it is most laughable to
others. Hegel does not emphasize the comic value of intellectual understanding at the expense of deeper intuition and
feelings, as Bergson later did. Instead he finds satire an extremely arid genre, in part perhaps because it is more intellectual. In developing Schiller's stress on self-possession and
on the freedom of the reflective person within positive
worlds of his or her own devising—or indeed in quite substantial worlds as was the case with Aristophanes—Hegel
lays the groundwork (as Anne Paolucci has convincingly
shown) for a much fuller comic theory than he actually de-
livered in his aesthetic lectures.

In line with the English humorists, Hegel seems to treat
the comic as in the main a function of characters. He does
say of situations, however, that a certain contradictory quality heightens the comic effect, as when earnest preparations
fail signally to achieve their intended end. This had been
Kant's explanation of the phenomenon of laughter. It does
not take us very far; what enriches Hegel's thought on comedy is the dialectic itself, which fills his terms "contradiction" and "antithesis" with meanings applicable to the
comic in general. His comments on comedy are not reduc-
ible to the vague notion of incongruity already to be found
in Hazlitt and before him in Maurice Morgann. Instead, he

---

material, I have made modifications. Henry Paolucci's translation is nearly
complete in this area, in *Hegel on the Arts* (New York: Ungar, 1979), pp.
89–108: see pp. 181–184, 191–193, 197–199. See also the very valuable article by Anne Paolucci, "Hegel's Theory of Comedy," in *Comedy: New Perspectives*, edited by Maurice Charney (New York: New York Literary Forum,
1978), pp. 89–108.

insists on the need for a comic resolution or final reconciliation. The contradictions must be resolved, however, with no
damage to "substantive being or the personal life" of the
comic characters. Hegel then makes a very strong claim for
the comic personality: "In the essential self-stability of the
individual characters the exalted principle remains which in
its freedom . . . continues itself in its character of self-security and self-blessedness."[6] To begin with Hegel is gathering
and preserving the ideas we saw in Congreve and Hazlitt:
the idea of humor as a very personal quality, nourished in
freedom and not to be found without it; and of "keeping"—
or as Hazlitt also defined it "the truth of absurdity to itself"—which truth-to-itself must be "kept up" and continued in the comic. Hegel adds the two elements of security
and "blessedness," with little more by way of explanation.
The continuity, the survival-as-himself, of the comic *character* is thus the key to transitional and early romantic concep-
tions of the comic, even in Hegel.

The use of the word "substantive" above requires comment. Whereas Dryden used the phrase "a substantial ass"
as a metaphysical flourish to praise Sir Fopling Flutter, by
Hegel's time its philosophical meaning no longer suggested
the "substantial union" of body and soul in the identity of a
human or divine person. To Hegel it meant something like
"established firmly by social sanction and internalized."
Hegel should not be read, therefore, as if he were under the
impression that authors create comic characters and give
them personal life. Rather he seems to be distinguishing the
fates of comic and tragic figures. Unlike the tragic, the comic
hero is not punished "substantively" by exile or ostracism or
any such deprivation of established components of his identity as defined in the Greek city. His self-sense is to be continued and if anything enhanced in the development of the
play. Hegel regards the world of comedy as man-made and
fully conscious. In it purposes are "thrown awry" and "lack
substance" because they reflect purely human knowledge
and achievement and subsist on a finite human basis. In the

[6] Lauter, p. 354; German text, p. 537.

comic world, therefore, Hegel can say that "it is the purely *personal experience* that retains the mastery in its character of infinite self-assuredness,"[7]—or in practical terms that the individual does not run afoul of genuine oracles, religious creeds, or profound communal constraints. For the experiences of comedy, clear human vision is enough to constitute a horizon. The personality only needs to be reconciled to its world through experience and to recognize its own limitations. Compared to the human spirit as an absolute, the vision of comedy is narrow, a vision of "the victory of the intrinsically assured stability of the wholly personal soul-life, the laughter of which resolves everything through the medium and into the medium of such life." The personality and its purely personal experience are everything in comedy, Hegel implies.

Using strictly personal terms, he presents three possible types of the comic, all confined to ethos:[8]

1. Someone who seeks intrisically mean and empty goals with earnestness and many pains and when he fails "does not experience any real loss because he is conscious that what he strove after was really of no great importance, and is therefore able to rise superior with spontaneous amusement above the failure." Here is a weak situation, for it can only apply to failures who cease to care that they failed. Furthermore, Hegel uses the term "amusement" without any explanation or justification, unless we supply the weak Kantian explanation of the cause of laughter. Hegel's case would be more typical if we substituted the word "relief" for "amusement." Yet his case is not properly comic at all, but an instance of mild rejoicing after one is relieved of a delusion. What seems to be suggested is either the rather sentimental *Bildungsroman* type of mellowed worldly wisdom, or the typical blocking character who sees the light, changes his will, and goes along with the happy ending. Neither development touches the essentially comic in a novel or play.

2. Hegel's second type is the reverse, he says, of the first. It

---

[7] Lauter, p. 350; German, p. 533.
[8] Lauter, pp. 350–353; German, pp. 535–536.

occurs "where people vaguely grasp at aims and a personal impression of real substance, but in their own individuality, as instruments to achieve this, are in absolute conflict with such a result. In such a case what substance there is only exists in the individual's imagination," and therefore effects a comic contradiction. He gives the example of Aristophanes' *Ecclesiazusae*, where the women's effort to frame a political constitution breaks down when they exhibit typical feminine characteristics. We might suggest, as even better examples, Falstaff and Don Quixote. Some valid basis of reality does subsist in the function of the Lord Chief Justice which Falstaff seeks to take up, and in the service of chivalry as Quixote sought to embrace it. The institutions themselves are made problematic compared to the two comic figures, who are as solid as literary creations can be.

3. There is very little to recommend the third of Hegel's three comic types in which he finds there is "a comic contrast" between the personal character and the "varied and extraordinary development" of external conditions and accidents. Again we find the question-begging term "comic" in place of an explanation or justification that would show us the nature of the contrast between "objects desired and their achievement" or what is "equally comic" in the resolution. This third case suggests a rather promiscuous category wherein *Tom Sawyer Abroad* would take a fairly high place; it tells us little about the comic. It seems possible that Hegel was not sufficiently impressed aesthetically by most comic writing to avoid falling into a certain blandness.

Yet Hegel does treat comedy as a genuine art. As an art, he declares it may not misrepresent the rational as if it were inherently perverse and useless. Neither may it allow folly and absurdity to triumph, but must rather show that in so far as they are real at all they are made up of false contradictions instead of productive and dialectically directed oppositions. It is perhaps fair to surmise that Hegel preferred tragedy, where such productive oppositions were the subsisting conventions and content of the drama. Above all, the close link of tragedy to history suited his ideas of dialectical progression and negation. The only strictly comic writer whom he discusses with his habitual insight is Aristophanes: "The masculine art of Aristophanes . . . does not turn into ridicule what is truly of ethical significance [but places before us] those elements directly opposed to a genuine condition of political life, religion, and art . . . in their suicidal folly."[9] Again, and even more pointedly, we are left with the question, what then is comic (and not suicidal folly) in Aristophanes? Hegel's only answer—and it is anything but clear—is that the comic works against "the appearance and imagined presence of what is substantive" and "the essentially perverse and petty," and thus asserts "the essential self-stability of individual character." Soon this seeming presence of the substantive vanishes leaving the comic personality behind as master, but only over its disillusionment, "at bottom unbroken and in good heart to the end."[10] Aimed probably at Falstaff, this is more applicable to Prospero, who is hardly a good choice for the comic archetype; and it still leaves us with an account of the comic character rather than of the comic.

It is true that Hegel did not wish to extend to the nonpersonal ("the comic") what he referred to as "the more exalted principle" that "continues itself in its character of self-security and self-blessedness" in the comic personality. This principle was the character's "subjective life," which alone, perhaps, might be said to possess freedom, even in a literary work of art. But as we have already seen with the help of Ingarden, one cannot pretend to speak of fictional characters in such a way. It is also unnecessary to do so, for their "keeping" of their own character gives a sense of spontaneity to their behavior that is an adequate fictional equivalent of free will in persons.

With this modification, the elements of Hegel's analysis of the comic will serve to support the view reached in this book. I would reject, of course, his limitation requiring that

---

[9] Lauter, pp. 353f. (modified); German, p. 536f.
[10] Lauter, p. 354; German, p. 537.

comic oppositions must always reflect vain or inane imagi-
nations. On the contrary, good comic characters choose
quite substantive goals and sometimes reach them. A figure
who aims at something that his author allows to lack *literary*
substance will prove to be a negligible character, weak in
personality and void of the comic force. The hapless victims
presented by Jonson and Molière may go about achieving
their aims in foolish ways, but the aims themselves are
usually substantive: a fortune, a faithful wife, a quiet house-
hold. Falstaff and Tartuffe seek substantive position and
power.

3. KIERKEGAARD'S CONTRIBUTION

Hegel's ideas were brought to bear on the comic from another angle and with much broader feeling for the subject by
Kierkegaard. Like Congreve, he was about twenty-five when
he began the academic essay now called *The Concept of Irony*,
which contains a remarkable analysis of Aristophanes' comedy, *The Clouds*.[11] In the book, Kierkegaard's main theme is
the character of Socrates as a historical individual. Plato attributed too much to him, i.e., he made Socrates the inventor
of his own positive dialectic aiming at the Idea. But Aristophanes perceived Socrates correctly, as far as he went, as
an ironist. He parodied his character, his negative dialectic,
and his "standpoint" (attitude toward life as a whole) from a
comic angle.

At this early stage of his own thought, Kierkegaard was
already convinced that the comic does not merely dissolve
(as Hegel thought), but transcends and judges the ironic,
even though the latter judges everything else. The ironist
hugs human happiness to himself in its weakest form, that
of merely remaining alert to the many ways in which the actual fails to be the ideal. Comically, the ironist is proud of
himself for detecting the disproportion and is content to
stop at that point.

[11] Soren Kierkegaard, *The Concept of Irony*, translated by Lee M. Capel
(Bloomington: Indiana University Press, 1968), pp. 158–184.

In Hegel's *Lectures on Aesthetics,* as we have seen, we find great praise for Aristophanes. Kierkegaard had not yet read these lectures, but he was familiar enough with the other materials already published by Hegel's students to organize his own critique of *The Clouds* along Hegelian lines but with a far livelier response to the comic than Hegel's. He does not make Aristophanes' comedy over into an exposure of the "suicidal folly" of Greek democracy. Though he says little about the comic as such, he exhibits a clear working knowledge of what it is and how it differs from the satiric and the ironic.

In Hegel's view of history as Kierkegaard presents it, pre-Socratic Greek society did not consist of individuals who were free in the modern sense of the word. On the contrary, their consciousness was immediate, that is, unreflecting and unexamined. It was also substantial because it was grounded in certain value principles of unquestioned authority that were thoroughly "established," as we too should say, in the everyday life of the community by reward or punishment, esteem or disesteem.[12] Such people, however, were hardly free individually in the full sense, though being Greeks they might have had a strong sense of political independence as citizens of their *polis.* Hegel called this condition a "concrete ethic," and distinguished it both from the "higher concrete ethic" he found in Aristotle and the new state of mind whose first real spokesman was Socrates.

Socrates submitted these "natural" constraints of Greek society to an all-pervasive examination. He created the strange possibility, which Hegel attributed to his own notion of "conscience" (i.e., an arbitrarily personal index of right and wrong), that anything may be evil to a person if his thinking makes it so. Coming after this Socratic negation, Aristotle was able to effect the Hegelian *Aufhebung.* He abrogated the naively given attitudes of the older Greek society in a series of philosophical inquiries. His argument also imposed a rational form of constraint upon the newly awakened conscience. It fitted together with the life it examined

---

[12] P. 248.

so as to make a totality, but this totality only assumed its full character in the individual and his freedom. Only in the magnanimous man, a person combining mind, passions, and ethos, could human life achieve wholeness.[13]

When we go over this now familiar ground with the comic in mind, it seems that the totality of some "natural concrete ethic" forms the moral setting for the great bulk of comic writing. The activity of eccentric conscience, on the one hand, though generating a few ironists such as Mr. Bennett in *Pride and Prejudice*, tends to be more productive of quacks, hypocrites, and humours eccentrics. On the other hand, the magnanimous man of Aristotle's higher concrete ethic is almost by necessity absent from fiction altogether, and for a reason perceived by Kierkegaard at a later date: he is not interesting, and could only become so if he were to depart from the norm of serene freedom and leisure that he incorporates. Literary critics have had to extrapolate him contextually as the "implied author." Even then, he has seldom if ever seemed comic in himself.

With regard to an ethos of the comic in literature generally, therefore, we may conjecture that it will appear in fiction as a natural concrete ethic. Such an accepted model of values, "substantial" in Hegel's sense of the word, is an almost necessary background for the comic, all the more if highly eccentric or nonnatural objectivities are to be developed. An excellent example is *Alice in Wonderland*, and Alice herself, as has often been said, is a perfect specimen of the "natural" concrete ethic of Victorian England, besides having the genuinely natural value feelings of childhood then and now.

Hegel did more than anyone else to establish "self-determination" as the essential meaning of "freedom," and in his *Lectures on Aesthetics* he also made self-determination an important aspect of comic character. We can see, however, that in his view early Greek comedy was incapable of presenting characters who were morally free. With Aristophanes he

[13] Pp. 249–251.

recognized an evolution. For one thing (and this insight deeply impressed Kierkegaard), Aristophanes' comic figures have enough self-awareness to know they are comic, though probably not enough to laugh at themselves.

As part of a long deconstruction of Hegel, Kierkegaard ascribes his own critique of Socrates to Aristophanes and proceeds to interpret *The Clouds* accordingly. He justifies his critical formula, "sophistry in the sphere of action,"[14] by showing that it is posited in the play by the brilliantly developed objectivity of the "Thinkery" (*Phrontisterion*) over which Socrates hovers in the notorious basket, "freely above" the virtues—and everything else. With his negating dialectic Socrates loftily dismisses Athenian law, customs, and reality, preferring to worship wide, empty air and the resourceful tongue of man. The comic hero Strepsiades seeks instruction in order to learn ways of negating his large debts, and is introduced to the chorus of Clouds as the protecting goddesses of the Thinkery. To the uninitiated old man, however, they are only fog and mist. Kierkegaard interprets this cloud symbol as one of the main devices used by Aristophanes.[15] He denies the Hegelian interpretation that its effect was to vindicate "the substantial consciousness of the state" against "the vacuity of this modern nuisance" of sophistry. The Hegelian interpretation, he says, is "too ponderous." Kierkegaard argues that "it would limit the comic infinity which as such knows no limit," referring to the specious freedom that irony has.[16] Irony is structurally comic because it maintains itself against the threat of being engaged with any positive totality.

His objection revolves around his strongly positive reconstruction of the Clouds as an objectivity. It "concerns the whole inner economy of the work" that neither chorus nor spectator should fail to see that the Clouds continue to be clouds, whether they are called centaurs, wolves, or god-

[14] P. 250n.

[15] Pp. 163–168.

[16] P. 161. This Hegelian interpretation had been recently presented by a certain Rötscher, a disciple of Hegel; p. 160n.

desses; clouds are just right as a symbol for the substance-
less "substantiality" of the community of sophists and idlers
at the Thinkery. "Socrates" in the play is not fooled by
them; he worships their formlessness, "like so many predicates . . . all coordinated without being connected to each
other, without inner coherence and without constituting
anything." Through its "inner economy," then, Aristophanes' play has constituted something positive out of
something purely negative, and what it puts before us "is
nebulosity itself, which is an excellent description of the
Socrates Idea."[17] Therefore it is a device of the "utmost
comic force" to give Socrates a creed ("I believe in wide
Space . . . in the eloquent tongue") suited to this deity, and
later to make him swear in keeping with it.[18] If Hegel is right
in saying the Greek chorus is "the actual substance of the
heroic life and action," then Aristophanes has made a comic
substance out of insubstantiality by turning his chorus into
polymorphous clouds.[19]

4. SATIRE AND IRONY DISTINGUISHED
FROM THE COMIC

The Hegelian interpretation of *The Clouds* would "ponderously" reduce a comedy to political propaganda by tying
it to an actual polemic, either by Socrates against the Athenian establishment or by Aristophanes in its favor. On the
contrary, Socrates' irony was only directed against the old
Hellenism because of the built-in opposition between the
actual and the ideal, and not because he wanted to supplant
it with some other kind of social life. In truth Socrates was
no polemicist, only an ironist; hence his standpoint "continually cancels itself." And this, Kierkegaard finds, is "in its
deepest root comical. As irony conquers everythng by seeing its disproportion to the Idea, so it also succumbs to itself

[17] Pp. 165, 163, 166.
[18] Pp. 166–167n.
[19] P. 162 and translator's note 9, p. 385.

since it constantly goes beyond itself while remaining in itself."[20]

Irony partakes of a movement toward the Ideal and always implicitly suggests the direction of such a movement.
But it never suffers the change involved in making the movement. This is its identity, its substance. Therefore, according
to our argument in this book, irony has a comic aspect. One
would think it could not resist grasping at the Ideal, but this
is the threat to which irony never yields. It enjoys itself by
never asserting itself; its essence is not to struggle for something better.

The comic, however, always asserts itself. It uses irony as
it uses all disguises, not to go beyond itself but to assert its
own positive qualities all the more strongly by contrasting
them with assumed ones. It conquers disproportion by being
proportionate to itself and either finding or creating its own
proper setting. This is what Kierkegaard sees Aristophanes
doing with his conception of Socrates. He feels that the portrayal includes a surprisingly high proportion of observed
fact; yet here too "comic conception is also a moment, in
many ways an infinitely correcting moment, in the total illustration of a personality or tendency."[21] The truth of the
comic is a correcting truth that comes from presenting the
subject with returns in from all the precincts, as we say at
election time. This entire truth is likely to include elements
of degradation that are still less caricature than parody, for
everything human or mortal has a side that is "all too
human," all too personal, and all too mortal. Self-discovery
of this side of a person's life can effect a sort of conversion
and engender a comic self-knowledge we can literally call
"wholesome." The same is true of the perception of institutions and ideas; when they are seen as objectivities in a
broad perspective, an element of self-parody—for example
a senility or second childhood—often seems to emerge from
any one of them as a comic truth. Such is the case Kierke-

[20] P. 161.
[21] P. 158.

gaard makes for the Socrates of *The Clouds* and the ironic negativity of his dialectic, as Aristophanes has comically presented them.

Without making a point of it he also accounts brilliantly for the positive, independent comic creation of other objectivities within *The Clouds*. He notes that the comic character of Socrates is mainly confined to the earlier part of the play and is artistically balanced against the later development of Strepsiades, who stands for the older type of Athenian; that is, the objectivities are not merely verbal or abstractly symbolic but are presented concretely: they take on substance, they become what they are on the stage. In doing so, they are not polemic but comic. Socrates is made a complete dramatic character, a speculator and a charmer. His disciple Strepsiades' "keeping" endears him as well to Kierkegaard, who praises his commitment to the new wisdom of the Thinkery.

There is a striking dynamism at work in the practicality of Strepsiades' demand for wealth. An outstanding quality of irony is that it becomes overtly comical as soon as one attempts to relate it to a result. Here Kierkegaard hits upon the important device Cicero listed, the comic outcome of our taking a figure of speech literally and developing it as if it were an objectivity on the factual level. Socrates' ironic standpoint amounts to the adoption of a figure of rhetoric, irony, as a way of life. The old rhetoric divided figures into "verbal figures" and "figures of thought." Socrates' use of *ironea* made it a "figure of thought," as was only proper; but to make any one figure of rhetoric a standpoint or habitual way of looking at life is to invite the comic. The event that finally disabuses Strepsiades affords a fine example. His son Phidippides, a finished product of the Thinkery, is "in his debt" for a traditional Athenian upbringing that included many a thrashing. Father and son engage in a sophistic discussion that proves to Strepsiades that he should now be literally beaten so that his son may discharge the figurative "debt." So long as the contest is figural, all is in order. But when Strepsiades begins to feel the blows on his own skin,

he quickly realizes the difference between metaphor and actuality.

The point is not made by Kierkegaard in this way, of
course. He does, however, call attention to another event
with obvious though puzzling metaphorical significance, and
explicates it with his usual insight. To show Strepsiades the
power of the new way of thought, an initiate of the Thinkery
tells how Socrates can control things. When they needed a
meal, Socrates "bent a spit; he grasped it compass-wise/And
filched—a mantle" from a pile of clothes at the nearby gym-
nasium.[22] The joke makes no sense verbally, and it set the
ancient critics off on a false trail of textual emendations;
Kierkegaard, however, grasps the main point, that the spit-
compass, whether as a tool for actual cooking or for construction, is misappropriated by Socrates for thievery, in the
first place, and for inappropriate thievery at that, for one
cannot make a meal out of a mantle. But if we recognize the
image as a sight gag and visualize it, we set up a very amusing sequence of cancellations for the mind's eye. First the
spit, a tool for spearing a piece of meat. Socrates, however,
bends it in two, not like a spit, but like tongs, also used for
handling food. Yet Socrates bends it, after all, not like tongs
either, but like a compass, a more noble instrument, suited
not to a greasy cook by the fire but to an architect, perhaps
an Archimedes, who will use it to scribe the plan of a build-

[22] See p. 169 and note, referring to line 177 of *The Clouds*, and especially
Kierkegaard's note on p. 172. Herewith is my literal translation of the passage, based on the text in the edition of Aristophanes by Victor Coulon
(Paris: Collection des Universités de France, 1967), p. 171, ll. 177–180 (I
have suggested the double meanings in parentheses):

> *Disciple:* Sprinkling thin ashes over the table, bending a small spit
> (persuading a compass leg), then taking a compass ("a pair of com-
> passes," like a pair of scissors), he filched (seduced) from the palestra
> the garment!
>
> *Strepsiades:* What, then, must we wonder at of the famous Thales?

The tendentious wit of the passage relies on the fact that the Greek for
"bending" can also mean "persuading," for "filch" also "seduce," and for
"spit" any pointed instrument, especially the leg of a compass. The thrust
is plain: Socrates' rhetorical skills are useful mainly for useless thievery
and seduction; his wonder-working science is all a deceit.

ing in the ground. Another surprise, the noble instrument becomes a thieves' tool, and, last surprise of all, "filches" a perfectly impertinent garment. A gross abuse of reality and the tools of real life is effectively brought out, though the sequence of images is pure mental farce. On the stage, one must also imagine, the actor would mimic the utterly fatuous credulity and admiration of the Socratic disciple who tells the story. The comic objectivity, as we saw earlier, only takes its full shape in the completion of these performances by the reader, who in this case must pretend also to be a theatergoer.

We may point out (against Hegel) that the comic can reside in nonhuman objects, as it does here, so long as this kind of "concretizing" performance is set to work in the reader. The principle is still self-maintenance despite the threat of alteration. We can call a long stick of wood a "spit" or a "tongs" or a "compass," depending on the shape given to it or the use made of it. But if it is mealtime, the stick of wood called a spit has a character quite out of keeping with compasses. If we further employ the bent stick to grasp something, there is a strong expectation that it will be edible. But the mantle is neither edible nor of any use in construction. The joke is of a very familiar type, one which Freud will classify for us later. It depends on our giving to the word *spit* its determinate character of a food-handling tool, because of the mealtime objectivity, and then threatening that determinate identity. Only the bland, idiotic acceptance of the disciple can complete the joke by maintaining the claim that Socrates did in fact find a way of solving a mealtime problem with this food-handling tool. It is what Freud calls a bad joke, but it does have the effect of reminding us that a meal is a meal and a mantle is a mantle, no matter how sophisticated our logic may be. That is its "comical truth."

Kierkegaard's concern for realilty, as we know, took an existentialist turn. His insight is that the Ideal, as the Socrates of *The Clouds* conceived it, lacked the positive Ideality Plato later developed; in the Socrates of *The Clouds*, "the Idea is true. . . . But what is true in this way never passes out into any predicate, it never *is*." For this reason he feels Aristophanes' portrait of the historical Socrates is just in characterizing his dialectic but quite inadequate in presenting him as he was personally, a "divine missionary."[23]

Kierkegaard's attitude is typical of the realist movement during the romantic period. In fact all the great realists seem to achieve the effect wherein the idea passes out into its predicates, as Hegel would say. By rounding off their fictional presentation of events, institutions, and characters with unnecessary, even insignificant, pieces of factual existence that are perhaps mere detail, perhaps even grotesque excrescences, they often succeed in bringing reality to light in the comic aspect that a broad perspective gives to serious things. Whether this effect is a mere "reality effect," a form of illegitimate closure, as Roland Barthes contends, or actually a movement toward openness is something to be considered in each instance. There is an opposing strain of romantic writing, however, that is as inherently uncomic as it is unrealistic. Poe and Hans Christian Andersen are outstanding examples. Kierkegaard began his writing career with an attack on Andersen for disregarding the claims of reality that were specifically imposed by his story material.[24] He accused Andersen of lacking a developed view of life. The mature Kierkegaard wrote of humor as a necessary threshold or stage in the development of a full conception of human existence.[25]

Kierkegaard felt the present threat to realism (in the sense ordinary language gives to the word "real") as few modern philosophers have done. He referred to "that development which modern philosophy acquired in Kant" as "a subjectivity raised to the second power, a subjectivity of subjectivity, corresponding to reflection on reflection." The first time

---

[23] P. 255.

[24] See Capel's note 37, p. 387.

[25] For example, in his analysis of Don Quixote as well as in his developed notion of humor as the threshold of the religious stage of existence in *Concluding Unscientific Postscript*, translated by David F. Swenson and Walter Lowrie (Princeton: Princeton University Press, 1941).

this revolution happened, i.e., with Socrates, "the old disap-
peared and everything became new."[26] After Kant there
came another disappearance of the old and a new modernity. Its effect was to generate what Hegel called the "unhappy consciousness" and to undermine the higher concrete
ethic of the European classic culture. A further effect (as I
argue) was to render a naively natural concrete ethic impos-
sibly remote and yet at the same time sentimentally interesting and desirable. With it all, the comic correction would
become extremely complex, for its "natural" base in a concrete ethic had come to be doubly distanced by two stages of
reflection, the classical-philosophical and the romantic-
ironical. This is one of the secrets of the comic power in the
modern age, when writing has persisted in discovering and
exhibiting naive bases for the most complicated individual
and social behavior. In an age whose mark is nostalgia for
the naive, it is no wonder that comic writing, in its many
modern forms, is the richest fictional genre. The comic is
forever showing things as true to themselves immediately,
and false only as the product of deceptive reflection.

It is also true that in the modern age a consciously aesthetic outlook has become very prominent, replacing for
many educated people the substantial sanctions of received
religion and the formal ones of a higher concrete ethic. At
the beginning of his career, even Kierkegaard paid tribute in
The Concept of Irony to Hegel's romantic idea of "living poetically."[27] He acknowledged that Hegel had "mastered" irony,
and in a final chapter entitled "Irony as a Mastered Moment:
the Truth of Irony" he developed the idea that "what is valid
for an existence as a poet" is also "valid in the life of every
particular individual." Validity is closeness to actuality: "the
poet only lives poetically when oriented, and thus assimi-
lated, into the age in which he lives, when he is positively
free within the actuality to which he belongs." Alone, irony
permits a person to be free only negatively. When mastered,

---

[26] P. 260; see also p. 292.
[27] P. 290.

irony remains irony but is no longer the "infinite absolute negativity" of Hegel's definition. Instead it is for the personal life what doubt is for philosophy: "no true philosophy is possible without doubt . . . no authentic human life is possible without irony."[28] The rest of the paragraph consists of praise of irony that could be placed alongside Cicero's praise of poetry in the *Pro Archia*. It leads up to Kierkegaard's statement that irony (i.e., mastered irony) is used as a control over the merely aesthetic norm of behavior, just as humor acts as a control over the merely rational and ethical norm. To Kierkegaard, humor is based on "the disproportion between the self and the Idea of the self" (so far a strictly ironic formula) "as discovered by the self"[29]; in other words the ironic self is discovered to be comic when seen by the realistically oriented self, once it is across the threshold described above. As we shall see, Freud's view of humor was very similar. We see an ideal dynamism of personal life that insists on moving toward a broad perspective of the actual, and in its movement passes through irreplaceable phases of the ironic and the comic.

With this deepened insight into the ethos of the comic in its romantic form of personal interiority and humorous self-awareness rather than self-complacency, we can appreciate the originality with which Kierkegaard appropriated Hegel's rather cursorily developed ideas on the comic in general. For one thing, Hegel had not been prepared to admit that Socrates' irony was a genuine form of dialectic. He thought of it as a manner of speaking, a way Socrates had of setting up a personal relationship with people.[30] It was only a subjective form of dialectic. Socrates' essential greatness, Hegel thought, was in his professed ignorance of abstract terms and his careful explications aimed at making them concrete. Kierkegaard deconstructs this argument with a vengeance, insisting that the movement of Socrates' whole *life* was al-

[28] P. 338.

[29] P. 426, n. 14 (quoting *Journals*, III, B 19).

[30] Pp. 256, 283f., where Kierkegaard quotes Hegel's *History of Philosophy*; also Capel's note 27, p. 416.

ways to begin anew with what he and each of his successive
interlocutors actually were. To Hegel this repeated personal
reaffirmation was too temporal and unsystematic, a mere
façon de parler. To Kierkegaard, however, "indirect" *personal*
communication is the only kind to use if one is concerned to
make the ideal actual.

This concern with making language personal and concrete
was universal during the earlier romantic period; Hegel
himself conceived of philosophical language as affording the
reader actual moments of verification as he thought along
with the text. The function of his own writing, Kierkegaard
said, was to be "the transubstantiation of the given content" whereby the merely given might be transformed not
only into the personal reception of each true gift but also
would become a task of making data actual in the life of the
historical reader.[31] We can see why he stressed the importance of a fictional and particularly a comic approach, and
why Hegel's "ponderous" and "reasonable" approach might
actually be less "serious" to him than Socrates' personal and
conversational one. Hence the importance in the comic of
elements of indirection, implication, imagination, and un-
stereotyped characterization, which are among the best ways
of appealing to the mind to do its work to achieve both the
constitution of an objectivity and one's own free insight into
it.

This work by the reader is necessary in irony. As Kierkegaard points out, "The ironic figure of speech cancels itself. . . , for the speaker presupposes his listeners understand him."[32] When this presumption on the speaker's part
is based on coterie sympathy or mere fashion, however,
Kierkegaard is astonishingly severe. Such ironists he finds
elitist, smug, and exploitative. They concern themselves
with *naifs*, but never to instruct them, only to confound the
wise and to enjoy both the relish of the naive and their own
superiority over it. These are the "romantic ironists," whose

[31] P. 388, n. 47; p. 293.
[32] P. 265.

outstanding feature is their need for a "subjective freedom" that allows them to feel "above actuality," as if in their air-borne baskets they were at every moment able to cancel the past and make an entirely new beginning. They lack charac-ter, especially comic character, as we have presented it, in its "keeping."[33]

Once mastered and adopted as a standpoint, however, irony produces a determined character, one steadfastly directed, like the Socrates of Kierkegaard, against the whole given actuality of a certain time and situation. As has been suggested, the effect is no longer that "the ironic figure of speech cancels itself," for it is no longer a case of the mo-mentary or supposititious as with any mere figure of speech. Instead the ironic standpoint becomes comic when it is con-tinued. One should not speak, therefore, as Hegel does, of Socrates' "tragic irony," but of the irony of the world play-ing off its darling Socrates in mockery of the Athenian state.[34] To Kierkegaard, Socrates' continual assertion of the same character and role gave him importance not only in his own city but as a figure in the history of the world. This continual assertion and survival as the same being even against the threat of death would make Socrates a comic rather than a tragic figure.

Aesthetically, the comic appears to involve a painless contradiction from the point of view of the spectator or reader, as Hegel said. In identifying this contradiction as be-tween personal inwardness and outward expression, Kier-kegaard introduced a very important concept of the meaning of humor. According to him, the comedian's seeming pain-lessness often conceals pain; all humor, in fact, is concealed pain. Humor is different from the comic in being conscious of sin and not merely based on a natural concrete ethic. Fur-thermore, humor knows that all are guilty, not just the rogues and fools. This knowledge underlies Hamlet's sar-donic humor: "Use every man after his desert, and who

[33] Pp. 292–302, 305. One is reminded of Hazlitt's complaint about mod-ern comedy.
[34] P. 284.

should 'scape whipping?" Just so, humor dissolves particular guilt, person to person and human to divine, by hiding it within the general category or type. Humor is inclusive, tolerant—hence the audience's complicity and willingness to pardon all offenders, for they too are all offenders.[35]

If this development of the comic ethos toward the depths of inwardness via humor cannot be ascribed to anyone in antiquity, there can be no doubt that it became a striking phenomenon in eighteenth- and nineteenth-century fiction and theater, and in the midst of ostensibly tragic works. One has only to think of Ibsen's Mrs. Alving and Hedda Gabler, both tragic heroines viewing themselves with a sense of humor. More than anything else, perhaps, this comic inwardness has helped to erode tragic structures in the theater and fiction of modern times.

[35] See *Concluding Unscientific Postscript,* pp. 242, 259, 490ff., 533.

⌐5⌐

THE MODERN COMIC ETHOS:
BERGSON'S *LAUGHTER*

AFTER SCHILLER'S presentation of comedy as a new, reflective genre peculiarly associated with the ideal of freedom, and the successive developments of Hegel and Kierkegaard, the latter nineteenth century seems far richer in practice than in theory. Even Meredith's famous essay offers little that is new in the way of theoretical insight. Except for Nietzsche, whose impact came later, we must wait until the beginning of the twentieth century for a second wave of original thought on the comic. Then, with *Laughter* in 1900 and *Jokes and Their Relation to the Unconscious* in 1905, we gain in Bergson and Freud the two most important writers on our subject. Their originality is great enough to make us reconsider whether we can continue to present their contribution under the rubric of ethos. Still, the Hegelian concept of the natural concrete ethic remains indispensable, even when we deal with Nietzsche, Bergson, and Freud on their own ground. The idea of the substantive and established ethic as that which lends weight and seriousness to social behavior and helps us to distinguish between different types of ethos is more useful than ever, because it is exactly what each of these innovators calls into question. Nietzsche enlists the comic against substantive ethos, Bergson makes laughter a social defense, and Freud sees in jokes and humor mankind's necessary anodyne against society.

Ethos will continue to be a valid focus for our investigation if we recognize that in 1900 morality and society had al-

ready become problematic concepts, and that the relationship of art to each of them has become ambiguous enough
since 1900 to require redefinition with each new artist or
thinker. The beginning of the twentieth century marked a
conscious schism between artist and society, in that art
began to play an overtly critical rather than a reinforcing
role in Western culture. One could say that the price of imperialism began to be paid when Judaeo-Christian and European ethnocentrism laid itself open to every kind of inroad
from other cultures, and the new human sciences began to
undermine accepted habits of perceiving "natural" behavior, "human nature," and the "nature" of the world. In this
situation we find Bergson belying, with a sequence of central
images, his own system of exact rules according to which
laughter supported the present conditions of society. Coun-
ternaturalizing imagery authorized Freud to postulate
an amoral inner psyche and to encourage forms of infantile
release. It provided the apocalyptic scene on which
Nietzsche could appear and reappear as the profound
prophet and guiding spirit in modern philosophy and art.

With the twentieth century there came a reversal of the
accepted relation between society and human nature in
which the former was ideally an extension and fulfillment of
the latter. Before then comedy had seemed to celebrate a
communion that was inherent in everyday life. It had aimed
at follies that were clearly antisocial and had appealed to
common sense and good nature (that is, to the natural concrete ethic) for a sufficient sanction to justify laughter. Except in their social aspect, it had let positive evils alone.
When it had asserted freedom against various forms of servitude, its targets had seemed much less deadly than other,
major threats to human liberty. Comedy, as Schiller declared, was freer than any other form; but until it faced up to
real evil it somehow seemed trivial. Such at least was the
frame of mind Bergson adopted when he limited himself to
vaudeville.

Laughter must be one of the most ambiguous books ever
written. The fact that it is one of the most charming books
ever produced by a philosopher has probably helped to

conceal its deeper purport. Seemingly quite conformist, its theory puts laughter at the service of society, attaching it to the ridicule of socially unfavorable behavior. One suspects that Bergson is being ironic when he writes: "To the credit of mankind . . . there is no essential difference between the social ideal and the moral. We may therefore admit as a general rule that it is the faults of others that make us laugh, provided we add that they make us laugh by reason of their *unsociability* rather than of their *immorality*."[1] But Bergson goes on to develop a social ideal much closer to pliancy than to freedom and based on mere accommodation to others in the tightly packed urban life of modern man. He tells us rather contradictorily that the one thing modern society finds ridiculous in its human members is the rigidity it builds into its machines. As stated in the most important of Bergson's laws:

> Life . . . never goes backwards and never repeats itself. . . . A continual change of aspect, the irreversibility of the order of phenomena, the perfect individuality of a perfectly self-contained series . . . are the outward characteristics . . . which distinguish the living from the merely mechanical. . . . the counterparts of these . . . *repetition, inversion,* and *reciprocal interference of series* . . . are also the methods of light comedy, and . . . no others are possible.[2]

If we carefully examine the other laws (also called axioms, theorems, and rules), we shall find that Bergson regards as unsociable, and therefore proper targets for comic attack,

[1] Henri Bergson, "Laughter," translated by Fred Rothwell, in *Comedy*, edited by Wylie Sypher (Garden City, N.Y.: Doubleday, 1956), p. 150; this is the most widely available edition in English, and includes Meredith's "Essay on Comedy" (1877) as well as Sypher's "The Meanings of Comedy," valuable in its own right for the study of absurd and black comic writing of recent decades. In the French original, *Le Rire: Essai sur la signification du comique* (Geneva: Skira, 1945), see p. 90. (Chapters will also be given, in roman; this is from Chapter III.)

[2] II, 118; French, 62ff., where Bergson refers to his rule as "la formule abstraite, cette fois générale et complète, des procédés de comédie réels et possibles."

whatever is machinelike, materialist, antipersonal, oversys-
tematized, repressive, banal, meaningless, or automatic. Yet
one cannot overcome a feeling of amazement at the highly
systematized and inflexible procedure of Bergson himself as
he works out his rules. He insists tyranically upon his thesis:
"Disregard this arrangement [i.e., the famous "mechanical
encrusted upon the living"], and you let go the only clue capable of guiding you through the labyrinth of the comic";
again, "Let us now attempt to frame a full and methodical
theory, by seeking . . . the changeless and simple archetypes
of the manifold and transient practices of the comic stage . . .
to discover the abstract formula . . . a general and complete
one, for every real and possible method of comedy."[3]

It could easily seem that Bergson, after fifteen years of
philosophical examination, had come to agree with Aristotle
that laughter is fundamentally unworthy of the ideal person,
and that writing comedy was no longer a liturgical service to
the city and the gods but a rote-learned activity fit for a combination of scrivener and beadle. *Laughter* is a full-scale rhetoric of comic composition, probably the longest and most
detailed of the recognized treatments of the subject at the
time it appeared. It is the outstanding exception to the
often-noted unwillingness or incapacity of twentieth-century critics to lay down prescriptive rules. True, Bergson
sought to justify his approach by declaring that his ostensible field, light comedy in the French theater, was not a genuine art. Yet writers of the first rank did not take long to follow his rules (Gide was one of the earliest) and were at their
artistic best in doing so.[4] It is strange that among them were
some whose views of society were corrosively ironic, for
Bergson repeatedly proposes that laughter is a mere ferula in
the hand of society: "Laughter is, above all, a corrective";
"Its function is to intimidate by humiliating." He continues,

[3] II, i, p. 116; French, pp. 61, 62.
[4] See John Keith Atkinson, *"Les Caves du Vatican* and Bergson's *Le Rire,"*
Publications of the Modern Language Association of America, 84 (1969), 328–335.
The "external proof" Mr. Atkinson desiderates (p. 335) is unnecessary
here, where it is a question of the application of general principles, not of
the history of influence.

however, in a rather different strain, showing that he had not forgotten the *Philebus* and perhaps recalled Nietzsche as well: "Now it would not succeed in doing this, had not nature implanted for that very purpose, even in the best of men, a spark of spitefulness or, at all events, of mischief . . . a degree of egoism and, behind this latter, something less spontaneous and more bitter, the beginnings of a curious pessimism which becomes the more pronounced as the laughter more closely analyzes his laughter. Here, as elsewhere, nature has utilized evil with a view to good."[5]

Before going any further, let us recognize that *Laughter* as a text is a work of art and that vaudeville, though dealt with very effectively, is not its real subject. First one must notice that Bergson, like Plato and many others after him, at once disclaims any attempt to define the comic spirit, which he associates with life itself; it is essentially flowing and elusive of fixed boundaries. Instead he claims to offer a line of inquiry like a broad road leading through the forest with occasional crossways where the traffic of imagination branches off from a common central image. These *images centrales*,[6] though perhaps less useful as rhetorical tools than the laws, are far more revelatory of Bergson's view of the true role of art in society. They shape the progress of the essay to a far greater extent than do the Euclidean set of axioms, postulates, and deductions. The rules, in fact, form an amusing counterpoint to Bergson's central insight, which the images strikingly present.

Bergson's most important image is a cosmic one in which social life, after being linked with the total environment of man in a "primal scene" of the earth cooling off after its fiery genesis, is then internalized in a new world picture of the macro/microcosm:

[5] II, v, pp. 188f.; French, pp. 122-123, reading *malice* for translated "mischief"; with the rest of the passage, this tends to lead us back to Socrates in the *Philebus*, where the word was φθόνος for an instinctively malicious ill-will.

[6] I, v, p. 84; French, p. 35. I believe Bergson may have originated the important concept of *images centrales*, which he had already used before *Le Rire*: see, e.g., the beginning of *Matter and Memory*.

Man must live in society, and consequently submit to rules. And what interest advises, reason commands: duty calls, and we have to obey the summons. Under this dual influence has perforce been formed an outward layer of feelings and ideas which make for permanence, aim at becoming common to all men, and cover, when they are not strong enough to extinguish it, the inner fire of individual passions. The slow progress of mankind in the direction of an increasingly peaceful social life has gradually consolidated this layer, just as the life of our planet itself has been one long effort to cover over with a cool and solid crust the fiery mass of seething metals. But volcanic eruptions occur. And if the earth were a living being, as mythology has feigned, most likely when in repose it would take delight in dreaming of these sudden explosions whereby it suddenly resumes possession of its innermost nature. Such is just the kind of pleasure that is provided for us by drama [i.e., *drame*, or serious theater]. Beneath the quiet humdrum life that reason and society have fashioned for us, it stirs something within us which luckily does not explode, but which it makes us feel in its inner tension. It offers nature her revenge upon society. Sometimes it makes straight for the goal, summoning up to the surface, from the depths below, passions that produce a general upheaval. Sometimes it follows a flank movement, as is often the case in contemporary drama; with a skill that is frequently sophistical it shows up the inconsistencies of society; it exaggerates the shams and shibboleths of the social law, and so indirectly, by merely dissolving or corroding the outer crust, it again brings us back to the inner core. But, in both cases, whether it weakens society or strengthens nature, it has the same end in view: that of laying bare a secret portion of ourselves, what might be called the tragic element in our character.[7]

[7] III, i, pp. 163f.; French, pp. 101f.

This cosmic image of the earth's crust and its fiery core is reflected in the first of the "crossways" images Bergson employs, something mechanical encrusted upon the living. The same fundamental image lies behind the entire set of laws in accordance with a process Bergson himself explains as follows: "Any simple image . . . is capable of worming its way into other images of a more complex nature, and instilling into them something of its . . . essence."[8] Bergson's simple image is of society as a cold hard crust or hide (*pellicule solide et froide*) pressing upon human life from above and outside. He makes some striking uses of this image, particularly in applying it to our intimate world where life takes the forms of imagination and dream. The imagination, he says, has its own logic, usually hidden by an "outer crust of carefully stratified judgments and firmly established ideas." The nature of this logic in the depths of our minds is a "flow of an unbroken stream of images which pass from one into another. This interpenetration of images . . . obeys laws, or rather habits, which hold the same relation to imagination that logic does to thought." There are habits of the imagination, there is a logic of the dream, not in the individual—for according to Bergson we are all as incapable of knowing each other's dreams as we are of knowing each other's minds—but a logic of the dream of a whole of society.[9]

No doubt the reader recalls that the long quotation given earlier applied this cosmic image only to art and to drama and not to light comedy. Nevertheless comedy does fit in, though in a more humble role. In the geological perspective of Bergson's imagination, he describes its evolution: "Comic fancy is indeed a living energy, a strange plant that has flourished on the stony portions of the social soil, until such time as culture should allow it to vie with the most refined products of art."[10] Here is language that makes no sense historically; Aristotle was far more accurate than this in placing the actual origin of comedy in its relation to Greek society. It

[8] III, ii, p. 173; French, p. 110, with *vertu* for "essence."

[9] I, v, p. 87; French, p. 37, with *croûte extérieure* for "outer crust."

[10] I, v, pp. 102f.; French, p. 49.

would be a serious mistake, therefore, to interpret Bergson's image historically and to try to relate it to the development of a future art form. His book shows not the least interest in the history of drama. Bergson means to say that comedy is not really an art because it does not come from the fiery interior nor give us knowledge of our individual inner selves. Comedy comes from the stony surface of the outer crust; its life is vigorous but strange and somehow inhuman, and only a prolonged craft tradition and the special indulgence of a high culture in society enable it to "vie with" but not really to attain the high status of art.

Bergson makes explicit use of a topographical structure to locate comedy in a zone between nature and art that he calls artifice. In this zone of artifice belong the wit and the comic playwright. Bergson goes so far as to assert that the imposition of the moral upon the mechanical is the specific function that permits comedy to be called "a living energy." But comedy does not belong in the region of art itself, Bergson makes clear, because it has to do with the general and the socially useful, whereas "art . . . has no other object than to brush aside the utilitarian symbols, the conventional and socially accepted generalities, in short, everything that veils reality from us, in order to bring us face to face with reality itself."[11] Comedy, on the contrary, looks outward, it observes things, it stays midway between body and soul. Thereby "comedy . . . turns its back upon art, which is a breaking away from society and a return to pure nature."[12] (An extraordinary definition of art, if ever there was one!) If the comic is allowed to pass for art, the reason is that the artifice of comedy is matched by the artificiality of society. Yet if it were not useful to an extraordinary degree comedy could hardly have achieved such a promotion; the service it renders must be very important socially.

One concession made to comedy by the image is that growing in stony ground it cannot be called parasitical.

[11] II, i, p. 162; French, p. 106.
[12] II, i, p. 170; French, p. 108, *simple* for "pure."

Bergson explains that the best comedy endows laughter with moral life, especially in the discovery of great characters when each becomes a new general category within human-kind—Alceste, Don Quixote, Falstaff. This is a great and paradoxical feat of artifice to Bergson, for laughter has "nothing very benevolent" in it. "It seems rather inclined to return evil for evil," and "it would fail in its object if it bore the stamp of sympathy or kindness."[13] The object of laughter, and therefore of comedy in Bergson's scheme of images, is to be a destructive force in relation to its own specific environment, the stony outer crust that is society. Like some poisons, laughter is used medicinally as a counterirritant.

Bergson's second central image is similar to the first. It transfers the macrocosmic, geological vision of a fiery earth enclosed in a cold crust into the psychic topography of an inner world, the depths of our mind, "a secret portion of ourselves," "the tragic element in our character":

> This is indeed the impression we get after seeing a stirring drama. What has just interested us is not so much what we have been told about others as the glimpse we have caught of ourselves—a whole host of ghostly feelings, emotions, and events that would fain have come into real existence, but, fortunately for us, did not. It also seems as if an appeal had been made within us to certain ancestral memories belonging to a far-away past—memories so deep-seated and so foreign to our present life that this latter, for a moment, seems something unreal and conventional, for which we shall have to serve a fresh apprenticeship. So it is indeed a deeper reality that drama draws up from beneath our superficial and utilitarian attainments; and this art has the same end in view as all the others.[14]

This is an identification of inner reality exclusively with its tragic aspect, and thus it leads to a rejection of comedy in

---

[13] III, v, pp. 185, 186, 187; French, pp. 120, 121, 122.
[14] III, i, p. 164; French, p. 102.

favor of bourgeois *drame*. It would again seem that Bergson paid little attention to the history of drama or to critical discussion of its generic structure, for he seems not to distinguish the sentimental *drame* of the contemporary French theatre from classical tragedy.

Nevertheless, written between the lines of the long passage I have quoted in two segments is a prophecy clearly outlining what comedy has steadily become in the course of the years since 1900. It is almost as if the writers of comedy had sought to achieve the tragic as Bergson pictured it but by using the rules he gave them for vaudeville.

Moreover this second central image is startlingly close to Freud's topology of the psyche, presented five years later in *Jokes and Their Relation to the Unconscious*. The conscious self is represented as harboring secret depths from which it is protected by its social defenses, an "outer crust of carefully stratified judgments and firmly established ideas"; but consciousness is moved from within by personal and ancestral memories, feelings, and events whose reality when only glimpsed causes our everyday conscious existence to appear unreal and insignificant.

The third central image helps to explain Bergson's ambivalence toward society throughout the book, and it suggests the close connection between his attitude and that of others, such as Albert Camus, who were convinced of a profound ambiguity in existence itself. His third image is that of a smooth lake, equivalent to ideal existence or "true life" in the sense of the visionary, peaceful, and completely sociable mode of living to which, Bergson speculated, nature originally destined mankind; at the same time, and as part of the same image, appears a vision of a turbulent ocean—actual life—its depths totally out of our sight except as bits and pieces of the bottom are whipped up to view by the tempests that sweep the surface.

In another astonishing image closely related to the three already presented Bergson makes it clear that his vision of comedy is germinally the same as that of even the most extreme writers of *humour noir*. The image appears during his brief discussion of humor, where one would expect him to acknowledge what every writer on the comic has seen since the term "humor" was adopted universally: a certain quality of humane feeling or sentiment, particularly identifiable in the novels of Fielding and Sterne. But Bergson, who insists that every vestige of feeling be excluded from laughter and from the comic, treats humor as equally unfeeling. Humor, he says, is a form of satire, like irony. It meets evil with evil, as all laughter does: "Humor is the more emphasized the deeper we go down into an evil that actually is, in order to set down its details in the most cold-blooded indifference. . . . A humorist is a moralist disguised as a scientist, something like an anatomist who practices dissection with the sole object of filling us with disgust."[15] This image suggests nothing so much as the extreme procedures of the school of sick comedy and *humour noir*. It opens the door to the recognition of the Marquis de Sade as *chef d'école*. It suggests, on Bergson's part, a revulsion of a most deep-seated kind against laughter, the comic, and humor itself, coupled with an attitude of the deepest distrust toward the society that according to him is the source of these three "artifices."

One might wonder how conscious Bergson was of his rather sinister view of laughter, the comic, and humor. When he wrote this sentence in the final pages of *Laughter*, he left no room for doubt: "Laughter," he said, "is simply the result of a mechanism set up in us by nature, or, what is almost the same thing, by our long acquaintance with social life." But as we have learned from the whole stream of images, if laughter is really the natural child of "mechanism," it is born to laugh its parent to death. If laughter evoked by comic artifice is the artificial product of a society, it exists to become nature's revenge upon society. "Here as elsewhere, nature has utilized evil with a view to good."[16]

It does not seem likely that writers like Gide, Céline, Beckett, and Ionesco have misunderstood their great con-

[15] II, ii, p. 143; French, pp. 83f.
[16] III, v, pp. 188f.; French, p. 122f.

temporary, gifted as he was with a marvelously clear style. They seem to have recognized what is only implicit in the early essay on laughter, perhaps aided by ideas that took firm shape in Bergson's later works, especially *The Two Sources of Morality and Religion*, and most of all by the idea of the contrast between closed and open societies. The later Bergson seems to have given a new and more recognizably humane turn to the Nietzschean Will to Power. He continues to be preoccupied with mechanization of life, seeing it no longer as the unavoidable bane of human existence but rather as its potential servant. Replacing a war-making mystique, freed from the service of imperialism and its machine of state, the operation of power becomes beneficient. Mechanization will implement "a very special 'will to power,'" Bergson said. "This will be a sovereignty, not over men, but over things, precisely in order that man shall no longer have so much sovereignty over man." It is time, Bergson says, to get the inventive instinct of man back on the tracks; for too long "machinery, through a mistake at the points, has been switched off on to a track at the end of which lies exaggerated comfort and luxury for the few, rather than liberation for all."[17]

For Bergson as for Thoreau liberation, which, as we have seen, is crucial to the whole romantic view of the comic, comes from obeying the injunction to "simplify, simplify." "Humanity must set about simplifying its existence with as much frenzy as it devoted to complicating it," Bergson insists.[18] Laughter can now be seen in its true light, as a natural instrument of self-destruction which, when harbored by the closed society, helps it move toward its own dissolution on the route to that open society that is the true destiny of mankind. The role of laughter is to act as an incentive, perhaps an irritant, prompting our necessary search "for the bedrock of sociability, and also of unsociability, which would be perceptible to our consciousness, if established

[17] Translated by R. Ashley Audra and Cloudsley Brereton (Garden City, N.Y.: Doubleday, 1954), pp. 311, 309.
[18] Ibid., p. 307.

society had not imbued us with habits and dispositions which adjust us to it. Of these strata we are no longer aware, save at rare intervals, and then in a flash. We must recapture that moment of vision and abide by it."[19] From these expressions of 1932 we can take the assurance to declare "sick comedy" a misnomer, for it is society that is sick; comedy is its medicine, helping to make it less sick and eventually more sociable. Above all, the "absurd comedy" of the fifties and sixties can be seen, with Bergson's help, as a "search for the bedrock of sociability and also of unsociability." This search, along with its necessary destruction of habitual adjustments to established society, was intended as an extreme means of "recapturing the moment of vision."

The fuller sense of what Bergson had in mind, brought out by *The Two Sources*, is still rather disquieting. His view of comedy remains regressive, seeming to correspond with seventeenth-century notions of chastising the ridiculous. Bergson's manifest aim for drama may have been an enhancement of the freedom of man, but we have seen that his latent image structure limits this function to the tragic alone and denies it explicitly to comedy of the lighter sort. His systematic rhetorical approach and his presentation of comedy as a finally distasteful instrument of reform and nothing more are quite contradictory to the romantic idea that freedom is the essence of the comic. Yet one cannot deny that the text of *Laughter* provided writers, before and after *The Two Sources* appeared, with the seeds of comic innovation. If we review the impact of the original laws, however, we shall find a revealing disparity in the way good writers have treated them. Some rules have been faithfully and frequently applied, while others have been ignored.

First, it seems clear that the notable writers refused to accept Bergson's view that the comic was an art of the surface and therefore not an art at all. The thrust of the existentialist movement, like that of the parent phenomenological move-

---

[19] Ibid., p. 275. Note that "bedrock" maintains the much earlier central image of *Le Rire*.

ment in philosophy, is to accord a high degree of significance to the surface, to phenomena, to whatever is laid open
to human perception by our common human experience.
The result is a corresponding lack of stress on the purely individual inwardness, which alone, to Bergson, qualified as
the reality that was the subject of art. So when he remarked
that it was the generality of its subject matter that set comedy apart from the other arts, Bergson was really saying that
to him comedy was no true art. Both in fiction and drama,
however, writers have now been dealing for several decades
with states of mind and of existence rather than with highly
personalized characters and their inwardness; they have
been looking not exactly for the typical but for applicable
structures that art can find for the essential experience of the
human situation. Insofar as comedy now lends itself better
than tragedy to the discovery of such structures it has come
to seem more worthy of the writer's effort.

Secondly, there has been an overwhelming rejection of
Bergson's original assumption that comedy, and laughter
generally, is aimed at correcting inadaptiveness to established social patterns. Writers agree that life needs tension
and elasticity, but they do not draw the conclusion that an
increasingly delicate adjustment of wills is necessary if we
are to continue to live together in modern society. They pay
attention instead to Bergson's call for simplicity. In 1900
Bergson felt that his society had reached the point where, no
longer worried over self-preservation, its members had
begun to regard themselves and society itself as a work of
art. They then began unconsciously and even immorally to
use laughter not to check eccentric rigidity alone but to stifle
what they regarded as the more insidious "slumbering activity with separatist tendencies."[20] Separatist art no longer
slumbers, but has long since taken the form of opposition to

---

[20] *Laughter*, I, i, p. 73; French, p. 25: "Toute *raideur* du caractère, de l'es-
prit et même du corps, sera donc suspecte à la société, parce qu'elle est le
signe possible d'une activité qui s'endort et aussi d'une activité qui s'isole,
qui tend à s'écarter du centre commun autour duquel la société gravite,
d'une excentricité enfin."

everything established. Society is now profoundly worried over its preservation. So when Bergson says "comedy . . . turns its back upon art, which is a breaking away from society and a return to pure nature," we can make the statement meaningful today by revising it to read "comedy, like the other arts, turns its back upon society in favor of a return to simple existence." The fictions of Beckett and Pinter, for example, may have the effect of attacks upon bourgeois morality and social values, but their essential artistic structure is to represent states of unsociable existence antagonistic to all specified or historical forms of established society. In their contradiction or extreme distortion of social reference they assert their freedom. They thus unite Bergson's claim for genuine art, that it gets beneath the outer layer of established habit, with Schiller's claim for comedy, that it enables an author "to be free of passion," to be "always clear, to look serenely about and within himself, to find everywhere more coincidence than fate, and rather to laugh at absurdity than to rage or weep at malice." The clarity of Beckett is almost total obscurity when we attempt to see through it by means of accepted concepts instead of looking at it phenominally, simply, and immediately. Beckett's work, as Schiller suggested of the modern, "battles on behalf of an ideal that it does not always articulate."

On the whole writers have rejected Bergson's most fundamental figural artifice for comedy, one that consists of a clockwork arrangement of human events that at the same time preserves an outward aspect of probability. His example was a stage filled with puppetlike characters. It seems stillborn, except perhaps in Ionesco's *Rhinoceros* and *A Stroll in the Air* or in such froth as Waugh's "bright young people" or Pynchon's "whole sick crew." Minimalism, rudimentary plots and amorphous characters rather than clockwork complexity and machinelike precision, have been the rule in the new comedy. Since his essential insight is that nature abhors sameness and life never repeats itself exactly, Bergson made the essence of comedy out to be the attack by ridicule upon exact repetition. Unfortunately he fails to distinguish mechanical repetition from symmetry and rhythmical cumulation. He cites the plot and subplot of *Amphitryon* with its powerful running contrast between gods and men as if it were a case of mere repetition. Even the running gags of farce are combinations of sameness with difference, and it is the difference that really counts in making the repetition funny. *Waiting for Godot* is the one play that appears to follow Bergson with regard to insistence on repetition, yet it fails to meet his requirements for complexity and precision. Pynchon, with *V.* and *Gravity's Rainbow*, seems to be one of the few who have made a determined effort to put all three of the principles we are discussing into effect.

His second figure Bergson calls *inversion* (it has been translated as "topsyturvydom"). This is the logical complement of repetition, for the same recurs in the form of its own reciprocal. Bergson mentions several common comic themes, "the biter bit," "the robber robbed," "the cheater cheated," claiming that any mishap befalling one through one's guilty intention can qualify as comic. Such an inversion of the roles of victim and aggressor is sometimes still seen in modern comedy but almost never in connection with guilt and retribution. Typically, comedy now rejects the normal relations of cause and effect completely, and above all it tends to dissolve the notion of crime and punishment or poetic justice. It is suggestive of Bergson's bias that he injects an old-fashioned notion like poetic justice into his handling of comedy; it follows from his insistence upon laughter and the comic as a mere corrective force serving society.

The third and only other logical possibility is the figure Bergson calls the "interference of series." Here repetition is not temporal but synchronous and relational: "A situation is invariably comic when it belongs simultaneously to two altogether independent series of events and is capable of being interpreted in two entirely different meanings at the same time."[21] Many authors have made comic use of this

---

[21] II, i, pp. 118, 123; French, pp. 63f., 67.

rule since Bergson wrote. The most striking example is in Evelyn Waugh's *A Handful of Dust*. The comic hero, Tony Last, is utterly absent-minded, hence laughable in Bergson's primary sense, for he has allowed his feeling for his wife to become mere mechanism. Brenda has consoled herself with John Beaver, and has herself become absent-minded in family matters. The death of John Andrew, their child, in a trivial accident is reported to Brenda by Tony's best friend in a way that allows the two series to interfere. This is her reaction when she realizes John Beaver, her lover, is still alive: "She frowned, not at once taking in what he was saying. 'John . . . John Andrew. . . . Oh thank God. . . .' Then she burst into tears." One could not ask for a better illustration of Bergson's essential conception of the comic and of humor, bitter aftertaste and all. Yet even a sophisticated reader will scarcely find Brenda's mistake comic except in retrospect when the whole novel has been read. Absent-mindedness and interference of series are not enough, separately or together, without a certain essential note that the comic ending of *A Handful of Dust* brings out.[22]

Writers have found quite different ways of employing the Bergsonian "interference of series." Robert Scholes, in *The Fabulators*,[23] has called attention to one of them in John Hawkes's *The Lime Twig*. In adjacent rooms, there is a scene of lovemaking and a scene where an inoffensive girl is beaten for her lover's betrayal of the gang. It is suggested, rather gruesomely I think, that the coincidence is comic.

[22] It is interesting that the human ties that bind Brenda to both her son and her lover contravene Bergson's principle of life as "complexity in space," where "coexisting elements" are "so exclusively made for one another that no one of them could, at the same time, belong to two organisms: each living being is a closed system of phenomena, incapable of interfering with other systems." This "perfect individuality of a perfectly self-contained series" fails Brenda when she bursts into tears, but she is more a living being than that closed system, Tony, whose wooden "self-containment" in his Victorian Gothic existence is the most continuously comic thing in the novel. This could hardly be the case had Tony not been surrounded by figures much more living than he, and less ironically presented.

[23] New York: Oxford University Press, 1967, p. 87.

Using Bergsonian premises, Scholes tried to overcome the normal reaction of repugnance by arguing that the beaten girl should not evoke sympathy. Bergson's precepts are here being expounded in a way that I think would have horrified Bergson himself. They have certainly been detached from the parent body of his theory and used as mere limbs of rhetoric. Yet Scholes may be justified in arguing that the Hawkes text itself mixes Bergson with Sacher-Masoch and Sade. Hawkes's "interference of series," however, is anything but comic; that it must inevitably be laughable is a fallacy that regrettably Bergson was the first to proclaim.

The application across the board of the "interference of series" technique for comic effect is undermined by Bergson's own very limited sense of its validity. As an example of an interfering series he suggests "an inconvenient past"—merely the farcical discovery that Monsieur X, indignantly accusing Madame X of having an affair, has had one of his own. This sort of thing gave rise to farcical chases through the bedrooms of an inn or a resort hotel, with a wealth of stock situations and running gags. Oddly, the Hawkes story makes use of the "adjacent rooms" of this farce technique; it thus qualifies for the appellation of parody that is all too frequently invoked, on doctrinaire grounds, as a guarantor of the comic. But parody works from the more dignified to the less so, not from farce to supposedly serious (and yet comic) art.

To anticipate for a moment here our discussion of black comedy, Bergson seems to have afforded writers in one related image an inversion of his own that turned the concept of humor inside out. It offers a theoretical basis for a large portion of recent comic writing, especially after World War II began to inspire the same acute disillusionment as World War I had done and Céline's *Voyage au bout de la nuit* came to be invoked as a model. The physician-hero of that book, and its title as well, seem superficially to coincide with Bergson's description quoted earlier: "Humor is the more emphasized the more we go down into the evil that actually is, in order to set down its details in the most cold-blooded indifference."

The keynote of this pronouncement is "cold-blooded." Scientific detachment, Bergson contends, can make anything humorous, even vice; cruelty, therefore, could be made amusing or comic. There seems to be a flaw in logic here, to say the least: it is one thing to say that laughter is incompatible with emotion, as Bergson often does, and quite another to suggest that the mere absence of emotion will change something painful or destructive into something laughable. What is a condition *sine qua non* elsewhere in Bergson becomes a specific technique in the course of his brief reference to humor. But the truth is that Bergson suggests in many places (especially in indirection and through imagery) that all laughter actually expresses a mixed feeling of pleasure and pain akin to spite or even cruelty itself: "an unavowed desire to humiliate . . . our neighbor."

Finally, we may end our consideration of *Laughter* with a few comments on wit, which Bergson regards simply as amusing word play and a means toward the development of comic characters. Since he excludes feeling altogether from every possible form of the comic, he defines wit as the equivalent of poetry without feeling on the odd assumption that anything can be poetic in the total absence of feeling. Only intelligence, he says, is present in the metaphors of the comic imagination, where the concrete is insisted upon to the exclusion of its emotional significance. Wit attempts a comic domination of the world by means of words; it "claims to accommodate things to itself instead of accommodating itself to things."[24] In so doing, word-play always betrays some arbitrary lapse of reference inherent in our language. As if encouraged by this suggestion, comic writers who are interested in language have made a widespread practice of spinning out lengthy sequences of words and phrases with almost no reference to real things. Once more, Pynchon affords examples, some quite good reading in themselves like the passage in *V.* beginning "Any sovereign or broken yo-yo," which is Bergsonian in inspiration and

[24] II, ii, p. 139; French, p. 80.

detail. But the crowning example is Lucky's famous outburst in *Waiting for Godot* (anticipated in some strange way by Sganarelle's outburst in act five of Molière's *Don Juan*).[25]

Despite his extraordinary contribution to twentieth-century comic writing, I can only re-emphasize, by way of conclusion, the fact that Bergson himself failed to look at the comic in a positive way. He regards laughter and the comic as a corrective, and proceeds to concern himself exclusively with the corrigenda: the mechanical, the routine, the absent-minded. These are negative, opposed to life. To conceive of comedy as the art of discovering and presenting such stimuli for the necessary (i.e., automatic) laughter of mankind is to degrade the comic art to the level Bergson suggests it really deserves and to relegate laughter to the sphere of ill-nature where he feels it belongs. It would be far better, I believe, to think of comedy as maintaining a positive entity, even that displayed in a Victorian Gothic anachronism like Waugh's Tony Last by means of the positive life that surrounds him and infuses itself into him as the literary creation that he is. I should repeat that the terms used here, *entity* and *life*, fall within the limits mentioned earlier with regard to fictional constitutions in general. A character, a situation, a world, or a narrative is comic only if it first be successfully constituted and then submitted to a sufficient series of testings to persuade the reader that it remains itself-and-the-same in different situations and under different stresses. Once he has persuaded us of these positive identities, the author's comic achievement has its necessary basis.

[25] These elaborate passages might be thought to produce the effect of a Rabelaisian catalogue, but the lack of reference is quite unlike Rabelais, or Joyce (to take a modern instance).

~6~

MODERN COMIC ETHOS
CONTINUED: FREUD

To Sigmund Freud, Bergson's *Le Rire* was doubtless a stimulus in his own studies, already under way, which took shape in *Jokes and Their Relation to the Unconscious* five years later (1905). Though Freud attempted throughout his book to be as scientific as possible, he too is lively; and if not so charming, he is a great deal sounder than Bergson on the comic itself. In addition, he presents some ideas on humor that avoid Bergson's peculiar aberrations and yet have proved equally applicable to the development of comic writing. It was in *Jokes* that Freud first clearly outlined his topographical scheme of the psyche, distinguishing the unconscious, preconscious, and conscious selves and setting up an inner mechanism, the censor, remarkably like Bergson's *pellicule* or *croûte* of socially acquired habit in its function. The power of the joke to slip past the vigilance of this censor and bring to light the hidden contents of the unconscious is a dramatic deepening of Bergson's image of the comic as a mere surface phenomenon. It helped to promote the comic over the tragic as the more serious literary approach to human reality. To put the matter in Bergson's terms, Freud showed that forms of the comic had means of penetrating the outer crust and exposing the inner turbulence where art takes its rise.

Freud made use of a methodological assumption that allows his contribution also to be considered as an ethos of the comic. In order to legitimize psychoanalysis as a positive science, he equated psychic forces with physical energy, and postulated the same measurable properties that were accepted in physics, conservation and expenditure of energy, in the hope that psychic forces could be measured as accurately, eventually, as natural ones, in their own equivalent of volts and B.T.U.s This led him to deal with psychic factors in terms of physical movement; and since he was already concerned with both abnormal and normal behavior, almost everything he said took shape in a practical ethos. Furthermore, despite its "scientificity," it is a strongly valued ethos, as we shall see. To understand the appeal of the Freudian world picture today, however, it is important to realize that he tried to make psychoanalysis a science on the model of economics. Polymorphous libido becomes a medium of exchange of psychic force, like money in economics. The unconscious becomes the repository of psychic capital. The rationale in psychic life as a whole, what made it possible to treat the inner self scientifically, is a principle of economy. Expenditure in the form of mental or emotional activity is regarded as work; pleasure involves the saving of such expenditure. With all this we have in Freud an even greater identification of himself with the bourgeois society of his time and place than we find in Bergson. We have, therefore, the same paradox of a potentially anarchic central insight (the unconscious) overlaid by an excessively regulated superstructure. Freud's capitalist economy is even more conventionally structured than Bergson's. Both seem to have been based on the topological notion that everything that is (life, matter, space, light) is open to the same interactive forces throughout in a totality of exchange, wherein (as Bergson saw it) the human psyche is unique in offering a special kind of resistance or delay.

FREUD's approach to the comic itself, like all the others', is quite gingerly.[1] First, he restricts his treatment to the relation

---

[1] *Jokes and their Relation to the Unconscious,* translated and edited by James Strachey, standard edition (New York: Norton, 1963), Chapter VII, "Jokes and the Species of the Comic," pp. 181–236.

between jokes only and "the species of the comic." Then he
repeatedly confesses the extreme difficulty of explaining the
essential nature of the comic and his intention to avoid any
such attempt. He proceeds to reject superiority and malice
as in themselves explanations of comic laughter, and gives a
much fuller account in line with his own ethos, based on an
axiology of maturation from carefree infancy to responsible
adulthood. The cause of laughter at the comic, Freud says, is
witnessing "an expenditure that is too large." One tends to
form an idea of the movement perceived in any behavioral
act, whether our own actions or, by empathy, those of
others. This whole area of "ideational mimetics" offers
pleasure because ideation "displaces far smaller cathectic
energies and holds back the main expenditure from discharge." We thus manage, by using our minds rather than
bodily movements, to effect an economy of physical effort
through much lighter mental work. We can laugh heartily,
therefore, even when all alone, and without any particular
malice, at a picture of a man with a big nose because the size
of the nose suggests a disproportionate amount of effort to
grow it and to keep on wearing it. The more general case,
though, involves a relationship fundamental to Freudian
thought, that of child to adult. The movements of children
are marked by imprecision and excess. We do not normally
laugh at them because they are quite natural to children. But
when we find an adult's movements marked by the same excess, we laugh because we have made a comparison between
his large expenditure (say in an overceremonious bow) and
the more efficient one appropriate to an adult. Laughter results because the behavior of an adult reminds us of the
overexpenditure of a child. (Freud, of course, has much
more than this to say of childhood and the comic, as we shall
discuss later.)

On the whole Freud agrees with Bergson in conducting his
study of the comic by primary reference to laughter. He too
considers a laugh to be the necessary effect of the comic
pleasure. Neither makes the clear Aristotelian distinction
between the laughable and the good-natured wit and socia-

ble delight of the magnanimous man. Moreover, Freud lowers the importance of the comic in several new ways peculiar to his own general theory. Most of all, it was Freud who made the unconscious so important that it has come to seem the only genuine basis for serious art; but Freud, like Bergson, severs the comic as such from the unconscious. Unlike jokes, which require at least a momentary dip into the unconscious, the comic reaches only into the preconscious. Besides being less spontaneous, the comic is also more remote than jokes from the original infantile pleasure-source. But it is very interesting to observe that Freud places himself firmly in the romantic line of comic analysis by basing his judgment of value upon the degree of freedom implied. Jokes are superior in that they preserve, in a moment of release, one's unconscious freedom from rational process; polite comedy, on the other hand, offers an exposé of irrationality; we take it in with amused detachment, but without that rhythm of delicious involvement and liberation offered by a full return to the infantile unconscious.

Freud therefore denies that jokes can be defined as merely the comic use of speech. On the contrary, jokes are consistently without intent to offend, whereas a comic comparison can often be recognized as a case of degradation, that is, a reminder of the childish (not infantile) pleasure we took when an adult lowered himself to play with us like a child. Only "bad" jokes resemble comedy; indeed "bad" jokes make good comedy because they make obvious use of the associational illogic that goes unobserved in jokes. Freud's example, the "herring on the wall" riddle, is a very good case in point:

> "What is it that hangs on the wall and that one can dry one's hands on?" It would be a stupid riddle if the answer were "a hand towel." But that answer is rejected.
> "No, a herring."
> "But for heaven's sake, comes the infuriated protest, "a herring doesn't hang on the wall."

"You can hang it up there."
"But who in the world is going to dry his hands on a
herring?"
"Well," is the soothing reply, "you don't have to."[2]

As Freud comments, this is a bad riddle, yet it is "irresistibly
comic." The exposure of the displacement process consists
in the teller's making conscious use of the unconscious illogic that good riddles, like good jokes, uncritically accept.
This degradation of the unconscious produces a bad riddle,
and, Freud suggests, an inferior form of the joke, though one
that works in a comic (i.e., manifest) way. One cannot picture Aristotle's fine-spirited man telling this kind of riddle,
yet the story itself is a splendid illustration of the nature of
the comic. The comic, as I suggest, may be defined as the
continuation of something as itself, despite threats to its
substantial self. In this case, it is a herring that continues. Everyone has seen a mounted fish (though never a herring)
hanging on a wall, and every fine-spirited person has experienced a sense of impropriety: there is something about the
nature of a fish that unsuits it for this form of interior deco-
ration. Sometimes things hang on walls because they are
useful rather than ornamental, towel-racks for instance. But
the wildest exertion of one's imagination cannot suggest any
use for a fish hanging on a wall—not even that most widely
used of all fish, the herring. Hence the force of the riddle: the
nature of fish as fish and herring as herring has been vindicated by the comic against the attempts of vain sportsmen,
interior decorators, or aggressive utilitarians to pervert that
nature.

Since we all have a large stake in the continuation of
things, it is the sense of the survival of an identity, the reas-
sertion of a continuity that has been subjected to a challenge, which pleases us here. It is the concrete image that is
comic first, before the psychological process induced by the
question and answer. The psychological process is the same

[2] Ibid., p. 215.

as in the response to all art, indeed in all keen perception: an intensified awareness, heightened in this case by surprise. The function of the comic in one of its important aspects is, like romantic art especially, to heighten our awareness of what we tend to overlook simply because it does continue. (I should add that the concept that Freud invokes here, of a bottomless reservoir of infantile illogical delight, is a particularly transparent instance of romantic nostalgia for "lost childhood.")

One might also find a transparently autobiographical element in Freud's analysis of the pleasure principle and its relation to infantile and childhood experience. In a way this is a strength rather than a weakness in his understanding of the comic, since his childhood experience was in large measure characteristic of that of any bourgeois in the culture through which ours has passed. But Freud associates serious mental work (especially in science and art) with hard labor, and he sees it as a form of bondage that the mature individual accepts but the child escapes, especially when an infant. In itself, this is a highly romantic idea, and only its monumental importance in Freudian thought prevents it from being regarded as rather sentimental. Seeing that it was Freud who directed attention to the rich eventfulness of infant experience, it seems ungrateful to point it out, but his manner of relating comedy and the comic to infantile experience is more than usually reductive.

The peculiarities of Freud's attitude to the comic center in the essential place he gives to economy of psychic expenditure. Paradoxically, he regards ideational mimicry as offering a saving of energy over bodily imitation, because it requires measurably less energy to go through movements in one's mind than with one's body; yet at the same time he obviously regards mental effort along scientific lines and according to the rules of logic and the laws of rationality as an activity performed only at great cost by the repressed, adjusted mature person, after he has seemingly overcome the wasteful behavior due to inexperience and immaturity. Thus his measurable economy of expenditure is accomplished at the immeasurable cost of lost pleasure. Jokes, however, enable the mature person to go off guard, to take revenge upon logic and the laws of reason by slipping, surprisingly and innocently, into the illogical and the infantile. The suspension of the practice of economy is the specific source of the keenest pleasure. Laughter then is a movement of prodigality and spendthrift abandonment. The rest of life is a severe effort to economize and to save, and it is most painful of all perhaps in science, where the theorist tries always to subsume ever more facts within the same general rules, always in difficulties to "save" those random events and experiences which, like unbudgeted disbursements, throw his accounts into disorder and threaten his system with wasteful revision and extension. The mature pleasure of good company and good talk, and comedy as a more formal entertainment suited above all to the experienced understanding, do not find a legitimate place in Freud's reduced scheme, except as types of forepleasure. He seems to have developed in his own noble work a sacrificial mood that drastically limits his treatment of the comic.

We may wish today to discount the part of his treatment that seems to reflect, ironically and painfully, his bourgeois milieu: that is, his casting of the comic as a form of bookkeeping in which expense accounts are kept and compared and the pleasure comes when we see a profit accruing to ourselves by comparing our own thrifty ideational mimicry with the wasteful expenditure of another. The whole conception of cathectic expenditure and saving, despite its pretension to a quantitative basis, is really only a metaphor, and Freud never succeeds in translating it into physical units. Judged on more appropriate grounds, i.e., aesthetically, the metaphor is old-fashioned and unattractive, indeed rather self-contradictory, since it is the prodigal expense rather than the saving that relates most truly to our sense of the comic. Nietzsche's anticapitalist metaphor of "spending" is closer to comic experience than Freud's economical one. But this does not mean that Freud's theory that laughter comes from the mimicking of childish overexpenditure has failed to inspire fiction writers. Pynchon's use of exaggerated ebullience of movement, for instance in Oedipa Maas's romp with the former child star Metzger, alias Baby Igor (*The Crying of Lot 49*), fits this principle of Freud's so perfectly that one suspects that the theory has been preceptively applied.

Freud also endorses Bergson's chief claim, that the comic is directed against the *méchanisation de la vie*.[3] He explains the process, however, in accordance with his own theory, first as a case of what he calls degradation, and secondly as an instance of the release of a differential surplus of ideational-mimetic energy, since one's understanding of an inanimate or mechanical object is arrived at with less expenditure than that required to understand a real, living person. Thus Bergson and Freud both laid it down as a necessary general principle that the persons of comedy must approximate mechanical puppets. It is therefore more than likely that the antihuman characterizations of black comedy and sick humor are in large measure the result of a conjunction of these two most potent influences upon the rhetoric of comic writing in the twentieth century.

On the whole, however, Freud appears to be consistently less doctrinaire than Bergson. With his resigned acceptance of the bourgeois society that he knew, he is not drawn into the ambivalences of regarding the comic both as a policeman guarding the constituted order and a revolutionary destroyer of it as well; the result is that he has a less troubled appreciation of the social aspect of comedy than Bergson. His basic theory is psychological: the comic is a pleasure, its effect is laughter, its purpose the regaining of a cheerful mood; it arises from a comparison of different expenditures of mimetic ideation, leaving a free surplus of innervative energy that is capable of discharge as pleasure or laughter. Nevertheless his analysis of the factors conducive to the comic and those prejudicial to it places the individual psychological experience in a social context. Freud explains that

[3] P. 209.

for the comic to succeed we require a cheerful mood to begin with, like that provided by expectation when we go to a farce or see a favorite comic actor appear on the stage. Other types of forepleasure also establish the right mood, such as the many forms of conviviality. Opposed to the comic effect, he says, are abstract reflection, except when one's mental effort is suddenly interrupted; forewarned attention (the comic process must be preconscious or automatic rather than conscious); and especially affect: feeling generates the most intense interference with the comic, according to Freud.

On this question of affect or feeling, Freud makes what is perhaps his most original contribution to the understanding of the comic. Unlike Bergson, he does not simply state that the presence of feeling prevents all comic effect, though he agrees that this is normally the case. He points to the existence of a very powerful motive for laughter, based upon realization of a very strong feeling of difference between what a person has expected and what actually occurs (the old theme of *contra expectatum*, found in Cicero, emphasized by Kant, and discussed at some length by Hegel). But his example is unusual and excellent, taken from Schiller's play *Wallenstein*, where Colonel Butler finds that his forty years' faithful service to Austria has been thrown away—and laughs. Freud clearly divines Schiller's drift when he states that the colonel's reaction is an example of humor, which in sharp contrast to Bergson he finds to be "itself one of the highest psychical achievements." Humor is a way of finding the comic pleasure "in spite of the distressing affects that interfere with it." Humor puts itself in place of these affects. Humorous pleasure occurs instead of an expense of affect that has not occurred as expected. Thus Colonel Butler, instead of giving way to a feeling of outrage at the ingratitude of his imperial master, ruefully laughs at himself and his own expectations. In Freud's system, the expected anger would have required a very large expenditure of emotion related to large quantities of equivalent kinesthetic expression; the difference between this hurricane of wrath and the actual response of the colonel is made available, therefore, as a form of humorous pleasure. Freud goes on to point out that humor completes its course within a single person (here Colonel Butler), and then he makes an obvious but highly significant distinction between humor and the comic.[4]

In theater comedy, feelings of distress are the greatest obstacle to the comic. Damage, mischief, or pain end the possibility of a comic effect. In humor, however, the damage, mischief, or pain is displaced by a laugh—first the victim's, then the audience's. The good humor of the victim effects a great saving for the audience, who otherwise would have felt sorry for him. This is also the case with "gallows humor" apparently, although Freud offers a magnificent insight when he says "there is something like magnanimity . . . in the man's tenacious hold upon his customary self."[5] In keeping with his theory, he can explain audience laughter as the spending of a surplus arising from the inhibition of pity. Gallows humor, however, seems a clearer case of the positive delight of all humanity at a "man's tenacious hold upon his customary self." It is what Hazlitt called "keeping" and Coleridge "a peculiar sincerity of feeling in the person." It is what we relish in Colonel Butler's inhibition of self-pity and the realization that he is being himself and the House of Hapsburg are being themselves, whereas if he were to feel outraged he would forget himself and become like them.

In Kurt Vonnegut's *Cat's Cradle*,[6] the climax of the book is an amazing feat of rhetorically inspired combination wherein Bergson's cardinal principle, "an incrustation upon the living," is merged with Freud's insight into the magnanimity of gallows humor. The whole of our earth's surface, as if to make literal Bergson's metaphor, has been encrusted into solid matter by the compound "Ice-9," the invention of a scientist who is not mad but absent-minded and mechanical in the way Bergson prescribes. Mona, the heroine, sud-

---

[4] Pp. 220f.
[5] P. 242.
[6] New York: Dell, 1970.

denly sees what has happened; she takes in the fate of the
world and of mankind, and she laughs. The extraordinary
response of Mona can be explained only by recourse to
Freud. It arises from the truly mature person's sense, when
faced by a great disappointment, that "I am too big to let this
depress me."[7] Her sense of grown-upness is cocreated and
shared by the reader as the triumph of the adult over the
child in oneself. It can be called Freud's "maturation principle," and it has been perhaps the most accepted standard of
value among educated people in our culture during the
modern period. It may not be the most profound principle of
ethos, but it is widely applicable and widely used, having
been internalized to the extent that we may regard it as a
basis for our own natural concrete ethic in which good behavior is "adult" or "mature" behavior. In Vonnegut's fiction, the presence of a moralistic and edifying undercurrent
is to be attributed to the ethical content of the Freudian and
Bergsonian central metaphors that he is making literal in the
course of his narratives, "Ice-9" being the perfect example of
this long-recognized comic technique.

A doctrinaire trend in Bergson's *Laughter* has already been
pointed out. It exists in Freud too, in connection with the
privileged and yet rejected place he assigns to infantile and
childish experience in the genesis of the comic. It is this
transgressive relation that forces Freud to differentiate between the comic and humor as if they were altogether distinct and even incompatible experiences.[8] Freud compli-
ments Bergson upon the insight that led him to try "to trace
back a number of comic effects to the faded recollection of a
children's toy" (the jack in the box, subject of one of Bergson's laws).[9] Freud then undertakes to carry the insight further not by a study of toys but of children. Or rather not of
children, who are not comic in themselves (as we have seen),
but of the difference between their nature and adults'; for it

---

[7] *Jokes and Their Relation to the Unconscious*, p. 234.
[8] Ibid., p. 335.
[9] See pp. 222–227.

is the difference that is comic, not the child. (An hypostasis of the difference-relation seems common to all modern thinkers who are attracted to the economic model, from Freud and Saussure to Derrida.) By comparison with adults, children suggest a domination of the mental by the bodily in their excessive expenditure on their movements together with their small intellectual outlay; and furthermore children are naive. These are sources of the adult's pleasure in a child, for "so long as he retains his childish nature the perception of him affords us a pure pleasure, perhaps one that reminds us slightly of the comic." Freud includes watching the play of children among those "forepleasures" which conduce to the comic effect. The laughter of children at play, triumphing in their joy of motion, is not "glory" according to Freud, because the child is not comparing himself with anybody else. And if he laughs at someone who falls, this also is not a feeling of superiority but rather *Schadenfreude,* unashamed delight in shameful events. No, the true source of comic pleasure is "in the 'quantitative contrast' of a comparison between small and large . . . the essential relation between a child and an adult." The one thing that is needed for the child to become comic is for him to adopt some form of adult disguise and thus make "the quantitative contrast" evident.

Freud makes this principle even more explicit, and at the same time correlates the comic firmly with the physical phenomenon of laughter, when he gives as "the specific characteristic of the comic" this formula: "I laugh at a difference in expenditure between another person and myself, every time I rediscover the child in him." This is no mere experience of superiority in the adult over the child, however, for "the essence of the comic" is "a preconscious link with the infantile." It is true that when the link takes the form of recollected childish embarrassment, or privation, or inability, the adult will feel superior—yet not as a rival: he will not glory over the "childish" plight of the victim, but sympathize, retrospectively, in an amused rather than pitying way. The more mature person, after all, was once a child. Further-

more, the mature person will be the first to see through children's illusion of over-hopeful expectation of what people
will do or what events will bring forth, perceiving their
childish credulity, however, as a source of the comic rather
than of self-pity. "I am too big to let this bother me," the
adult will say. As Freud puts it, "Those things are comic
which are not proper for an adult."

It is remarkble that Freud, from such a different approach,
should have come so close to Schiller's description of the
essential feeling inspired by the comic, that of seeing everywhere mere chance and whim rather than the doom of ma-
lignant fate. The individual in his freedom once he has lib-
erated himself by the play of the mind from the thralldom of
"inevitable" destiny feels a superiority—not to fellow
human beings so much as to chance and the vagaries of existence. Freud's description, of course, is quite different as
regards the terms. He does not suggest that the mature person is ever free, or that for him the serious activity of the
mind is not always painful and laborious. But his description
of the feelings of comic liberation enables us to identify it as
the same feeling that Schiller described. It is marked, above
all, by a sense of freedom arising out of life itself when perceived from the right angle of the imagination, accompanied
by a double sense of limit, first of our being linked by bonds
of nature to a common humanity, and secondly of our rising
above "common" humanity by means of a certain amused
grasp or humorous perspective of it in its entirety. In other
words, we see ourselves as Puck saw us, and say "what fools
[read 'babies'] these mortals be." Both Freud and Bergson
agree with Hegel that the comic can arise only out of persons, and Freud's stress on the childish serves to emphasize
what we have most in common as individual persons—our
lives as children, wherein we are more similar to each other
than we can be as adults.

Freud concludes that jokes, the comic, and humor are
each "methods of regaining from mental activity a pleasure
which has in fact been lost through the development of that
activity." By these three means, "the euphoria which we en-

deavor to reach is . . . the mood of a period of life in which we were accustomed to deal with our physical work in general with a small expenditure of energy—the mood of our childhood, when we were ignorant of the comic, when we were incapable of jokes and when we had no need of humor to make us feel happy in our life."[10] This conclusion, too, seems to be in agreement with Schiller's distinction between the two ages of mankind, the naive and the reflective. The mature person of our time cannot be naive, and this deprivation fills him with nostalgia; but he may take great pleasure in reflecting upon naiveté, and indeed this is the quintessential romantic feeling: reflection upon the naive as an object of loss and gain. Freud makes the comic, jokes, and humor reflective techniques of projecting a "supplement" (in Derrida's sense, describing a basic romantic move) for the naive experience of childhood.

Freud's romanticism, perhaps even his sentimentality with regard to the happy life of children, may well have hindered him from carrying his speculations upon humor very far beyond their initial stage, where they are already of great interest. He observed that while it is closer to the comic than to jokes, humor is characteristically "broken" in the sense of generating "smiles through tears." Freud's explanation of this phenomenon, however, seems self-contradictory. First he insists that humorous "displacement" of otherwise painful affects is impossible under the glare of conscious attention; it must be preconscious, that is, automatic. But he goes on to say that humor "scorns to withdraw the ideational content bearing the distressing affect from conscious attention as repression does, and thus surmounts the automatism of defense." By comparing his present ego with his childish one, the mature person can say, "I am too big to be distressed by these things."[11]

What leads to this contradiction is the incompatibility of Freud's determinist economics with the existence of what

[10] P. 236.
[11] Pp. 232f.

Schiller called the play instinct, or what might be called the play of the imagination. This process is not properly called preconscious, because it is lighted up by intense conscious activity; it has an important element of the spontaneously free, which we associate with imaginative activity. This spontaneous element, it seems to me, is a sudden flooding in, while we are perceiving a given immediate situation, of a broad stream of personal experiences and attitudes amounting to a characteristic point of view, one which will decisively and personally govern the response to the situation in a way that is related to the person rather than to the situation, that is, one in which the person will dominate rather than be dominated by the event. This flooding-in is involuntary in the sense that applies to all characteristic feeling; it is not "willed" into being. But it is conscious, and indeed an augmentation of our ordinary consciousness. We never know ourselves better than in such experiences, nor is our delight in fictional characters ever so keen as when they cause us to undergo such separate realizations of our own selves in the course of our empathizing with them.

In Freud's somewhat positivistic view, however, it would seem that the world is only the world, a collection of largely disagreeable facts needing most of all to be faced up to. Against this "reality principle" the "mood of our childhood" can only seem, comparatively speaking, an illusion. But if the world is interpenetrated by human experience, changed by it and even in an important sense made by it, then humorous perception need not merely be a defense, but rather a simple grasp of an objective reality: the retentiveness things (or persons) have of themselves, especially when perceived in the perspective of "man's tenacious hold of his customary self."

These remarks may be regarded as unjust to Freud, because it was he who most powerfully drew our attention to the presence of libido and its continuing force in the best-controlled lives. From this point of view, jokes, the comic, and humor appear as more than mere defense mechanisms. Jokes, for example, according to Freud, whisper that "the wishes and desires of men have a right to make themselves acceptable alongside of exacting and ruthless morality."[12] The freedom that jokes vindicate, then, is not mere self-indulgence, but a sphere for the fulfillment of desire in its attempts to transcend the narrow limits of actuality. True, Freud's own vision of the extent of this sphere seems to have been rather limited, as this statement suggests: "So long as the art of healing has not gone further in making our life safe and so long as social arrangements do no more to make it more enjoyable, so long will it be impossible to stifle the voice within us that rebels against the demands of morality."[13] Evidently Freud saw the goals of art, science, and society as security and enjoyment. Morality seemed "exacting and ruthless" because it stressed security and denied pleasure. But beyond this merely unpleasant constraint, which may be blamed upon the slow progress of enlightenment, Freud saw a "rebellion against the compulsion of logic and reality" itself, which is "deep-going and long-lasting."[14] In his earlier formulation, the rebel is the ego or pleasure principle, enemy of the reality principle. The dynamism here is a relatively simple polarity, as the polarity of Nietzsche's Appollonian and Dionysian urges was a relatively complex polarity. Both dynamisms are alike, and both seem to derive from Schiller's polarity of the naive and the reflective.

Yet Freud, like Nietzsche before him, became aware of an integrated principle giving a positive basis for comic pleasure rather than the comparative one involved in the infantile/adult polarity. In Freud, this principle is *recognition*, which (like Aristotle in the discussion of anagnorisis) he declared to be pleasurable in itself (thereby linking his "ideational mimetics" to Aristotle's fundamental claim for mimesis). "The games founded on this pleasure," he said, "make use of the mechanism of damming up only in order to increase the amount of such pleasure."[15] As I have been

[12] P. 110.
[13] Ibid.
[14] P. 126.
[15] P. 122.

arguing, the comic may be regarded as the recognition of something continuing as itself, despite situations that tend to interrupt or obscure such continuance and thereby provide the "damming up" that Freud mentions.

THERE ARE other areas in which Freud made important contributions to the perception of comic possibilities: his relating of jokes to dreams and to what he called "dream work," including the absurd, is probably the most important. In addition, his analysis of "unmasking" and "degradation" has provided major techniques, especially for exploitation in black comedy. He was able to point convincingly to a saving of energy in caricature, parody, and travesty when we direct them against objects of authority and respect, enabling us to "stand at ease" before our betters. To Freud the "saving" of energy would be comical in effect. The serious problem here is that, along with the basic Freudian notion of an excess released by the comparison between great and small, the reduction of these familiar techniques from their aggressive roles in satire and polemic makes them into defensive forms of mere psychological escape. Freud can also state that the "effect of caricature is not essentially diminished by . . . falsification of reality."[16] Once the function is merely pleasure for the audience rather than work toward the goal of reform in society or government, accuracy of resemblance to persons or practices living or dead, even in seriously critical satire, would become unproductive. So too, "parody and travesty destroy the unity . . . between people's character and their speeches"—as if satiric technique consisted simply in producing the uncritically ridiculous, without concern for its being characteristic of the persons or states of affairs that are being ridiculed. These judgments amply confirm Freud's general view of jokes, the comic, and humor as a source of individual solace rather than, as Schiller had argued, modes of apprehending reality or representing it critically. This is a retreat from the optimistic idea of the relationship between

[16] P. 201.

reality and the ideal that characterized so much of romanticism. It means that Freud disagrees with Hegel on the achievement of Aristophanes in presenting the genuine essence of Athenian political and social reality (and with Plato as well, who would have foreigners study Aristophanes' plays in order to know the Athenians). We have seen at length how Freud's view is contradicted by Kierkegaard's.

If Freud's other central principle is the therapeutic or defensive value of recognition, we need to ask the phenomenologist's question, recognition of what? The answer appears as the reality principle, seen in opposition to the ego or pleasure principle. The essential relationships come out more clearly in the paper on "Humor" that Freud published much later, in 1927, when the "reality principle" had given way to the "death wish." Here Freud plainly states his concern with jokes "only from the economic point of view," repeating that "the essence . . . is that one spares himself the affects."[17] He is quite firm in saying that "like jokes and the comic, humor has something liberating about it." Now, however, he is intent upon underlining the superiority of humor over jokes and the comic. "Humor is not resigned; it is rebellious." It is a triumph of ego and the pleasure principle, it even rejects the claims of reality. Humor is one in the "great series of methods which the human mind has constructed in order to evade the compulsion to suffer." Another of these methods, it is very important to note, is madness. Humor has a further dignity, lacking in many jokes, in that it is not merely an aggressive form of behavior. He then correlates the ego (or pleasure) with the child, and the superego with the father, and declares that in this structure "humor would be the contribution made to the comic through the agency of the superego."[18] And in another move toward Aristotle, he dissociates humor from laughter; he finds it never produces hearty laughter, nor is it as productive of pleasure as jokes. Yet he still insists that in humor

---

[17] *Works*, standard edition (London: Hogarth Press, 1953–), XXI, 162f.
[18] Ibid., p. 165f.

"the superego is actually repudiating reality" (as in gallows humor above all). And he concludes as if stating a great and profound mystery of life: "But (without rightly knowing why) we regard this less intense pleasure as having a character of very high value; we feel it to be especially liberating and elevating." It is "a rare and precious gift," with its "origin in the parental agency." "The main thing," Freud sums up, "is the intention"—using this word in the same sense as Kierkegaard's "standpoint" or perspective of human life and the universe—"the world . . . is nothing but a game for children—just worth making a jest about."

We may locate in these sentiments of Freud most of the stimuli that give its peculiar character to twentieth-century comedy and particularly to black humor. We may also uncover, it seems to me, the most striking new characteristic of the second wave of romanticism, already moving forward in 1900, the view that art itself is a major enterprise in the "great series of methods which the human mind has constructed in order to evade the compulsion to suffer" and that its activity is no mere evasion in the sense of escapism, but a rebellion and a liberation, aimed against all compulsion, including aggression. Art, like humor in "actually repudiating reality," offers itself as "a rare and precious gift" that will enable us to see the totality of things under perspectives the human mind has constructed, as if we adults were children again, and at play.

There is one area of the comic to which Freud concedes a measure of reality. "Unmasking" is a technique that "only applies when someone (or some abstract idea) has seized dignity and authority by a deception and these have to be taken from him in reality."[19] This analysis is perhaps not at all original, but it is so clearly and pregnantly stated that it affords many insights. The most interesting that occurs to me concerns the very difficult denouement of Shakespeare's *Measure for Measure*. When Lucio pulls off the "Friar's" cowl and exposes the Duke of Vienna, an unmasking in Freud's

---

[19] *Jokes and Their Relation to the Unconscious*, p. 201.

sense of the term does take place, for Duke Vincentio has no right to the dignity and authority of a Franciscan friar, and in addition he has usurped them to deceive his own subjects. The unmasking action is of great dramatic significance because the official dignity Vincentio should have as duke has been lost over the years by his own negligence. It is comic, too, because it is embarrassing to him to be discovered as himself, scheming and intriguing in the garb of a humble busybody when his proper place all along has been to command as his people's sovereign.

Perhaps the best-known area of the comic indicated by Freud has been that of the "absurd" as he associated it with the unconscious and with the infantile. To him the essence of jokes lies in a compromise between the demands of rational criticism and the urge to cling to one's childish pleasure in mere words and nonsense. Comic pleasure, also, arises from consciously giving free play to unconscious modes of thought. Since the latter resemble the illogical logic of dreamwork, we find Freud suggesting, as a technique of the comic, that writers adopt the methods of expression peculiar to dreams. These include an exaggerated indirecton, in which displacement shifts from any element to any other, and a replacement of internal relations such as those of similarity or cause and effect by external ones like simultaneity in time, contiguity in space, and similarity of sound. The important difference is that absurdity never, according to Freud, arises in the dream by chance; the dream represents embittered rejection and contemptuous contradiction of actual reality only rendered absurd in order to convey them past the internal censor. "Good" jokes, being socially acceptable, may use play or nonsense rather than outrageous illogic because they need make no effort to evade this rational censor.[20]

Recognizing the antisocial motives of almost all *humour noir*, we are not surprised to find that it vastly prefers "bad" jokes to "good" ones. And in creating its bad jokes it makes

[20] Ibid., Chapter VI, pp. 159–180.

overt use of the techniques Freud discovered in dreamwork: exaggeration, displacement, and replacement of structural logic by mere incoherent association. Thereby, black humor is striving for an effect that corresponds in every way to Freud's description of the qualities in dreams that differentiate them from jokes. Jokes are social, a form of developed play springing from no need but more from mere mental activeness, and are only secondarily connected with life, being above all aimed at the attainment of pleasure. Dreams are asocial, deceptively formed to remain secret, springing from deep needs as a means of wish fulfillment by regressive hallucination (i.e., by passing images back up from the unconscious to the preconscious). Painfully close to life, dreams originate in and are determined by life's unbearable stresses, and their aim is only to allay its unpleasure.

What has happened is that some artists of the twentieth century have seen the qualities of the dreamwork as infinitely more serious and worthy of exploitation than those of the joke, or for that matter of comedy or tragedy in their traditional forms. This preference, however, has sometimes led to confusion between the genuinely absurd, as in dreamwork, and the comic. Among artists and critics, especially during the fifties and sixties, there has been a refusal to accept the distinction Freud makes and an insistence upon regarding as comic (or at least as black comic) whatever is asocial, illogical, cryptic, hallucinatory, and wish fulfilling in that it rejects an unbearable demand. Black comedy can thus become an attempt to make chaos acceptable, or at least interesting, without allowing it to become orderly or meaningful.

TWENTIETH-CENTURY THEORISTS:
MAURON, CORNFORD, FRYE

THE PSYCHOLOGICAL WRITING of Freud stimulated a great deal of work on the comic, though it was not always of direct literary significance. The outstanding achievement is Charles Mauron's *Psychocritique du genre comique* (Paris: Librairie José Corti, 1964). Mauron's "psychocriticism" is a method of textual analysis that seeks "relations that probably have not been thought and willed in conscious fashion by the author," by means of "superposition of texts."[1] The method, of course, exposes much duplication resulting from literary imitation and convention, but this is left to historical criticism, in whose province it belongs; psychocriticism seeks for enigmatic repetitions of structure that suggest a common source in unconscious psychic experience. Mauron develops this complex formula for stage comedy in general: "A fantasy of triumph is projected, in the guise of play, on quotidian reality, and elaborated as comedy according to the laws of laughter and the comic art."[2] The triumph fantasy is not comic by itself; it must be projected upon reality by means of art. In a sense the psychocritic leaves the final stages, when the art of comedy is actually exerted, to others. His province, however, is still important because in it is to be found the peculiar power of the comic, and he can help to explain artistic misfires as well as bull's eyes so as to give practical criticism a surer foundation.

[1] Appendix A, p. 141, my translations.
[2] P. 131.

To Mauron, comedy is one of the defenses against anxiety, one of the most important in the whole sphere of play and the arts; and these, he believes, constitute the chief aids (along with love and procreation) in our maturation. Perhaps the most distinctive theme of comedy is Oedipal, reflecting the guilty anxiety everyone feels over longing for the death of one parent while trying to monopolize the affection of the other. The father-as-obstacle was probably the most common donnée of European comedy from Menander to Sheridan. Oftentimes his father's death is all that would be needed to put an end to the comic hero's difficulties. The comedy, however, by enabling the youth to triumph without this guilt-producing event, reverses the anxious fear that the father ordinarily inspires. In Plautus, the son's sexual triumph can be explicit, for he may carry off a girl to whom the father also has been laying claim. In the ancient world, social custom made this situation more of a real possibility than in modern times. So, according to Mauron, the simple triumph fantasy over the father had to develop by means of the dream techniques of displacement, substitution, partial suppression, and allusive attenuation into the new theme of cuckoldry of the husband. This imaginative development is the first stage of the specifically artistic process of comedy, the "projection on reality." It is persuasively explained by Mauron as developing out of the substitution in the Middle Ages of *amour-passion* for incest as the major taboo of society. The beloved woman was typically a forbidden object, and to possess her was the equivalent of tricking or robbing the father. Her husband thus became a father-surrogate in the Oedipal structure, and to cuckold him became a triumph-fantasy that entered European literature as early as the Latin farces of the twelfth century.

The other and perhaps even more lasting major theme of comedy is pre-Oedipal: that of the mother lost and found. Infantile glory in the maternal presence is the most fundamental of all psychic states. It affords in itself the principal affective basis for overcoming the fear of death. Our main defenses against destructive anxieties arise out of recalling her presence in one form or another. Thus Mauron says that in the comedy of Aristophanes the fifty-century Athenian city was the historical equivalent of communion with the mother. Not many years later, after the defeat and destruction of the Athenian political community, the center of communion was placed in the family rather than the city. Then, in the domestic milieu of Greek and Roman New Comedy, a marriage for love, which unites the pleasure principle with the reality principle, became the uniform denouement.

But there is a further range of triumph-fantasies, the narcissistic ones, which Mauron seems to relate on the one side to Oedipal anxieties such as identity-threats (twins, disguises, imbroglios) and on the other to images of the nourishing motherly presence (cooks, parasites, misers). It seems to me that this narcissistic category contains the great bulk of comic nourishment today. Both the father-as-obstacle and the communion-with-the-beloved themes, prevalent though they still are, are overexposed conventions that appear in comedy now with more frequency than comic force. The psychological critic suggests that the power of these themes is unconscious. Perhaps it would be more helpful to regard them theoretically as givens in the Hegelian sense of limits necessary to selfhood and therefore to one's free self-determination. Thus one ought not to be surprised to find that a comedy lacking these two elementary limits is weak in comic power because it fails to define the selves necessary for successful comedy. Still, the inability of as penetrating a critic as Mauron to round out the major themes of comedy without resort to an ill-defined combination of narcism and identity-threat seems indicative to me of a limit in Freudian criticism. Brilliantly contributory with regard to ethos and interpretation, it has little to offer in the determinations of art itself. The two most important contributions to ethos are first Freud's maturation principle, which seems to take its origin in a submerged central image of adulthood as represented by the enlarged, upstanding phallus and which develops into a full-fledged myth expressing the primary value of responsible paternity as the core of approved adult behavior; and secondly, the "family romance" as the basic structure of human interaction in society, the competition in which maturation is achieved. No other myth to be found in literature of the twentieth century is more important or omnipresent, or more value-laden, than the one that combines these two themes.

Mauron in fact acknowledges that the correlate of maternal communion we now seek in the theater is a mystery of a religious order. Tragedy and comedy are both mysteries manifesting the salvation of the unconscious personality. This is a helpful emphasis, in my opinion, resting upon the sense of the continuation of the self. Mauron's interpretation of Nietzsche's Dionysian urge is that it is "the oscillation between two semi-divine drunkennesses: heroic exaltation and satiric regression," that is, between tragedy and comedy. On its side, "the comic genius plays . . . with the abandonment to regression, satiric raillery, the taste of drunkenness, to liberate itself from the double servitude of instinctive tendencies and of social norms."[3] Unfortunately it appears to be impossible really to liberate, and thereby to save, the unconscious self, which always remains infantile in Freudian thought. One would think, too, that an infantile self would always be completely subject to instinctive tendencies, and indeed find the only positive delight there, as opposed to the retrospective reflection of the controlled and paternal superego, whose best outcome is solace.

Furthermore, Mauron agrees with Freud in placing the comic within the preconscious, particularly in stage comedy. As a form of play, he says, it triumphs over unconscious anxieties by re-enacting remembered dangers and humiliations voluntarily recalled in the preconscious because they were brought out of the unconscious and mastered there. Mauron honestly faces up to the problem of combining the conscious with the preconscious and the unconscious self as follows: "The familiar myth" (that is, what Mauron called "the personal myth"), "according to the anxieties and the defenses proper to the author, will be represented with that

[3] Pp. 23, 36.

affective incoherence . . . which assures the spectator against anxiety, pathos, and reflection (all unfavorable to laughter), and accords to the author the liberty of playing, like a witty man, with a mixture of sense and nonsense. . . . The spectator compares [the growing result] each instant with his own normal adult representation: the differences between the two representations nourish laughter."[4] Once the psycho-critic has established the author's personal myth, it is up to other kinds of critics to show how the play of "affective incoherence" becomes art, how sense and nonsense are combined to make comedy, and what kind of adult behavior correlates with the zany and outrageous activity on the stage. This is very barren soil for literary criticism to grow in, but it cannot be otherwise in view of the Freudian doctrine of separation between unconscious and preconscious and the heavy preference for the former as the one source of artistic power.

It would be unfair to end our notice of Mauron with the suggestion that he is a captive of Freudian doctrine. Freud's work provides him with a multitude of insights, but he can also criticize it effectively, as in his remarks on repetition. Freud had agreed with Bergson that the living never repeats itself, and that repetition (as in mimicry) is always a form of degradation. But Mauron points out that a good mimic reproduces especially the most original and living traits of his subject, waking in us a sense of triumph; and that rebirths and revivals in comedy are evocations of magic and mystery and even have the vital power to suggest miracle and divine liberty. The second Menaechmus, he remarks, always wins over the first;[5] the second Hermione, we might add, is more powerful than the first. So is the reborn Dionysus, to name that archetypal figure.

BEFORE LEAVING the discussion of our comic inheritance from the two major twentieth-century theorists, Bergson and

[4] Pp. 32f.
[5] P. 106.

Freud, it may be noted that while Bergson provided a well-articulated rhetoric and Freud a persuasive account of the human importance of the comic, neither was impressed by the effectiveness of comic theater in mounting a critique of society or of individual behavior. Bergson saw comedy as a reflection of social pressure—benign, we may feel, in an open society, oppressive in a closed one. Freud saw it as a blessed means of obtaining relief from social pressure and the other demands that real life makes upon us. In contrast, there has always been a conviction that the theater, especially, is an agency for effecting positive change in social and individual behavior. The neoclassical view looked to comedy to correct vice and folly, gently or severely, urbanely or brutally, in the conviction that both society and individuals would always need correction. This view was limited, however, to giving comedy a license to operate within rather strict bounds of "human nature" and a closed society. The change it called "correction" was not revolutionary change, but a return to well-understood norms. No more than the neoclassical critics, actually, did Bergson and Freud expect the comic or the comic theater to be an agency of positive change. At best they called upon it to improve the endurance and adaptiveness of its audiences.

Yet the comic writing of the twentieth century has been insistently critical not so much of individual behavior but much more of society's norms. This strong tendency goes under the name of satire; but some of its twentieth-century manifestations, especially in the vein of black comedy, drastically extend older definitions of the satiric. Satire now endeavors to destroy the structures of society and has thrown out the old recognized categories of human nature. No wonder that the effect of this satiric intrusion upon comedy, which always had a vested interest in the proprieties of nature and society, has been catastrophic.

As a strategic reserve against this debacle, we have kept till now what may be the most striking claim for modern comedy: that it may be performed as a communal ritual of redemption. This function was brilliantly disclosed from the then innovative anthropological point of view by F. M. Cornford in *The Origin of Attic Comedy*, published in 1914. The theory which emphasizes links between literary art and dramatic ritual owes a great deal to this exciting book, which was a worthy successor in its academic fashion to *The Birth of Tragedy*. Cornford does not invoke the Apollonian/Dionysian contrast overtly, but he does something much more effective: he gives the narrative form of an evolution, mythically continuous, to what Nietzsche presented as a historical process that had already reached its unhappy conclusion during the lifetimes of Socrates and Euripides. Cornford tells us that the drama, and comedy in particular, sprang from religious ritual originally meant to guarantee the fertility of the ranges, pastures, fields, and people of the tribe. The basic natural phenomenon, the cyclical alternation of the seasons, was dramatically represented by a struggle between a king and his destined successor, standing for the old year and the new year, as Sir James Frazer had argued thirty years before. The king, after being overcome (as nature demands), would somehow be reborn (as the needs of the tribe, and indeed of the human psyche, require). Cornford suggests that such a struggle once took place bloodily and gradually evolved into a more civilized dramatic representation of the sacrificial combat. Similarly, many lesser victims were offered by the tribe to propitiate the powers of nature and the divine. These *pharmakoi* included scapegoats, animal and human. They were sacrificed in the course of fertility rituals, in a gradually less painful manner as society evolved. The tragic hero thus arose as the successor of the defeated king, somehow reborn; the characters of comedy became the successors of the *pharmakoi*, victims of humiliation, punishment, and ridicule but happy in the assurance that they were helping to give continued fertility to the tribe.

Cornford was able to point out, in the evidence provided by the folklorists, a convincing set of descendants of these comic figures. They had already become fixed and stock folk-play characters in ancient Greece, yet they are found surviving into the twentieth century both among primitive peoples and in rural England. Thus the anthropologist accomplished on evolutionary grounds what the Freudians established on psychological grounds: he found a basis in the universally human for the powerful appeal of comedy (though not, it would seem, a clearer idea of what the comic is, except that it ought to include the note of fertility, redemption, and rebirth).

The qualities that appear in the comic-redemptive figure are first that he is a victim—beaten, humiliated, cast out. Secondly, he is strongly associated with regeneration, and even more strongly perhaps with generation. His sexual characteristics are marked.[6] (Cornford quotes a piquant instance of a *pharmakos,* while being led in procession to the place of sacrifice, being ritually beaten on the genitals with leeks.) Thus in the explanation-by-genesis that characterized the evolutionary outlook of early anthropology the stress of most later comedy upon physical abuse and sex is vindicated, as well as the toleration of so much disreputable theatrical behavior by civilized society. Comedy, Cornford demonstrated, still partakes of a religious ritual that we celebrate in reverence for the vital generative forces that enable us to survive and be happy.

ANOTHER redemptive theory, and far and away the most widely studied theory of comedy in America during recent years, is that of Northrop Frye. *The Anatomy of Criticism* (1957) dealt with the comic in two extended sections, as a "narrative category" under the name of "The Mythos of Spring" and also as a dramatic genre in stage or film comedy. Much of this argument Frye had presented earlier in the article "The Argument of Comedy" in the first issue of the *Hudson Review* (1948). These two have been the most frequently anthologized pieces of Frye's criticism. He admits to being an Odyssean critic, one who prefers to deal with the

---

[6] F. M. Cornford, *The Origin of Attic Comedy* (Garden City, N.Y.: Doubleday, 1961), pp. 106–112.

comic mode, and in 1965 he returned to it in a discussion of
Shakespeare's later comedy, *A Natural Perspective.*

Though Aristotle is the predecessor whom Frye praises,
his theory seems to me to have more important resem-
blances to Freud's, Bergson's, and especially Cornford's. Its
originality, however, is not limited to the Spenglerian superstructure of seasonal myths, ritual patterns, and fictional
cosmologies in which it is enclosed and which (as Frye
seems to admit) are rather machines for classification than
elements of a literary theory. Quite apart from these, Frye
offers a restatement of neoclassical comic form and an imaginative explanation of the pervasive emphasis upon community that is found in all comedy.

In "The Mythos of Spring" Frye defines comedy according to its movement toward an image of the world as a fictional form: comedy is a vision of the establishing of a desirable society.[7] His general scheme places comedy among
the four "narrative categories" (logically prior to literary
genres): comedy, romance, tragedy, and irony. Among these
four kinds of stories or myths comedy is the mythos that is
organized around anagnorisis—recognition of a newborn
society is the characteristic story line of comedy. The fictional worlds in which comedy is set range along an axis
from the more ironic to the more romantic through six types
of societies:

> 1. Ironic: "The redeemed society . . . in its infancy,
> swaddled and smothered by the society it should re-
> place."
> 2. Quixotic: The redeemed society "in adolescence,
> still too ignorant of the ways of the world to impose it-
> self."
> 3. Mature and triumphant: The old man (*senex*) gives
> way to the youth (i.e., the newborn society succeeds in
> imposing itself at the end).

[7] *The Anatomy of Criticism* (Princeton: Princeton University Press, 1957),
pp. 163f.

4. Mature and already established: The established society is neither old nor young, but mature.

5. Innocent order: From the beginning an order is settled; it is of a religious nature, drawing away from human experience toward a paradise or mythical over-world.

6. Imaginary withdrawal: Ghost stories, returns to the womb.

The remarkable thing about this scheme is that, while in one sense it is an axiological arrangement along a line from irony to romance, in another sense its first four social epochs are actually the embodiment of a myth: the Freudian maturation myth, so universal among educated Americans at the time Frye was composing his system (or, as he prefers to call it, his "synoptic scheme"). Further, this Freudian myth is con-flated with the myth of the ritual origin of drama in the overcoming of the old king by the new—though Frye disbe-lieves that the rituals of the theater have any source except the need to hold an audience's attention. The result is itself a quasi-mythic construct of considerable imaginative ingenu-ity, and one that is quite viable pedagogically. Its six phases constitute a life-story of society rather than a coher-ent axiology. Furthermore, the reason for six rather than the customary seven ages lies in the symmetrical appeal of a scheme in which each of the four narrative categories or mythoi is characterized by six phases, three parallel to the mythos that precedes and three to the mythos that follows it on the total circle of mythoi. Frye's hope was to create a the-oretical structure like that of the circle of fifths in music, so that a fictional motif could be identified and noted down in its place as a musical motif can be. It is doubtful whether anyone has taken this formal aspiration seriously, and Frye himself seems to have abandoned it in favor of a single scheme based upon topography (as Freud says his is based, in *Jokes and Their Relation to the Unconscious*), and including an underworld, an overworld, and the world in between.

Frye's more solid contribution in his earlier writing was to

describe the structure of classical New Comedy (post-Aris-
tophanean, or as Frye calls it, Menandrine) in terms that
combine a sometimes specious erudition with genuine critical insight. Old Comedy was a dying form in Greek, he says,
even when Aristophanes gave us our only extant specimens
of it. From then until now, comedy has normally followed
the Menandrine tradition. In it we have a basic comic Oedipus situation: a youth outwits an opponent, who either is or
stands for his father, in order to possess a girl (that she
stands for his mother may be hinted at).[8] Here Frye anticipated Charles Mauron. (It is ironical that Mauron, even in
his extensive and valuable bibliography to *Psychocritique du
genre comique*, should ignore Frye, who himself was cavalier
in acknowledging sources.) The "comic Oedipus situation"
seems so apt that one is astonished that Freud himself did
not deal extensively with it. A recognition is necessary to
make the girl marriageable, for normally she is a courtesan
or otherwise under a taboo. Thus it is the pattern of fulfillment of an unconscious infantile wish that accounts for the
lasting appeal of this basic kind of comedy.

Frye notes that Aristotle gave his blessing to New Comedy
and goes on to make what seems a most un-Aristotelian application of the master's four causes. The material cause is
said to correspond to sexual desire; the formal cause to the
social order, which is triumphantly renewed when the
youth, after defeating his old opponent, conforms to it; the
efficient cause is the intriguing slave; the final cause, the audience's applause. Aristotle, in speaking of tragedy, made
the material cause the language, music, and other means of
production, the formal cause the plot, the efficient cause the
poet, and the final cause the raising and purging of pity and
terror. When Frye identifies the formal cause of comedy
with the newborn society, he is simply making use of Aristotle's term to impose his own quite different scheme. That
the final cause should be the audience's applause seems very
odd indeed, since Aristotle had said that the actual success
of a tragedy at a given performance was not what mattered

[8] Ibid., pp. 185f.

but whether it was apt to move pity and terror, just as the actual success of an orator did not matter if his speech and arguments were such as deserved to win.

Frye's whole approach is profoundly un-Aristotelian. His handling of the *Tractatus Coislinianus*, for example, as if his explication of it were more or less legitimate Aristotelian doctrine on comedy, seems to me neither fish nor flesh, but indeed good herring. The *Tractate* is extremely remote from Aristotle in time (fifteen centuries), without external authority, and internally vague, confused, and inept;[9] moreover, it is cut off from contact with a stage tradition of comedy. This remoteness from the theater probably helps rather than hinders Frye in working his analysis of the *Tractatus* into his own romantic view of the comic. That eclectic view is tied to nostalgia for infantile joy (the Freudian component), nostalgia for the integral community expressing itself in valid ritual forms (Cornford and the anthropologists), and the central romantic (and Bergsonian) conviction that imagination, propelled by desire, can end by giving a body to what begins as a fiction.

Thus while Frye correctly says that comedy has been "remarkably tenacious of its structural principles and character types,"[10] he explains its structure in terms of a social dynamics that has little relation to history, but is in fact mythic. Greek New Comedy, which was the "basis for most comedy," Frye says was "not a form but a formula." Its elements were complex:

1. A movement from one society to another.

2. At the beginning, the characters in charge of society are obstructive; the audience recognizes them as having usurped their authority.

3. At the end, the hero wins the heroine in a "new" society.

4. The denouement, in which the hero triumphs, is

---

[9] Even as described by its "discoverer," Lane Cooper, in "An Aristotelian Treatment of Comedy," *The Poetics of Aristotle: Its Meaning and Influence* (New York: Cooper Square Publishers, 1963), pp. 69–74.

[10] P. 163f.

accompanied by an anagnorisis or cognitio, i.e., a revelation of some sort.

    5. There follows a party or festive ritual (e.g., a wed-
ding or a dance) with a pairing-off of characters.

    6. The audience joins in the communion thus en-
acted.

There is a heavy emphasis here on the social aspect of
comedy—or rather on the communal basis that Cornford, in
particular, developed. There is also a lack in Frye of concern
for literary form, occasioned in part by his view that comedy
is first of all a broadly narrative category, not a dramatic one.
Since it is arguable that "the tragic" exists outside of tragedy
and unquestionable that "the comic" exists outside of comedy, it is reasonable to draw up a formula including the recognized components, whether they are found in plays, films,
or fiction. This would explain the fact that Frye's formula is
even more descriptive of Greek romances than of stage comedy as we actually have it from Plautus to Wilde. True,
Frye's formula makes the hero's social role quite important,
and it stresses audience participation in a way that anticipates the environmental theater of today; but neither of
these emphases is well suited to a description of classical
New Comedy as we have it. Furthermore, his most basic
component, the social "movement," is much less frequently
present in Menandrine comedy than in Aristophanes, where
there is normally a reorganization of society in accordance
with a bright idea of the hero. The driving force behind
Frye's formula is his own conviction that human desire,
stimulating imagination and taking fictional shape by means
of imagination, can achieve the actual transformation and
redemption of society. This is a romantic ideal and, I believe, a sound one. It has, however, very little to do with the
comic, either in experience or in theory. Its intended application by Frye includes Dante's use of comedy to mean the
story of the world as set forth by the divine imagination and
even the Bible, which Frye believes has a comic structure.

    In the first and sixth of his comic phases where the dyna-

mism of social movement ought to be more tense Frye loses
sight of the comic altogether in pure irony or romance; and
in the middle phases no social movement is evident. In
phase one, "a more intense irony is achieved," he says,
"when the humorous society simply disintegrates without
anything taking place, as . . . frequently in Chekhov."[11] This
is to miss altogether the comic of immaturity in *The Cherry
Orchard*, where nostalgia for the nursery is ridiculed as an
overt object of fun rather than an unconscious source of
pleasure, where the children desert their home and the old
man Fers is left in possession of the stage while the horrid
new society prepares to build its villas. In *Three Sisters* the
old society disintegrates, but it is the society to which the
young heroines belong; and yet they survive (that is the real
point) along with their nemesis, Masha and Baby Bobik.
Aggressively alive as the latter are, we feel that the sentimental fragility and gentleness of the sisters, their quasi-
aristocratic ideals, will resist Masha's worst efforts.

At the other end of the axis, Frye writes: "The closing
scene of *The Winter's Tale* makes me think . . . of bodily met-
amorphosis and a transformation from one kind of life to
another . . . both far-fetched and inevitably right, outraging
reality and at the same time introducing us to a world of
childlike innocence which has always made more sense than
reality."[12] This can only be a surprisingly sentimental evo-
cation of Freud's infantile world before we were guilty, coupled with a rejection of the real world as absurd. When Frye
comments that "we see the action . . . from the point of view
of a higher and better world" he is extrapolating the rare
grace and clemency of Shakespeare into a category of comic
fiction that hardly exists aside from a few masterpieces. It is
a fault of Frye's method that he cannot acknowledge the individual and sometimes unique accomplishment of separate
works, but must derive their force from a totalized system.

In Frye's handling of this "higher and better world" to-

[11] P. 178.
[12] P. 184.

ward which comedy is said to move, there is too much ambivalence over what is real. In romantic thought there is a legitimate sense in which the ideal, as imaginatively projected,
is more complete, integral, and genuine than any realization
of it can ever be. But to suggest that this romantic notion of
the ideal/real has much connection with the fictions of comedy—even romantic comedy—is to disregard the evidence
of comic writing. Even in Shakespeare, the comedy of Bottom and company, of a better world perhaps, is not of a
higher one. The figure of Shylock seen from a higher and
better world would cause tears, not laughter. Falstaff is far
better off reposing in Arthur's bosom than in Abraham's.
Indeed, Frye's account of Falstaff is merely an anthropological catchall: "In Falstaff . . . we can see the affinities of the
buffoon . . . with the parasite . . . a development of what in
Aristophanic comedy is represented by the chorus, and
which in its turn goes back to the kommos or revel from
which comedy is said to be descended."[13] In *The Tempest*,
Caliban, Miranda, and Ariel are all childlike, but they vary
greatly in innocence, and it is the guilty child Caliban who is
by far the most comic and who makes us laugh the most.
Prospero shows us what to think of the "higher and better
ordered world" that his spells have created, and its point of
view, when he breaks his staff and drowns his book of magic
before returning to Milan, "where every second thought
shall be my grave."

Shakespearean comedy, like comedy in general, encourages us to face commonplace reality and to live with it. This
ability has much to do with our being able to transform it;
survival is a more practical program than revival. Frye, on
the contrary, insists upon the ideally real of the romantics:
"Shakespearean comedy illustrates, as clearly as any mythos
we have, the archetypal functions of literature in visualizing
the world of desire, not as an escape from 'reality' but as the
genuine form of the world that human life tries to imitate."[14]

[13] P. 175.
[14] P. 184.

Seen in its Hegelian evolutionary "form," such a transformation process perhaps "makes more sense than reality."
This formalism does not alter the fact that comedy in general and Shakespearean comedy in particular pays much less
attention to process than to reality.

Actually, much of Frye's writing on comedy does show an
appreciation of its concentration on everyday reality and
unchanging behavior. As we have seen, he recognizes that
comedy is "remarkably tenacious of its structural principles
and character types," and like Cornford he specifies the pe-
rennial stock characters of the *eiron, alazon, bomolochos,* and
agroikos. These skeleton types arise from functions performed in the play; they are still as evident in comedy today
as they were in ancient Greece. As usual, Frye pours many
kinds of new wine into these old bottles. The *alazon* is not
simply the clever impostor so dear to the Greek temperament; the type includes "blocking characters" in general,
like the *senex* or old father. The *eiron* includes not only self-
depreciators but also the hero and heroine, the clever slave
and the parasite, and that hard-worked but dim figure, the
Vice. Clowns are divided into *bomolochoi* (buffoons) and
agroikoi (rustics), and these broader categories are made to
include the more numerous personae described by Cornford.[15]

Frye limits the ways in which comedy may be developed
to two: either by emphasizing the blocking characters, or by
emphasizing discovery and reconciliation. Yet the latter emphasis is the only one that fits his definition of comedy, his
repeated references to the general atmosphere of reconciliation, and his stress upon the reborn comic society. For instance, he states as a general truth that all right-thinking
people come over to the hero's side at the end, and "a new
social unit is formed on the stage." This is the comic resolution, and is equivalent to "the birth of a renewed sense of
social integration." The ritual pattern of hero and society
dead and reborn is hinted at, Frye suggests, by the threats of

---

[15] Pp. 171–176.

death that are often found in New Comedy. But the superficial nature of this whole classification of comedy developed by emphasizing discovery and reconciliation, or rebirth and redemption, is apparent in a couple of Frye's obiter dicta. "As the main character interest in comedy is often focussed on the defeated characters," he says at one point, "comedy regularly illustrates a victory of arbitrary plot over consistency of character."[16] As for the hero whose society was said to triumph in comedy, Frye states that his character is generally neutral so that we can empathize with him and sometimes so unimportant that he is not even brought upon the stage. These remarks show that comedy normally inheres in the all-too-actual blocking characters and buffoons rather than in the hero's desire or his ideal society.

Frye agrees with Bergson, in part, in the view that what is comic in these blocking characters is the absurdity of repetition.[17] There is a Bergsonian note, too, in Frye's view that the general movement of comedy toward accepting the hero's version of society is a movement from illusion to reality. To Frye, illusion has a fixed character; anyone who perceived it would rebel, saying, "Whatever reality is, it's not like that!" As opposed to the illusory, closed society, the final reality is one to which the audience can reconcile itself because it is "a kind of moral norm, or pragmatically free society."[18] Aside from the ambivalence of the term "reality"—as Frye uses it, it fits Aristophanes' plays better than New Comedy—these remarks are valuable, especially when supplemented by a statement in the earlier essay implying that freedom is shown pragmatically when a society tolerates variety. "The tendency of comedy is to include as many people as possible in its final society."[19] It is this inclusiveness—the law of comic form, according to Frye—and not the poet's supposedly more religious outlook that accounts for the stress in Shakespeare's later comedies on reconciliation. As for the

[16] P. 170.
[17] P. 168.
[18] P. 169f.
[19] P. 165.

"moral norm" (what, following Hegel, we have called "the natural concrete ethic"), it need not be very demanding. Comedy does not require the moral stress applied in *Volpone*, for instance; better for everyone to dissolve at the end in laughter, as in *The Alchemist*.

Whatever its inconsistencies of treatment and principle, Frye's discussion of classical and neoclassical comedy is fresh and stimulating. His most characteristic contribution, nevertheless, is elsewhere, in his notion of a "second world," a community of nature and man that has been usurped and supplanted by "this world" in a primeval Fall. Comedy increasingly evokes the primal Green World as it moves along the axis away from irony toward romance. Just how thoroughly romantic this conception is appears in Frye's early statement of its principle: "In order to pass from the physical world to the spiritual world man has to use his imagination and train himself, with the help of works of art, to reverse the natural perspective" ("Yeats and the Language of Symbolism," 1947).[20] The title of his book of lectures on Shakespeare's late romantic comedies, *A Natural Perspective* (1965), is taken from the Duke's speech near the end of *Twelfth Night*, "A natural perspective, that is and is not." Frye's aim as a critic is to reverse the natural perspective and to move with the help of literature away from what is in the direction of what is not, toward what he calls "the Bottomless Dream of mankind."[21] The language of this dream is myth and metaphor, the universal language of poetry as distinguished from the ordinary languages of the nations and tribes of men. We seem to have another Copernican revolution proposed here: instead of poetry imitating nature we have nature imitating poetry, which has given structure to categories developed within the human imagination. Indeed, Frye's view is quite continuous with the original Kantian starting-point of the German romantics. His stress on edu-

[20] In *Fables of Identity* (New York: Harcourt, Brace and World, 1963), p. 233.

[21] See *A Natural Perspective* (New York: Harcourt, Brace and World, 1965), p. ix.

cation through the imagination is like Schiller's in the early 1790s, and like Schelling's, Hegel's, and Arnold's thereafter. His slight regard for everything merely physical, however, is characteristic of the German rather than the English wing of romanticism.

As in his earlier work, Frye is convinced that comedy acts for the recognition of free identities of two kinds: social, in the birth of a new social community; and individual, in the self-recognition that releases a character from mechanical forms of repetitive behavior. These two kinds of recognition are in fact only one, for the old society, with its arbitrary laws and whims, is essentially mechanical and repetitive ("closed") too. Clearly recognizable here is Bergson's explanation of the laughable as whatever points up the mechanization of behavior. But since Frye is not narrowly concerned with the problems of society today, what he says about the mythical or the primitive basis of comedy is much more important than his diagnosis of the evil of mechanization. This comic force, he says, is "a movement toward the rebirth and renewal of the powers of nature . . . expressed in the imagery more directly than in the structure." The cycle of natural death and rebirth is the backbone of all literature. Its first half is the passage from dawn to dark, birth to inevitable death; this half permits the tragic alliance of nature and reason. "Comedy, however, is based on the second half of the great cycle, moving from death to rebirth, decadence to renewal, winter to spring, darkness to a new dawn." Its suggestion is of "something unpredictable and mysterious . . . the imaginative equivalents of faith, hope, and love" rather than of reason and the inevitable. It suggests that "it is *death* that is somehow unnatural, even though it always happens."[22]

Frye deeply respects this force. If in Freudian terms it is wish fulfillment, it is nevertheless "a power as deeply rooted in nature and reality" as the "reality principle" and, at least in comedy, it can be seen "taking over and informing the

[22] Ibid., pp. 119–122.

predictable world."[23] Here one thinks of two famous comments on poetry, Sir Francis Bacon's that it "doth raise and erect the mind by submitting the shews of things to the desires of the mind" and Omar's

> Ah Love! could you and I with Him conspire
> To grasp this sorry Scheme of Things entire,
>   Would not we shatter it to bits—and then
> Re-mould it nearer to the Heart's Desire!

But Frye is not reflecting Bacon or Fitzgerald, one may be sure; rather he is in the American midstream of William James's *Will To Believe* according to which if one wants a dream to come true ardently enough to imagine it and to act vigorously upon one's imagined projection of it, one's belief in a fiction will seriously affect reality and may indeed bring the dream into being as the new reality.

Comedy, Frye says, tends to support the notion of divine providence; but he adds that this is what might be called an accident of literary convention. A more serious fact is that when the comic society is born at the end of a play it has succeeded in internalizing the mechanical law that held at the beginning by giving it an "inner source of coherence" instead of abolishing it. A "barrier to action" becomes "an inner condition of behavior." This movement in Shakespeare's romantic comedies amounts to a dialectical renewal. In moving from the old society to the newly born one, it lifts us to a "vision of something never seen," "a higher world," and it "separates that world from the world of the comic action itself." The comic peripeteia or "real turning around" is completed "when the comic action defines the world of its conclusion [i.e., the new society], and separates itself from the world of confusion and chaos below it."[24] At this point the playgoer perceives his critical recognition. In the projected vision he recognizes what Frye some-

---

[23] P. 123.
[24] Pp. 133,140.

times calls the Green World, a world that is a proper place
for man, an Eden—like the one from which he insists on believing he fell. His ordinary world is abolished because he is
no longer a mere spectator, for he possesses an internalized
vision. It affects his own sense of identity with his own possible world and leaves to his own imagination the challenge
to participate in and not merely to watch the further elaboration of that possible world.

In explaining his dialectical vision Frye invokes religious
comparisons though in a rather different way from that of
the American biblical exegetes in their literary criticism. He
says there is a parallel between romantic comedy and "the
comic framework of the Bible, where man loses a peaceable
kingdom, staggers through the long nightmare of tyranny
and injustice which is human history, and eventually regains
his original vision."[25] A further parallel appears in the simplified cycle of nature from spring to winter to spring again,
and this in turn corresponds to "three modes of reality."[26]
The first spring is Eden, "the nature that God intended man
to live in, the home." The winter is the ordinary world of
fallen man wherein he has learned to seek an inward equivalent of Eden by means of law, religion, morality, but especially in education and the arts. Below the winter world is
nothing—the mere abyss of disorder and madness and the
tempest that symbolizes devouring time. Images of chaos in
comedy take the form of confusions of identity. The comic
world separates itself from this abyss into a forest world, a
dream world, an upper human world toward which the
comic action moves. It stands as a symbol of natural society,
the proper home of man, the world he is trying to regain. It
is a world of magic art and music.

At this point of realization where it might be wiser to stop,
Frye pushes on. He proceeds to annihilate the ordinary experience of the world on which he, like many others in recent years, passes a severe judgment. With the vision of the

[25] P. 133.
[26] Pp. 136f.

Green World, he says, "the world of ordinary experience disappears, for the separation has finally been made between . . . a world ransomed and a world destroyed." Mere time is no more, for we have been caught up in "the rhythm of existence, the recovery by man of the energy of nature." The world below—not chaos at this point in the dialectic but Middle Earth, our present world—is "nonexistent."[27] So drastic an internalization has probably parted company with the experience of comedy or the comic. It has left nothing of substance in human nature or the world; when all is changed, the comic least of all can survive. If Frye's dream were to come true, the comic would be transformed into romance.

[27] Pp. 158f.

NIETZSCHEAN VALUES IN
COMIC WRITING

1. Tragic and Comic in Nietzsche

AMONG NIETZSCHE'S transvaluations of value, one of the most prophetic was his overturning of Aristotle's original dictum that the comic avoided the "harmful." Nietzsche coupled delight and destruction; he found them inextricably mingled in the creative behavior of the human who is a producer and a product of modern culture. Written at the start of the movement toward black humor, a passage like this stands as a manifesto:

> Man no longer needs a "justification of ills"; "justification" is precisely what he abhors: he enjoys ills *pur, cru;* he finds senseless ills the most interesting. If he formerly had need of a god, he now takes delight in a world disorder without God, a world of chance, to whose essence belong the terrible, the ambiguous, the seductive.
>
> In such a state it is precisely the *good* that needs "justifying," i.e., it must be founded in evil and danger, or involve some great stupidity: then it still pleases. Animality no longer arouses horror; *esprit* and happy exuberance in favor of the animal in man is . . . the most triumphant form of spirituality.[1]

---

[1] Friedrich Nietzsche, *The Will to Power*, translated by Walter Kaufmann and R. J. Hollingdale (London: Weidenfield and Nicolson, 1968), §1019, p. 527. Most of the translations used in this chapter are so widely accepted that it seems adequate to cite originals by section only.

The "justification of ills" Nietzsche rejects here is the formulation of evil as a mystery with perhaps a divine but certainly not a human solution. He tells us that it is useless to
make evil into a problem soluble only by God, for evil is a
part of existence itself; existence is ambiguous, both good
and evil by its nature, and necessarily so. Instead of accepting the ambiguity of existence, human beings one-sidedly
rejected it in the past, and produced their concept of God so
as to give him the responsibility of coping with evil. The
"world of chance" that follows upon the rejection of this
God ought to suffuse humanity with a sense of new and
vastly increased power, enough to encourage them to take
upon themselves the evils of existence as their own responsibility. Perhaps these evils are subject to human control—if
not through science and technology then through human
wisdom and endurance. In this view, the good in its former
sense of grace shining forth in the actions or character of a
human as a touch of the divine would no longer have God as
a ground. The good would seem adventitious, unnecessary,
not to be relied on. Thus, as Nietzsche says, it would need to
seem out of keeping with its environment ("founded in evil
and danger"), or it would appear self-contradictory and
weak ("involve some great stupidity"). Good, not evil,
would then need to be justified, for even to detect its existence would be no easy matter. When it appears as "happy
exuberance in favor of the animal in man," however, good
strikes many people as evil, and then they notice it. Though
Nietzsche does not make the application, this bit of irony
helps to explain how sensuality, obscenity, and pornography
came to be so heavily emphasized in black comedy.

    Some of Nietzsche's most fundamental ideas had been an-
ticipated by Schiller, who stressed the importance of freedom and its immediate relationship to mere chance, especially in the comic. Schiller also accepted destructiveness, at
least in satire, and he recognized the coexistence in Lucian
and Swift of a destructive as well as a playful vein of writing
that had qualities of the comic besides the purely satirical.
But he differed from Nietzsche in stressing "the beautiful
soul" or "the beautiful heart" of a free spirit like Lucian.

When this ordinarily playful satirist deals with the corrupt life of Rome, Schiller says, he reaches sublime heights of condemnation and repudiation. Nietzsche on the contrary, only scoffed at "beautiful souls."[2]

Though Nietzsche never appeared concerned to distinguish tragic joy from comic joy, he firmly denied that the modern age was capable of the tragic. He rejected not only Wagner's *Parsifal* but all modern tragedy. In the "Self-Criticism" of *The Birth of Tragedy*, which he wrote in 1886, while he failed to make clear his own notion of stage or literary comedy, Nietzsche excluded "the tragic view of life" in favor of a comic—or at least a laughing—one. Fifteen years earlier in section 18 of *The Birth of Tragedy* he had credited Kant and Schopenhauer with an insight that inaugurated a new culture, which he then ventured to call "a tragic culture." He had followed that tribute with an enthusiastic paragraph written with Wagner in mind:

> Let us imagine a coming generation with such intrepidity of vision, with such a heroic penchant for the tremendous; let us imagine the bold strike of these dragon-slayers, the proud audacity with which they turn their back on all the weaklings' doctrines of optimism in order to "live resolutely" in wholeness and fullness: would it not be necessary for the tragic man of such a culture, in view of his self-education for seriousness and terror, to desire a new art, the art of metaphysical comfort, to desire tragedy as his own. . . .[3]

In 1886, making fun of "metaphysical comfort," Nietzsche answered his own question: "No! you ought to learn the art of *this-worldly* comfort first; you ought to learn to laugh, my young friends, if you are hell-bent on remaining pessimists."[4] And he repeated the passage from book 4 of *Thus*

---

[2] Ibid., §100, pp. 63f., where Nietzsche attacks Rousseau, the spokesman for the *bel âme*, for his moralizing and his need of God.

[3] *The Birth of Tragedy and the Case of Wagner*, translated by Walter Kaufmann (New York: Vintage, 1967), §18, pp. 112f.

[4] "Attempt at a Self-Criticism," Ibid., §7, p. 26f.

Spoke Zarathustra that ends, "Laughter I have pronounced holy: you higher men, *learn*—to laugh!" (section 20). In denying that European man in the nineteenth century was capable of expressing in life or in art anything like the tragic sense of terror or of joy that the Greeks once knew, Nietzsche gives the same reasons that black and absurd comedy used to establish its condemnation of inanity, banality, mechanization, and meaninglessness in modern society. His critique of the modern world and modern man has been so widely accepted in its negative aspects that it has for some time now lain under the same curse of banality, overacceptance, and overinternalization as those humanitarian pieties that he attacked. Alienation, overeducation, overconceptualization, museum culture, denial of the body, destruction of real communities and substitution of "lonely crowds," *ressentiment*, and in general a decline of whatever is excellent toward its least common denominator: Nietzsche pilloried all of these. But he found a joy in his destructions, a joy he knew how to express.

"Laughter I have pronounced holy: you higher men, *learn*—to laugh!" This command of Zarathustra's is aimed at freeing his disciples from his own Devil, his worst enemy, whom he repeatedly calls "The Spirit of Gravity": "I found him serious, thorough, profound, and solemn: it was the spirit of gravity—through him all things fall. Not by wrath does one kill but by laughter. Come, let us kill the spirit of gravity."[5] This command strikes down all those who have embraced the tragic vision and the tragic view of life as their religion; clutched as "a solace and a stay," to use Matthew Arnold's phrase, the tragic view of life hardly seems the affirmation, the "saying yes to life," that Zarathustra stood for. When the sixth seal is broken, his word is "My sarcasm is a laughing sarcasm . . . for in laughter all that is evil comes together, but is pronounced holy and absolved by its own

---

[5] *Thus Spoke Zarathustra*, translated by Walter Kaufmann, in *The Portable Nietzsche* (New York: Viking, 1954), "On Reading and Writing," part 1, p. 153.

bliss." And the Seventh Seal reveals the light of antino-
mianism: "Are not all words lies to those who are light?
Sing! Speak no more!"[6] Nietzsche's celebration of joy in destruction has attracted many more artists than Arnold's
"culture." Paradoxically, Nietzsche's attitude seems accept-
ably mystical to them and Arnold's too pragmatic.

It is not immediately obvious that Nietzsche's thought
should be applied to the comic on stage or in fiction; few
critics have tried to do so. Not formulated rules but
Nietzsche's own example, especially in *Thus Spoke Zarathustra*, will give us the clue. As a beginning, we can establish a
conceptual basis by taking up some of his remarks on
beauty.

In *The Will to Power* we find a passage (§§416–417) written
sometime between 1883 and 1888 in which Nietzsche gives a
quick resume of the steps he took in reaching his ultimate
insight: the eternal recurrence of the same. His first solution,
he says, had been the perception of "Dionysian wisdom,"
which he defines as "joy in the destruction of the most noble
and at the sight of its progressive ruin: in reality joy in what
is coming and lies in the future, which triumphs over existing things, however good. Dionysian: temporary identification with the principle of life (including the voluptuousness
of the martyr)."[7] This early awareness Nietzsche must have
had along with his conviction that the proper pursuit for
man was not happiness before he wrote *The Birth of Tragedy*.
Already in that first book he had subordinated beauty to the
orgiastic delight in the agon that tragedy then was to him: a
mingling of pleasure and pain. Beauty is only a temporary
form, a delay. "I took the will to beauty (i.e., to persist in like
forms) for a temporary means of preservation and recuperation," he continues. "Fundamentally, however, the eternally
creative (like the eternal compulsion to destroy) appeared to
me to be associated with pain."[8] This pain that is a part both

[6] Ibid., part 3, "The Seven Seals," §§6, 7, pp. 342f.
[7] *Will to Power*, §417, p. 224.
[8] Ibid., §416, p. 224.

of the creative and the destructive forces must be a sign that an expenditure of ourselves is required; according to Nietzsche, man's basic urge is not to pursue happiness but to expend himself. Beauty cannot overcome or permanently keep at bay this pain of existence, but it can be a means of temporary delight in allowing us to enjoy forms that appear, by some perfection in them, to persist as themselves. Such forms, however, call for a participatory giving of oneself that involves some individual sense of struggle.[9]

The complement (and more than just the complement) of beauty is "the ugly," which has a remarkable genesis. "The ugly is the form things assume when we view them with the will to implant a meaning, a new meaning, into what has become meaningless: the accumulated force which compels the creator to consider all that has been created hitherto as unacceptable, ill-considered, worthy of being denied, ugly."[10] The character of Nietzsche's thought comes out in these definitions that do not define entities so much as the ways in which we might regard our experience emotionally as well as intellectually as part of the whole process of becoming, so that nothing would stand as permanent being. Beauty—or rather "the will to beauty"—stabilizes certain forms in that they continue to give delight. The nature of the ugly appears to be more complex: there is no "will to the ugly," but rather a will to meaning that leads us first to see as ugly that to which we already feel a need to give some new meaning. The ugly is something that is perceived to be in need of change and that cries out to be changed. The strength and pathos of this appeal prevents the ugly from being a mere contradiction or absence of beauty. The ugly had indeed been viewed as the partial content of a certain powerful aesthetic quality, the sublime, as defined by Burke, Kant, and Schiller; to Nietzsche the sublime is the cloak of the ugly.

While Nietzsche's thought presents pain as a broader,

[9] *Thus Spoke Zarathustra*, part 2, "On the Tarantulas," pp. 213f.

[10] *Will to Power*, §416, p. 224.

more ambiguous and complex aspect of experience than pleasure, he refuses to allow either pleasure or pain an ultimate place in his scheme of human values. Joy, however, is fundamental. It mingles pleasure and pain; happiness is subordinate to one's sense of fulfilling the general will to power with its simultaneously destructive and creative aspects and therefore its joy.

This thought expressly mingles, if it does not totally confound, the tragic with the comic view of life. Since Nietzsche's thought was second to none both in its prophetic insight and actual influence over new movements in literature, we should not be surprised by what we find today: not old-fashioned tragicomedy—a combination of two distinct and contrasted moods, one expressed in the main plot and the other in the subplot—but instead black comedy; not nineteenth-century *drame* but a mingling of the ugly to-be-destroyed-for-now and the beautiful to-be-preserved-for-awhile. The question about this thought that is so difficult to answer, whether the new meanings come first and reduce the old to ugliness or are brought into being only as the outcome of desire or need and prompted by the insufficiency of the presently existing, is just as hard to answer with regard to the art of the twentieth century. Destruction of forms seemed to come first, but many traditionally minded people still cannot see that any meanings have arrived.

Still, criticism has clarified many new attitudes and in their light has described new genres (fiction without plot or character, ritual drama, absurd or asocial theater, particularist verse, minimal art, and many others). Critics have helped us to realize that parody—not a genre in itself but a reflective way of playing with genres that exploits a sure but critical sense of their generic characteristics—is the most prevalent formal principle in the comic writing of the modern age. Joyce, for example, parodied the Homeric archetype of all Western epic, using prose and a very unheroic hero; and then he wrote *Finnegans Wake*, a parody not only of the forms of fiction but of literary language itself. Eliot's *Waste Land* is a parody of Juvenalian satire, mixing in elements of the pastoral as Schiller predicted would happen. One might even risk the speculation that *Madame Bovary* (hardly a tragic book) is a parody of the novel of romantic fulfillment, a black comic equivalent for the nineteenth century of *Don Quixote.*

In all of this destructive activity, tragedy was at first the "ugliest" form in that it was the most in need of change. Its terror was swallowed up in solace—in pity, which Nietzsche feared and detested; its meaning ended in a stoic pose or in making excuses founded on the myth of progress. To Nietzsche terror was basic to existence, pity only degrading to pitied and pitier. The reason he put so high a value on Greek tragedy and such a low one on the tragic writing of his own era appears in the entry already quoted in part, where he continues the account of the genesis of his own thought thus:

> 1. My endeavor to oppose decay and increasing weakness of personality. I sought a new *center.*
>
> 2. Impossibility of this endeavor recognized.
>
> 3. Thereupon I advanced further down the road of disintegration—where I found new sources of strength for individuals. We have to be destroyers!—I perceived that the state of disintegration, in which individual natures can perfect themselves as never before—is an image and isolated example of existence in general. To the paralyzing sense of general disintegration and incompleteness, I opposed the *eternal recurrence.*[11]

The point of this development for us is that, while Greek tragedy was born out of strength and integration, nineteenth-century tragedy maintained itself only as an expression of weakness in an age of disintegration. The absence of limit precluded the tragic; but it freed individuals to seek a perfection of their own. He realized that this absence of limit and this struggle for perfection were an image of all existence. Nietzsche then received his mysterious revelation of

[11] Ibid., §417, p. 224.

the eternal return. He saw that acts are not performed as in tragic plots, once for all time. Better, then, to take up the tone of laughter and to avoid the "serious, thorough, profound, and solemn." Best of all, to avoid the comforting, and rather to shock, offend, terrify, ridicule, madden, and intoxicate oneself and one's audience. Nietzsche, however, never suggested it was possible for art to use these means exclusively, and his own practice in *Thus Spoke Zarathustra* indicates that he was aware of limitations on the use of the offensive and the terrible in art.

Laughter itself is a limit in that it is a release. Especially when one laughs at himself, one sets a limit to one's self-importance and to the importance of one's claims or sufferings. At least this is true of sane laughter. Nietzsche's most important image by far is Zarathustra, and his laughter is the most striking thing about him; this laughter is always eminently sane. Zarathustra is gentle rather than terrible. His madness and intoxication are under the signs of hospitality and conviviality. He shocks us in the formally destructive, but to us delightfully recognizable, disguises of literary parody.

As a total structure, *Thus Spoke Zarathustra* parodies the form of the "life and sayings of a holy man," as we find it in the Gospels, the *Life of Buddha*, or the *Little Flowers of St. Francis*. Zarathustra, of course, is Nietzsche's own invention. He is presented as a dancer, jester, and comedian, specifically in order to do away with the aura of seriousness that might otherwise surround so great a prophet. The language throughout, Walter Kaufmann tells us, "abounds in allusions to the Bible, most of them highly irreverent."[12] It also abounds in puns and coinages: Nietzsche ridiculed and parodied not only Luther's German Bible but the German language itself. He also parodied the Sermon on the Mount, the Last Supper, and the mass. Today this parody seems more playful than vindictive. Although we must allow for a greater shock value when these irreverences first appeared in the 1880s, parodies of a much more ribald and outrageous

---

[12] *The Portable Nietzsche*, p. 108.

sort were rife in the Middle Ages and were actually granted academic and ecclesiastical sanction. Of course, Nietzsche disbelieved in the texts he parodied, and therein lies a great difference. But while Nietzsche's parodies effectively present his anti-Christian ideas, they are constructively fictional and unpolemic to an outstanding degree. Kaufmann's comparisons to Joyce's *Ulysses* and the second part of Goethe's *Faust* are therefore well taken.

It would be too hasty to say at this point in the argument that Nietzsche's practice in *Thus Spoke Zarathustra* illustrates something like a comic theory. Let us only repeat then that the book is anything but tragic. It is reasonable to assume that the comic form of this work might turn out to be the obverse of what the youthful author raved over in *The Birth of Tragedy*. It is a work of art throughout, obviously intended as such. Nietzsche meant it to achieve beauty in forms that persist in their own likeness (to use his own language), for the sake of the preservative and recuperative power that such forms possess. He thought of Greek tragic art as all the more joyous because Greek experience was full of pain. The depth of pain was measurable not by expressions of anguish but reciprocally by the degree of sublimation of pain in the joy of the whole Dionysian celebration of which tragedy was only a part, and comedy too. Nietzsche's paradox about laughter, that it was invented by the most suffering of animals, man, extends this reciprocal character of artistic expression in the direction of the comic.[13] Because man is strong, he turns sorrow into laughter. According to Nietzsche, he does not laugh at the sorrows of other weaker men, nor did human beings invent laughter as a way of expressing superiority over the rest of creation, as if they were gods rather than mortals. "Learn to laugh at yourselves,"[14] is the word of Zarathustra to his convalescing higher men. Laughter is a sign of strength in *Thus Spoke Zarathustra*, and also a way of becoming strong.

The laughter of Zarathustra, besides being the most im-

[13] *Will to Power*, §990, p. 517.
[14] *Thus Spoke Zarathustra*, part 4, "On the Higher Man," §15, p. 404.

portant trait of his fictional character, is a highly effective
image in itself. It is a revealing sign of his sunny outlook on
all of life, more frequent even than his singing, dancing, or
jesting. Perhaps Nietzsche wished to acccentuate this difference between his Zarathustra and Aristotle's magnanimous
man, who smiled a bit but never laughed out loud. Zarathustra is as courteous and generous as Aristotle's model
man, and in a more delicate and psychologically inner way.
Indeed, Zarathustra may be exposed a little to the charge of
overcomplexity and refinement. He is too indulgent to the
"human, all too human" to be comic all the time, too much
given to sudden fears, questionings, emotional affirmations,
even sermonizing. At other times he is too inhumanly
strong, superior, reliable. If he were meant to stand on his
own feet as a comic character, Zarathustra would have to be
purged of these qualities. The whole structure of *Thus Spoke
Zarathustra*, however, indicates that he is not meant to stand
by his own inner force alone, but that he may be taken as a
parody of the figure of Jesus in the Gospels.

  Thus Spoke Zarathustra consists of four books, like the four
canonical Gospels. Nietzsche intended to write more, but
the story of Zarathustra is complete in the four books that he
finished, and in them the parallel to the earthly life of Jesus
is rounded off. After a period of obscurity Zarathustra enters
upon his public life, preaches to the people, travels away
from his chosen town into the countryside, attracts twelve
disciples (of whom one is "loved"), performs works of
power, rebukes a great city, goes away into the desert, is
tempted, returns, upbraids the lukewarm, the hypocritical,
and the pharasaical, is transfigured before his disciples,
holds a final festival supper with them that he commands
them to observe in his memory as a ceremony of mystical
communion in the (earthly) good, and finally leaves them to
go off into a new phase, where he is to find companions
more akin to himself. The style of *Thus Spoke Zarathustra*,
besides being similar in diction to the Bible, offers many
quotations, allusions, and parodies of biblical materials,
especially from the New Testament. As for Zarathustra's

own speeches, they have a strong similarity to the psalms in their more lyrical passages. There are further similarities (no doubt intentional) to other holy books, especially the *Life of Buddha*.

Nevertheless, Zarathustra never loses the force of authority—of the nonauthoritarian type, that is, required by Nietzschean thought. He is a living model, an image invented to present Nietzsche's ideas without recourse to a merely conceptual and systematic framework. His new "psychological" thought was aimed at transcending the horizon of science and the rules of logic. He created a figure capable of presenting philosophy as personal behavior, with an ambiguity suited to reality. The interrelationship of the ideas and image is neither irrational nor arbitrary; it is personal. Ideas are never presented as intellectual judgments, but as modes of action in a context of subtly controlled feeling and with the strong flavor of aesthetic promotion or rejection.

As Nietzsche invokes laughing Zarathustra to overcome the Spirit of Gravity, the image of the agon now becomes a comic one. For Zarathustra, "Whatever in me has feeling suffers and is in prison; but my will always comes to me as my liberator and joy-bringer."[15] Suffering and frustrated (i.e., "in prison"), the self is more recognizably the self; its imprisonment only calls attention to its individuality. According to Nietzsche self is the body, first of all and most importantly; only secondarily is it the ego. His view was not unlike Freud's in some ways, and insofar as Nietzsche tended to value actions performed unconsciously or spontaneously as the only "perfect" activity,[16] his romantic view of the unconscious has tended to supplant Freud's more rigorously defined one in the outlook and writing of modern artists and critics. Nietzsche's self was unscientific, anti-Darwinian, and undetermined except that, as Zarathustra laments, "Alas, much ignorance and error have become

[15] Ibid., part 2, "Upon the Blessed Isles," p. 199.
[16] *Will to Power*, §289, p. 163.

body within us."[17] Nietzsche would not look for systematic explanations of change, like evolution; it was necessary to him that the changes become subject to human aspiration and will.

2. THE BLACK COMIC TECHNIQUE

The comic possibilities of the Nietzschean self arise out of his image of willing. As if he were reversing the old apologue of the body and its members, Nietzsche takes the fable out of political philosophy and internalizes it. It then serves as a psychological account of what happens within us, to explain our feeling-states and our behavior from moment to moment. Nietzsche's image is that of a little political community, rather like a Greek city-state, with a public-spirited elite and a well-integrated *demos*. Power would normally flow through such a body politic without inhibitions. Mutual confidence, common aims, and the familiar expectations of command and obedience would guarantee an easy continuity of intention and execution. Willing would not seem to originate at any one point in the power process, or within any single segment of the community; it would spring from the whole body. Those who actually gave the orders would rejoice in the beneficial execution of plans for the common good as well as in their own exercise of command as individuals. Nor is the pleasure of superiority the issue, either; rather it is the sense of expenditure in a willing participation. The sense of having shared in willing what one saw being fulfilled would undoubtedly heighten one's delight in the entire process.

Delight Nietzsche finds to be our response to the overcoming of obstacles when our willing is effective and not frustrated. In his playful vein, he suggests that our will is a good deal of a fiction, a way of looking (after the event) at the total psychosomatic process that occurs when a human being acts. Indeed, the Will to Power is not my will, or even Caesar's, but a force working through all of life. When I

[17] Part 1, "On the Gift-Giving Virtue," §2, p. 189.

have the sense of guiding this force, I am elated, just as the governing elite of a community might take pleasure in seeing social programs carried out successfully. This sense would be the more perfect the more the community was a perfect one, because of the greater degree of identification between commander and commanded. "In this way the person exercising volition adds the feelings of delight of his successful executive instruments, the useful 'under-wills' or under-souls, to his feeling of delight as commander. *L'effect c'est moi.*"[18] Although Nietzsche is not talking about art in this passage, it is impossible not to apply these words to participation in artistic experience. It is as if he were unfolding the meaning of Shakespeare's symbolic presentation of power and the power of art in *The Tempest.*

The analysis suggests two possible kinds of comedy, based either on the Will to Power or on its frustration. The first kind would be on outright magical fantasy (Kafka's Oklahoma Nature Theater in the unfinished *Amerika*). The second would limit itself to minimal means, focusing our perception on the dumb delight that can accompany our sense of physical well-being. Making us smile by showing pleasure frustrated, this kind would remind us of how lucky we are much of the time.

In Kafka's only expressly comic work, *Amerika,* one can open the book almost at random and find passages that illustrate Nietzsche's account of the inner experience of the sensation, thought, and emotion of willing, together with the notion of the commander "I" and the obeyers. Very rarely is the passage a fantasy of wish fulfillment, as it is in the excerpt that follows where Karl is seeking to make contact with the recruiting team of the Nature Theater:

"You all play very badly," said Karl, "let me have a turn."

"Why, certainly," said Fanny, handing him the trum-

[18] *Beyond Good and Evil,* translated by Helen Zimmern, in *The European Philosophers From Descartes to Nietzsche,* edited by Monroe C. Beardsley (New York: Modern Library, 1960), §19, pp. 816f.

pet, "but don't spoil the show, or else I'll get the sack."
Karl began to blow into the trumpet; he had imagined it
was a roughly-fashioned trumpet intended merely to
make a noise, but now he discovered that it was an instrument capable of almost any refinement of expression. If all the instruments were of the same quality,
they were being very ill-used. Paying no attention to the
blaring of the others he played with all the power of his
lungs an air which he had once heard in some tavern or
other. He felt happy at having found an old friend, and
at being allowed to play a trumpet as a special privilege,
and at the thought that he might likely get a good post
very soon. Many of the women stopped playing to lis-
ten; when he suddenly broke off scarcely half of the
trumpets were in action; and it took a little while for the
general din to work up to full power again.

"But you are an artist," said Fanny, when Karl
handed her the trumpet again. "Ask to be taken on as a
trumpeter."[19]

This passage of wish fulfillment is set in an episode of comic
anagnorisis replete with the imagery of sex fantasy; nothing
of this, though, would serve to account for the sense of freedom that, more than anything else, generates a comic effect
in the passage. The two *termini* are there—Karl's aloneness
and joblessness at one end, a "good post" with an old friend
among admiring women at the other. The sense of motion
between the two points is made actual by his blowing the
horn. The thought is threefold: finding an old friend, the
privilege of playing the trumpet, the likelihood of a good
job. The singleness of intention and the emotion are what
the artist feels when he succeeds in stilling the usual quotidian din long enough to gain a hearing, and gives expression
to the music within him, that is, what he makes of his expe-

[19] Franz Kafka, *Amerika*, translated by Willa and Edwin Muir (New York:
Schocken, 1962), pp. 277–279; *Gesammelte Schriften*, edited by Max Brod
(New York: Schocken, 1946), II, 269f.

rience, with the instrument at his disposal. Much more might be said about this recognition scene, but the main point is that its comic quality depends upon the fullfillment of the Will to Power, as Nietzsche describes it, and not simply upon the fulfillment of a fantasy.

More typical of *Amerika* is one of the numerous passages recounting Karl's frustration. This one, near the beginning of the story, actually coincides closely with Nietzsche's analysis of the complex state and process of willing. It comes when Karl has been enticed away from his uncle's New York apartment to the estate of a Mr. Pollunder, vaguely placed on Long Island. Karl is anxious to get back to his uncle's:

> But Karl had felt more and more restless the more clearly he became aware of his relation to his uncle during his speech, and involuntarily he struggled to free himself from Pollunder's arm. Everything cramped him here; the road leading to his uncle through that glass door, down the steps, through the avenue, along the country roads, through the suburbs to the great main street where his uncle's house was, seemed to him a strictly ordered whole, which lay there empty, smooth and prepared for him, and called to him with a strong voice. Mr. Pollunder's kindness and Mr. Green's loathsomeness ran into a blur together, and all that he asked from that smoky room was permission to leave. He felt cut off from Mr. Pollunder, prepared to do battle against Mr. Green, and yet all round him was a vague fear, whose impact troubled his sight. He took a step back and now stood equally distant from Mr. Pollunder and Mr. Green.[20]

This passage, above all else, deals with Karl's emotion. Freedom is presented with considerable emotional force in

[20] Ibid., p. 82; cf. the key phrases in the German text, p. 84: "der Weg . . . erschein ihm als etwas streng Zusammengehöriges, das leer, glatt, und für ihn vorbereitet dalag, und mit einer starken Stimme nach ihm verlangte."

Karl's image of the "strictly ordered whole" that will take
him so smoothly to his uncle's house; and the impact of the
emotion is heightened, in Kafka's way, by its actual damming up. Since Karl cannot execute the command his "I" is
giving him, he becomes frustrated and anxious. The people
around him, both apparent friend and apparent enemy, blur
together, and the room itself darkens. All of his powers
seem to desert him, like routed troops. So it is not simply
that Karl cannot leave Mr. Pollunder's, but rather that Kafka
wants us to partake of the full experience of the frustrated
will to power. Karl is not free; this is what it is like not to be
free in a commonplace human situation without the melodrama of a Bonivard and his dungeon by Lake Leman. Note
that it is precisely what Nietzsche specifies as the signs of
willing that are missing here: "the straining of the attention,
the straight look which fixes itself exclusively on one thing."
Karl is powerless, his attention equally divided between Mr.
Pollunder and Mr. Green; there is no "inward certainty that
obedience will be rendered"—what Karl feels inwardly is "a
vague fear"; and far from identifying himself with the others
present, Karl takes a step back from them and from the path
that he so desires to follow. Nor can Karl escape the sense of
self-division, above all because of the powerlessness of his
"I," split in two between Mr. Pollunder and Mr. Green.

Kafka's exploitation of the complex state of willing and its
frustration may plausibly be associated with the will to
power. Yet I am concerned even more with the question of
what if anything makes this passage comic. Many critics,
first among them Edwin Muir (Kafka's translator), have insisted upon Kafka's humor throughout the whole of his fiction. Furthermore, there is ample theoretical justification for
regarding such writing as ridiculous provided we are willing
to invoke the old-fashioned but once dominant superiority
theory. Reading Kafka's analysis of Karl's experiences, we
take a perhaps malicious, perhaps pitying pleasure (which
harms no one, for what we are concerned with is only fiction) in the boy's continual frustration, because it enhances
by contrast our own sense of power. The scenes of Karl's

frustration are sometimes remindful of our own misadven-
tures (for example, some remarkable pages dealing with the
functioning of a hotel information desk), but even these universal cases still allow us to feel masterful by comparison to
the inept Karl, whose inadequacy is pervasive and compulsive. Most of the time, also, one can regard Karl's hesitations
and anxieties as grotesquely exaggerated and therefore ridiculous. That many readers still relish this simplistic response might seem to be proved by the prevalence of such
antiheroes as Karl in recent plays, films, and novels.

Yet something very like Kafka's technique is described by
Nietzsche in such a way as to throw the sufferings of Karl in
Amerika into a new light for us: "It seems, a little hindrance
that is overcome and immediately followed by another lilttle
hindrance that is again overcome—this game of resistance
and victory arouses most strongly that general feeling of su-
perabundant, excessive power that constitutes the essence of
pleasure. . . . Pleasure and pain are not opposites."[21] In the
unfinished *Amerika*, Karl, of course, does not so much overcome his inhibitions as merely survive them. Perhaps the
reader who identifies himself with Karl is amused because
his sense of sympathetic frustration tenses and relaxes in a
pleasurable rhythm; perhaps other readers, refusing to
identify with him, laugh at him instead because they find
him ridiculous.

Nietzsche, in substituting his communal model of will for
old notions like that of will as a faculty of the soul directly
opposed to the body and its animal instincts, opened up the
microexperience of human existence to observation and
commentary, and thus helped writers of fiction to discover a
new world. It is an interior life of the soul rivaling the one so
carefully mapped out over the centuries by the moralists and
mystics. Self as body above all rather than as spirit is a more
intransigent subject for a writer, but a better one by present
notions, because it is more dense and more opaque. Rather
obviously, its possibilities seem to lie in the comic rather

[21] *Will to Power*, §699, p. 371.

than the tragic direction. Moreover, the thread of interest is still freedom: in Nietzsche's transvalued ethos, liberation from imprisonment for the feelings is as important as enhanced freedom for the spirit was to Schiller.

The more traditional writers of modern comedy (who are unwilling to work entirely in the area of those microexperiences) deal with our sense of experience either psychologically, in the form of aggressive neurotic forces presented through type characters involved in some strongly patterned combination of inhibitions (Pinter), or much more allusively by presenting a society that is schematized to the point of absurdity (so-called absurd comedy). The society (in Ionesco, for example) does not differ much from the characteristics Nietzsche attributed to his "last men," or even from this description written with tongue in cheek by Kierkegaard almost a century and a half ago:

> the whole romantic school related or thought they related to an age in which men had become ossified, as it were, within the finite social situation. Everything had become perfected and consummated in a divine Chinese optimism that allowed no rational longing to go unsatisfied, no rational wish unfulfilled. Those glorious assumptions and maxims drawn from custom and convention had been made objects of a pious idolatry. . . . One married, one lived for domesticity, one filled his position in the state. One had children and family cares. . . . One meant everything to his own, year in and year out with a certainty and precision always correct to the very minute. The world was becoming childish, it had to be rejuvenated.[22]

3. LIBERATION FROM THE SPIRIT OF GRAVITY

Black, absurd, and sick comedy aim at the special kind of Dionysian joy that revels in the destruction of a society of

[22] *The Concept of Irony,* p. 318f.

Philistine automata. But there is a more genuine Dionysian joy that is only to be found in the destruction of forms that are noble and good rather than ugly. One might be inclined to feel that this latter joy is far more likely to infuse successful works of art. In his own account, Nietzsche presented a kind of foolery as liberating—forms of lightheartedness, gaiety, prankishness, everything in fact that contravened the spirit of gravity. This joy does not always provoke laughter, nor is there an insistence on cynical or malicious ridicule. Certainly there is no suggestion anywhere in Nietzsche that we laugh at anyone's weakness of will in a spirit of hostility or superiority. The spirit of gravity itself is to be mocked, laughed at, and killed, not its unhappy victims. Freedom thus emerges in Zarathustrian comedy as something like the interplay of feeling and volition, proceeding so as to release our feelings from a sense of imprisonment. Free play would thereby achieve the moment of permanence that beauty maintains and would offer beauty's recuperative power. None of the opposed terms—Dionysian/Apollonian, Zarathustra/Spirit of Gravity—would be annulled, abrogated, or transcended in any final way. Their contest would be structured so as to achieve a series of moments of recuperative power, overcoming, or sublimation. The impulses in which we share and are most made aware of must seem to be given the freest play, and thereby to fulfill the Nietzschean notion of a simultaneously active communal will involving writer and reader. Nietzsche will thus appear as a thinker in the mainstream of the romantic epoch in that he assigns a central role to freedom.

4. The Nietzschean Image of Art

I shall now try to explain how a Nietzschean image for the mechanism of self-becoming has pervaded thought about the activity of the artist since his time and still provides us with our picture of the relationship of art to nature today. To clarify the process of selving and sublimation, Nietzsche invented a little parable: a lake "one day ceased to permit itself to flow off; it formed a dam . . . this lake is rising higher and higher . . . perhaps man will rise ever higher as soon as he ceases to *flow out* into a god."[23]

The image from hydrostatics was used previously for economics, to present the idea of capital accumulation; and it has since served as a metaphor to codify the terms of financial functioning in general. Even before Adam Smith it was already a very potent central image, having served to present the circulation of the blood (as Smith used it to present the circulation of wealth), and long before that the flow of the four humours within the body. Also, as tidal ebb and flow it connected the human temperament with the waters of the earth and the gravitational pull of the moon and thus with the universe as a whole. It was not until Nietzsche's lifetime, however, that the image received its most richly significative development. It was applied to the behavior of electricity in circuits, making detailed use of every metaphorical possibility: inflow, collection, tension, discharge, gap, open circuit, closed circuit, short circuit, high and low pressure (voltage), and strong and weak current, wave formation, cyclical rise and fall, and so on *ad infinitum*. Moreover, the notions associating electronic circuitry with work and therefore with economics continued to be strong: capacity, energy, output, resistance, consumption, efficiency of production, storage, and transmission of energy. When one adds the phenomena of radio, there is no end to such images; new ones are being made very day.

Nevertheless, the parametric form of the image for the arts was the psychological one originated by Nietzsche and developed into a cosmology by Freud. Aeons of human experience are stored up and extended still further back into the animal past. Our collective experience exists today as if gathered in a vast lake whose unfathomed depths are charged with every profound instinct and source of emotional energy known or yet unknown to us. The race as a

---

[23] *The Gay Science*, translated by Walter Kaufmann (New York: Vintage, 1974), §285, p. 232.

whole and every individual member of it draws upon powers latent in this reservoir, but by far the deepest draughts are drawn by the great genius, and particularly the great artist.

Bergson, as we saw, used the lake image and extended it to a picture of the stormy ocean. He also added a different version of his own, the deep, fluid, fiery core of life encrusted all over with its pellicule of social use and wont. Freud, as we all know, developed it into a well-mapped psychic world. His interior world-picture is more effectively ours today than similar images furnished by Galileo or Newton ever were in their time. Freud, as we also saw, clung to the hydrostatic version. Nietzsche's "power to flow" became cathexis and his "damming up" became the censor mechanism or the superego. The deepening lake became the unconscious, its primal state the libido. Also, the primary energies stored up became "capital," just as a "head of water" is a source of profitable energy when used to do work. Freud's imagery is highly convertible with economic coding, but for the discussion of art the most effective conversion has been into electric and electronic terms. Thus libidinal drives are given a much higher energy potential as a result of inhibitory mechanisms that we perceive acting like resistors and condensers in an electrical circuit. The result in art is imaged as a high voltage discharge across the gap between the unconscious and the conscious mind. This spark, linking one to one's unconscious, is what the genius artist communicates to the spectator or reader.

The notion of a gap suffused with electric tension that then acts as a carrier or bridge from a high potential source through a low potential medium is by now an omnipresent, if usually submerged, metaphor in the minds of all of us. Without it, twentiety-century literary theory (particularly in New Criticism) would shrink to half its compass. Recently, however, we have learned to redeem the image from a threat of elitism. When it ceased to be satisfactory to view the modern artist as the Promethean fire-bringer, the picture of the electromagnetic field in space came into play. The gap

ceased to exist in the sense of a space between high energy
and low energy polar opposites, or between poetic and ordinary language, or genius and consumer; in its place we have
a free play of forces intersecting in a text that has no author
as origin of significance but wherein an unfolding, or undu-
lation, is the carrier wave for meanings given it (as well as
taken from it) in an energy transfer of an open sort that we
call writing. This version of the image is not, however, a
transformation denoting a break with Freud, Bergson, and
Nietzsche. The new image is actually more faithful to
Nietzsche's original version than either Bergson or Freud
dared to be, for they both had a lively interest in the maintenance of European civilization, even though they were dis-
mayed at its actual state of unsuccess. Like Nietzsche, the
French critics who gave this theory and submerged image its
present currency aim at dispersing Western authority beyond recovery.

5. NIETZSCHE'S NOSTALGIA FOR THE NAIVE

The persistence of the romantic movement in Western culture has been due in significant measure to the German fas-
cination with idealized Greek antiquity, part of what
Nietzsche saw as the Teutonic yearning for the south. The
Germans, I should say, colored the first romantic wave
through Winckelmann's and Goethe's Hellenism, the second through Nietzsche's Dionysian/Apollonian contrast,
the third through Heidegger's concern for the pre-Socratic
Greek thought and mode of being. Each involved a special
kind of *Heimweh* or nostalgia, and always for the naive. The
first was for the genuine Greek taste, purified of the crass,
utiliarian, and vulgar Roman accretions. The second was for
the Greek nature, at one with the world in a union of *physis*
and *cosmos*. The third has been, and still is, a nostalgia for the
naive, where the almost unorganized simplicities of existence allow human imagination its most untrammeled
scope. The special longing for freedom that characterizes
these three different phases of one movement is a persistent

mark that helps to unify them. Whatever the terms used, the essential is self-determination: the self locates itself by seeking out its proper home. It finds its "limit" in the Hegelian sense, in a community, either immediate and political, or else in an ideally humane society. In either case the home is longed for as an alternative kind of life that permits substantive values to come into being and to endure. From the first, beginning with the thinkers and artists who looked to Greek antiquity as a uniquely privileged alternative, an original, primal home, all romantics have desired a setting such as the Greeks had. Its pristine communal world seemed peculiarly opposed to actual bourgeois conditions as they developed from the later eighteenth century until now.

The romantic escaped the imprisonment of "time and its 'it was' '' by turning feelings of revenge against the past into acceptance of whole alternative worlds,[24] fictional worlds created by a succession of great innovators in the arts. The first wave began to move in the last quarter of the eighteenth century with the idealized recovery of "Hellas" and "the Gothic." Goethe's *Götz von Berlichtigen*, Schiller's *The Robbers*, and the novels of Walter Scott conjured up past ages; Goethe's first and second parts of *Faust* seemed to equilibrate the Gothic and the ancient Greek worlds in order to afford a magical perspective on the modern one. These works provided acceptable versions of a past redeemed of its burden, while serving to free artist and audience, imaginatively at least, from the bondage of a bourgeois civilization that threatened to tie everyone down to the petty and the mean. By the mid-seventies of the nineteenth century, Richard Wagner had composed a more single-minded mythic alternative world and established it at Bayreuth. Half a century later still, the solitary writing of James Joyce in *Ulysses* created an entirely different sort of alternative world in which the recurrence of the past takes place in Nietzs-

---

[24] The terms are Nietzsche's; see *Thus Spoke Zarathustra*, part 2, "On Redemption," p. 252; Martin Heidegger, *What Is Called Thinking*, translated by J. Glenn Gray (New York: Harper, 1972), pp. 92ff., deals with their modern significance.

chean style as the present of the fictional dream, parodically the same as in the Greek past of Homer. Then, by means of a seemingly infinite control over the entire reservoir of language, Joyce in *Finnegans Wake* distanced the petty and the mean of individual experience by giving it universal forms.

With regard to our own inquiry, we may recall that Nietzsche first welcomed Wagner's innovation as a new "Birth of Tragedy," only to reject it fifteen years later in favor of laughter. Nietzsche repudiated Wagner, along with Baudelaire, as a decadent. He recognized clearly in them certain symptoms of a peculiar bourgeois unhealthiness, and he sometimes managed even to recognize the extent to which he shared the disease himself. Nietzsche's real problem was the one already recognized by Goethe, bourgeois meanness. In its place he created an illusion: the tyrant instincts—pitiless and dreadful passions—that call resistance into being and thereby generate power.[25] Thus he turned his own small need, as a means of successfully controlling it and freeing himself for self-direction, into a great need that he did not encounter at any time in his life except in his thinking and writing. His methods (adopted recently by French structuralism and the *Tel Quel* group) are suited to the magnification of the individual *penseur* into a world-shaker. Nietzsche himself went further and identified himself with a timeless aristocracy for which he had almost no personal or family qualifications. Like the true *parvenu*, he usurped aristocracy and was as loyal to his ideal as the greatest snob. This foible is comically apparent even in his early writing; in his decline into insanity it might easily provide a source of the cruel laughter he wrote about so often. Nietzsche's value as a critic of this kind of pettiness in himself and others, however, is enormous.

He is certainly correct in observing that, like Baudelaire, Wagner was among the first to reinterpret in vastly dis-

---

[25] *Twilight of the Idols,* in *Portable Nietzsche,* "Skirmishes of an Untimely Man," §38, p. 542. Cf. *Will to Power,* §§704, 705; also R. J. Hollingdale, *Nietzsche* (Baton Rouge: Louisiana State University Press, 1965), pp. 242f.

tanced myths the psychology of neurotic modern individuals living in an urbanized culture. His accusations of decadence, whether justified or not in their tone of prophetic de-
nunciation, outline the profile of bourgeois art since 1850.
He charged it, and its spokesman Wagner in particular, with
coupling perfect sexual union and death in a kind of androg-
ynous sterility that prevents its heroines from having any
children. Instead of working toward redemption, the decadent hero is content to fall into some form of annihilation.
There are no plans made for the future, for this world is
soon to pass away. Freedom is defined falsely as closeness to
the void. Past centuries are not borne as heavy burdens to be
abnegated, but reappear sentimentally as escapes from the
overpowering meanness and complexity of modern life.
Hence the preference for ready-made myth rather than history, for the turgid rather than the unambiguous style, for
extreme emotions rather than clear feelings: all three forms
of excess are meant to blunt the impact of actual existence.
In the place of desire for life there is a yearning to be carried
away into some form of extinction. Tragic suffering then becomes a suffering from the unbearableness of life itself, instead of a glorious contest in which the human agonist lives
the fullest possible life. Modern heroes are found willing
their own destruction. The death of desire and the extirpa-
tion of passion, like the imperatives of an exotic and sterile
religion, take hold of all "serious" and "profound" art. The
spirit of gravity is the god of the decadents.

Against this kind of tragic outlook and its "metaphysical
solace" Nietzsche finally set up the laughter of Zarathustra
as the laughter of freedom from all this, and—as we have
been arguing—established the foundation for almost all of
the modern black comedy that needs to be taken seriously.
This form of humor, as he said, is based on instincts that are
pur and *cru*, that is, primitively and puritanically destuctive
of the accretion of conventional modes of behavior; and it
can be both crudely and cruelly ridiculous. In terms drawn
from the history of the comic, the Nietzschean doctrine calls
for a recurrence of the *sauvage* spirit of Archilochus. One

then seems to desire the humiliation, degradation, painful suffering, and indeed the death of one's hated butt; and only the force of life inherent in the essential comic prevents the last of these desires from being accomplished.

In beginning with the early Greeks, Nietzsche was giving free rein to his own particular nostalgia. He longed for the naive in its pure Attic form before the decadence of Socratic reasoning had set in with the tradition of Plato. He never changed the conviction stated in one of his earliest essays, "Homer's Contest," that "man, in his highest and noblest capacities, is wholly nature and embodies its uncanny dual character. . . . The Greeks, the most humane men of ancient times, have a trait of cruelty, a tigerish lust to annihilate."[26] This "dual character" of Greek nature gives rise to the twofold mythic figure of Eris. The first is the goddess of discord; she is cruel and promotes feuds and open warfare, things necessary as paths to honor; the second or better Eris rouses men to deeds of contest rather than armed hostility; one might call her the goddess of competition. The better Eris, however, does not inspire people with laudable ambition only, but with envy, jealousy, and spite as well. "The whole of Greek antiquity," Nietzsche assures us, "thinks differently from us about hatred and envy."[27] Here, of course, he is quite mistaken, for he has actually drawn an accurate portrait of the cutthroat competitor who was the typical nineteenth-century capitalist tycoon.

Nietzsche insisted on incorporating the twofold Eris in his description of the Greek naive: wherever we find the "naive" in Greek art (e.g., the "naiveté of Homer"), he says in section 3 of The Birth of Tragedy, we encounter the twofold effect of culture: a terrible insight into the depths of reality, and a triumph over an intense experience of suffering.

He defined culture as unity of artistic style in all the expressions of the life of a people. The Attic smile on the visage of an antique statue of a warrior, therefore, indicated to

---

[26] Portable Nietzsche, p. 32.
[27] Ibid., p. 35.

Nietzsche an Apollonian triumph over horrors of war that both the living soldier and the living artist had tasted to the full. This naive is by no means innocent and Edenic—quite the opposite; it is a total life-style, founded in dreadful insight and intense suffering and overcoming these tyrants by means of illusions of power and joy.

In the unphilosophical sense of the term, we might say that Nietzsche idealized the Greeks, as Goethe and Schiller had done in the first wave of romanticism and Heidegger was to do in the third. We should realize, however, that Nietzsche was a leader in revolutionizing the present mode of thinking as it conceives of "idea" and "nature." He rejected the dualisms of ideality and reality, soul and body, form and matter, nurture and nature. He tells us that the Greeks originated the idea of unifying their culture and their natural environment. But they originated it by doing it; it is only we moderns in the Platonic tradition who must make an idea of it. For the early Greeks it was a naive matter of everyday concern for their real needs. This argument appears in an early almost programmatic essay, "On the Use and Abuse of History." It is prophetic not only for Nietzsche's own work, but for the characteristic outlook of the modern artist.

He began by setting up his favorite concept of the past as a burden that needs first to be assumed and then abrogated, by one means or another, so long as one gives full weight to the life-and-death importance of the task. And finally he brings a long richly suggestive argument to its culmination by citing the example of the Greeks. They "did not long remain the overburdened heirs of the entire Orient" (that is, of "Asiatic vague immensities" in Yeats's words). The ancient Greeks "learned to *organize the chaos*," says Nietzsche, by "thinking back to themselves, that is, to their own true necessities."[28] The outcome of their thinking was the idea of

[28] In *The Complete Works of Friedrich Nietzsche*, edited by Oscar Levy (London: T. N. Foulis, 1915), II (titled *Thoughts Out of Season*), 3–100; see p. 99. For the German, see *Werke*, edited by Giorgio Colli and Mazzino Montinari (Berlin: deGruyter, 1972), part 3, I, 329, where *das Chaos zu organisiren* is given emphasis.

culture as a new and better nature.[29] The Greeks and the
Asiatics inhabited the same geographical world, but the
Greeks went on to create a world of their own and to live in
it fully. Out of a totality of need (i.e., chaos) they summoned
the strength to give expression to themselves as a community organized by human will so as to respond to human desire. They lived humanly, even in the natures they gave to
the gods whom they envisioned in order to manage the universe humankind brought forth.

Nietzsche's personal culture and life-style was aimed at
exactly the same naiveté as he attributed to the early Greeks.
That which is most personal of all, his style of writing, has
been called "talking to himself," and "heightened conversation." In Nietzsche's own words, his goal was the "cheerful
and benevolent" overcoming of "any trace of suffering or
depression"—suffering that he continually describes in his
letters as infinite and intense, and depression verging on the
suicidal. The cheerfulness he cultivated was rather to be
called joy, joy as deep as the depths of the pain he endured
so willingly, despite all his complaints. Joy was his defense
in the agon with the "weakness and weariness which those
who dislike me will look for."[30] Quite evidently, the naiveté
Nietzsche saw as the chief mark of the early Greek style in
art and life was the mask he sought to present to the world
in his own activity as an artist and a man. It became the style
of his own self-creation. The discursive and still academic
structure of the *Untimely Meditations* from which we have
just been quoting soon gave way to the series of aphorisms
and paragraphs in which his later books took shape. The
style was an innovation in German that he himself put on a
par with Luther's Bible and the prose of Goethe. Its ease and
apparent informality were achieved at great cost to the artist.
These qualities were thus the equivalent of the Attic smile,
and they constituted a rebirth of the naive in an epoch of decadence. At last they became the strongest evidence for

[29] Cf. Hollingdale, pp. 122–125.
[30] Hollingdale, pp. 140, 144, 185.

Nietzsche's doctrine, centered as it was on joy, power, self-mastery, and genius as self-creation. No wonder that the thought of Nietzsche and his practice as a writer remained powerful throughout two successive waves of romantic nostalgia for the naive.

⌒9⌒

AFTER BARTHES:
DEATH OF THE COMIC?

IN THE PRECEDING CHAPTERS we have spoken of the romantic movement as essentially a nostalgia for the naive, occurring so far in three waves. We may now tentatively distinguish three forms of the naive. First, the primal natural community and the *bel âme* of Rousseau, well suited to the idealistic Hellenism of Winckelmann and Goethe, along with the worship of humanity, the spirit of joy, and the growth of freedom that Schiller celebrated and argued for, Byron fought for, and Hegel justified in speculative thought. After this idealist naive, we may speak of a realist naive, championed by Hugo and Balzac and also (as Nietzsche made clear) to be found in Baudelaire and Wagner. It was a naiveté trying to make something new and fresh out of industrialized, urban Europe. Even when one of these artists used the medieval ideals of religion and *amour-passion,* as Wagner did, the devices functioned to reinvigorate his decadent and self-destructive society—an inspiration all the more naive when he remained unconscious of the judgment he was passing on his contemporaries. What began in realism ended as decadence, a combination that persisted throughout what is now called the modernist period, until the 1940s. One can say, finally, that modernism, in this limited sense of a second wave of romantic nostalgia for the naive, has been succeeded by a more overt and extreme effort at achieving the naive without any taint of decadence at all.

WE CAN identify the third and present wave of romantic nostalgia for the naive with two powerful movements to-

ward simplification: the attempt to break away from ethnocentrism, and the voluntary limitation of artists themselves
to minimalist techniques in art, no matter what the medium
may be. On the part of late modern artists who renounce the
power of inherited techniques, minimalism can be seen as
both an anti-imperialist and anti-ethnocentric movement,
directed against traditional European structures. Such a
movement certainly seems to endanger the continued practice of the comic as it has been described in this book. Its
theoretical challenge can be studied best of all, I believe, in
the work of Roland Barthes, and its practical implications
may be discerned in a short novel by Donald Barthelme.

Barthes was for a while known as a structuralist. Since the
idea of structuralism arose in the twenties, it has been
widely adopted in the biological and human sciences. As
stated by a prominent biologist, its basic notion is that "any
set of primary data becomes meaningful only after a series
of . . . operations has so transformed it that it has become
congruent with a stronger structure preexisting in the
mind."[1] According to this definition, Barthes became an
anti-structuralist, for he opposed all pre-existing stuctures.
He was against structure and for structuration, just as
Nietzsche was against being and in favor of becoming.
Barthes aimed to destroy that structure pre-existing in the
mind of Western, Judaeo-Christian, Greco-Roman civilization; he called it "the kerygmatic civilization of meaning and
truth, appeal and fulfillment." His widely imitated prose
style was based on his conviction that, since the "diadic
unity of subject and predicate" is the "mother cell of Western Civilization," the diadic sentence is dated and foregone,
ancien, and must be replaced by much more paratactic writing.[2]

S/Z has a special importance among Barthes's works. The
outcome of a seminar held just before 1970, it marks his response to two of the chief developments of the sixties for

[1] Gunther S. Stent, quoted by C. H. Waddington, "Mindless Societies,"
New York Review of Books, August 7, 1975, pp. 30–32.
[2] *S/Z,* translated by Richard Miller (New York: Hill and Wang, 1974),
XXXII, 76; LXXX, 188; French edition (Paris: Seuil, 1970), pp. 83, 194.

French criticism, the events of May 1968 and the arrival on
the then structuralist and semiological scene of Jacques Derrida in 1967. May '68 gave Barthes an intensified commitment to freedom, and Derrida gave him a precise formulation of ethnocentrism, as the "stronger structure" inherent
in the Western theological and metaphysical view of a cosmos with its creator at its origin and present everywhere in
the system as center and finality, while being present also to
individual souls as an immediate interior voice. Derrida
showed the acute need of deconstruction when even the text
of Lévi-Strauss, whom one might have supposed to be im-
mune to Western ethnocentrism, was disclosed to share
with texts of Rousseau the ontotheological prejudice in favor
of the immediacy of the voice—the spoken word. On the
back cover of the French edition of *S/Z* Barthes dedicated
his enterprise with Balzac's *Sarrasine* to the new birth of
freedom:

> I have copied a text, ancient, very ancient, an anterior
> text, since it was written before our modernity; I have
> picked up, put together ideas coming from my culture,
> that is to say, from the discourse of others; I have com-
> mented, not in order to render intelligible, but to know
> what the intelligible is; in all that, I have continually
> taken into account what was being said around me.
>
> I hope to take part in this way, *en passant* (as all writ-
> ing should), in the pluralization of criticism, in the
> structural analysis of the narrative, in the science of the
> text, in the spread of dissertative knowledge, the en-
> semble of those activities taking place before my eyes,
> (and, all, around me, speaks of its urgency) in the (col-
> lective) building up of a liberating theory of the Signi-
> fier.[3]

---

[3] My translation. Here is the French text in full:
   Au moyen age, la gestion du texte antérieur était distribuée entre
quatre rôles dont aucun ne correspond à ce que nous appelons au-
jourd'hui le critique. Le *scriptor* copiait, sans rien ajouter. Ce que le
compilator ajoutait ne venait jamais de lui. Si le *commentator* mettait du

The question at issue is whether the theory I have already presented, linking the comic with the romantic and with freedom, can stand up to Barthes's *théorie libératrice du Signifiant*. Keeping this issue in mind in what follows, I shall hold Barthes's literary-critical praxis as developed in *S/Z* against the standard of greater freedom in its postmodernist guise of more and more open structures in the arts. Barthes's central image of the modern (in the sense of plural) work is that of a network with no particular outline that leads off in every direction, so that one cannot determine a center, a profile, or a single perspective for it. The net is folded upon itself here and there so as to produce repetition and thereby points of reference. This manifold productivity is unlimited, as also should be the interreferencing of points in any systems thus formed. They thus become meaningful in a potentially infinite number of ways. One does not want the appearance of any unduly strong structure that cancels out the outside and closes in the inside: what Barthes calls "closure."

In dealing with this question after 1968 and with the impact of Derrida, Barthes found himself in opposition to linguistic structuralism itself at its origin in the work of Saussure.[4]

---

sien dans le texte tuteur, c'était à seule fin de le rendre intelligible. *L'auctor* enfin, risquait bien ses propres idées, mais en leur donnant toujours l'appui de ce qui s'était pensé hors de lui.

J'ai essayé de me faire tout cela à la fois. J'ai copié un texte, ancien, très ancien, un texte antérieur, puisqu'il a été écrit avant notre modernité; j'ai pilé, pressé ensemble des idées venues de ma culture, c'est-à-dire du discours des autres; j'ai commenté, non pour rendre intelligible, mais pour savoir ce qu'est l'intelligible; et en tout cela, j'ai continument pris appui sur ce qui s'énonçait autour de moi.

Je souhaite participer de la sorte, *en passant* (comme il se doit à toute écriture), à la pluralisation de la critique, à l'analyse structurale du récit, à la science du texte, à la fissuration du savoir dissertatif, l'ensemble de ces activités prenant place à mes yeux, (et, tout, autour de moi, en dit l'urgence) dans l'édification (collective) d'une théorie libératrice du Signifiant.   R. B.

[4] Ferdinand de Saussure, *Course in General Linguistics*, translated by Wade Baskin (New York: McGraw-Hill, 1966); the original posthumously published in 1916 sums up lectures presented earlier.

There the strongest of all structures is *langue*, which is unchanging and unchangeable. *Langue* is neither a convention
nor a contract; in it solidarity with the system limits the liberty to choose, and continuity annuls freedom. *Langue* is that
part of *langage* that is socially acquired as a passive deposit in
the minds of native speakers. As such, Barthes rejects it in
favor of *écriture*, writing, which is not restricted to one natural language and can be extended to include every kind of
signifying activity from fashions to the DNA code. Since our
normal use of the alphabet is tied to phonemes bound by
langue, we do well to introduce into writing graphic and
other visual forms that do not have such limitations. For that
reason *S/Z* is an elaborately produced book with a rich variety of typefaces and an important frontispiece. To Barthes
the problem facing modern writing is to get away from origins, authors, utterances, speech acts, all that puts up walls
of ownership, acquisition, and appropriation—all property.
He brings a rather vague socialist internationalism to bear
against *langue*, the private property of national cultures, of
native speakers; the universal vehicle is not personal speech
(*parole*) but writing. Similarly he opposes writing to imperialism: "Only writing, by taking up the most vast plural in its
own labor, can oppose without recourse to violence the imperialism of each *langage*."[5]

Imperialist inscriptions, however, must be wiped out.
They consist of anonymous citations from a book whose archetype is the textbook used in the bourgeois educational
system. Histories of literature, art, Europe, treatises on medicine, psychology, ethics, logic, rhetoric, plus an anthology
of proverbs, in a manner characteristic of bourgeois culture,
appear to establish reality. Life, then, in the classic text becomes "a nauseating mixture of common opinions, a smothering layer of received ideas." Barthes's metaphors for this
social use-and-wont are similar to Nietzsche's ("a nauseating mixture") and Bergson's (a "smothering layer").[6] But

---

[5] *S/Z*, LXXXVII, 205f.

[6] Ibid., p. 206; French, p. 210f. In the French, "nauseating mixture" is *un
mélange écoeurante*, and "smothering layer" is *une nappe étouffante*.

being much less tolerant of bourgeois life than Bergson, Barthes means to mark it for extinction by codifying each set of stereotypes deriving from its institutions.

Historically, the desire to free writers and readers from the perception of stereotypes instead of actual reality belongs to the romantic movement as a whole, and it was perhaps most intense at the beginning of this century. Barthes's own move belongs to the postmodernist effort to do away with the passive *perception* of reality and to substitute its active *constitution*. To him bourgeois realism only created a "reality effect" in fiction by a truthtelling that was at once very precise and quite unsignifying.[7] Its only reason for being there was that things must really have happened just so. Indeed, the absence of any need for human signifying activity was assumed to be the strongest proof of the real. But to *homo significans* this is the opposite of freedom; it requires a brutal subservience to being and to things as they are.

The creativity of classic novelists has tended to be found most of all in the credibility of their characters but also in their convincing plots and natural settings—what adds up in a series of works to an author's world. Since such creativity is credited entirely to the author, Barthes finds that it affords no freedom to the reader, for the more consistent it is according to the standard that "all things are connected," the less there is of the plural that makes it possible for the reader to become a free cowriter. Barthes therefore provides a well-thought-out apparatus for freely deconstructing the characters, plots, and settings of classic fiction. (To some extent, the apparatus can also serve as a theoretical matrix to describe the new fiction.) First of all, the author is not a creator, not God. "He" is text; the anonymous voices of five nonauthorial codes weave themselves together and constitute the text we read. The action code (made up, of course, of names, not actions) derives either from the stock of human experiences or from the novelistic corpus, e.g., "the Declaration of Love, the Murder." These names of actions form "trees," as the linguist says of connected utterances,

---

[7] *S/Z*, LXXVII, 182; French, p. 188, *l'effet de réel.*

and are subjected to a logico-temporal order. Selected and linked grammatically, they constitute what synchronically Barthes calls an "armature of the readable," using a metaphor that combines the musical key, the electric motor, and sculpture. But because they are assembled from a lexicon and their diachronous organization is like an utterance in time, they can also be studied with procedures similar to those used in linguistics. Analytic reading will systematize each such sequence in its turn and give it an appropriate name; the student will thus have a vocabulary and a grammar with which to analyze the "words" and "syntax" of narrative structure. This procedure liberates when it serves not as a preceptive poetics but in a search-and-destroy mission against every form of behavior or experience that is unfree, i.e., already culturally determined.

Along with the action code (Barthes, with a taste for Greek that reminds one of Frye, calls it *proairetic* most of the time), goes the hermeneutic code, which Barthes illuminatingly develops as the code of the enigma: it has its suggestion, posing, development, and finally the revelation of its answer. The archetypal example, of course, is afforded by *Oedipus the King*, which Barthes takes as the germ of all storytelling in the West. The more deeply buried the truth is and the more delay there is in constituting its revelation, the more valuable, the truer, it is made to seem. There is no doubt that Barthes has put his finger on a characteristic modernist proclivity, namely to prize depth, profundity, and interiority. It was Georg Riemann whose topology made it possible to think this unvisualizable fact mathematically: all that is is continuously interacting in an energy exchange so that every part is both active and passive with respect to every other part. And it was first Nietzsche, then Bergson, who identified amid all of this action and reaction certain bodies, especially those of human beings, that had the ability to delay the passage of energy and to process it so as to act and to learn independently—to possess, that is, along with reactive perception, a certain freedom of active selection and retention. The picture is one of nontransparence, opacity, and also of an absorptive depth, a stored-up reserve, a capacity that forms the basis for spontaneity of action and freedom of response. Barthes retains the concept of deference, attaching it not to interiority but to repetition or coincidence, the "conducing" influence of signals from many sources that fade in and fade out. His model here is not film but radio, rich in metaphoric images with its waves and wavelengths, resisters and capacitors, transformers and condensers, feedback, resonant circuits (homologies), and so on.[8] Thus the concept and image of inner self is rejected in favor of space, field, openness, and nonsubjectivity.

Here is Barthes's account of characterization:

When identical semes traverse the same proper name several times and appear to settle upon it, a personage is born. The personage is, then, the product of a *combinatoire*; the combination is relatively stable (denoted by the recurrence of the semes) and more or less complex (involving more or less congruent, more or less contradictory traits); this complexity determines the personage's "personality," which is just as much a combination as the odor of a dish or the bouquet of a wine. The proper name acts as a magnetic field for the semes; referring in fact to a body, it draws the semic configuration into an evolving (biographical) time.[9]

There is clarity in this statement, but it is more metaphorical and impressionistic than directly applicable to the issues of reference in fiction and I shall argue later that it may be thought of as strongly suggesting one particular kind of postmodernist characterization found, for example, in Donald Barthelme.

Barthes's critical contribution, however, is to distinguish

---

[8] *S/Z*, XX, 42; French, pp. 24f., employing the English word: *"un* fading *brusque."*

[9] *S/Z*, XXVIII. The translation, p. 67, has been modified; it failed to make clear the distinction, further developed in XLI, between *personnage* and *figure*; see pp. 74f. of the French edition.

between *personnage,* based on the code of *semes* and the diachronic attribution of *semes* to a proper name, and what he calls *figure.* Barthes thus carries to an extreme the dualism of Saussure with the same privileging of the synchronous over the diachronous. The historical and biographical aspect of character is reduced to the repetition of a *combinatoire* that reinforces the same set of sensory impressions as a wine may be said to do—or rather, not a real wine, but a vintage as described in the *langue* appropriate to the merchandising of vineyard produce. Meanwhile, on the privileged side of the *barre* we find Barthes placing existence, a future, an unconscious, a soul, all given to the *figure* and denied to the *personnage:* "We occasionally speak of Sarrasine as though he existed, as though he had a future, an unconscious, a soul; however, what we are talking about is his *figure* (an impersonal network of symbols combined under the proper name "Sarrasine"), not his *person* (a moral freedom endowed with motives and an overdetermination of meanings): we are developing connotations, not pursuing investigations."

While denying to the *personnage* the psychic life that could be investigated by analysis, Barthes goes well beyond Freud in the insistence upon an economic model for the character in fiction so that it can be reduced to a more convenient package: "We are merely acting in accordance with the economic nature of the Name: in the novelistic regime (and elsewhere?), it is an instrument of exchange: it allows the substitution of a nominal unit for a collection of characteristics . . . it is a bookkeeping method in which, the price being equal, condensed merchandise is preferable to voluminous merchandise." Further, carried away by his metaphor (the weakness that saves Barthes for literature), he mocks characters, according to his modern economics, for adhering to the gold standard: "To say *Sarrasine, Rochefide, Lanty, Zambinella* (not to mention *Bouchardon,* who really existed) is . . . to insist that appellative currency be in gold (and not left to be decided arbitrarily)." Barthes's attitude is quite clear: not only is personality old-fashioned in the novel, like the gold standard in economics; to be subverted by the gold of fictional personality, to submit to it, is for the novelist and his readers to worship gold. Thus not for the only time Roland Barthes appears in the role of Moses, leading a reluctant people through the desert. The golden spoils of the Egyptian captivity are not to be worshiped in the form of any living creature; the "realms of gold"—classic literature—are to be left behind in the desert, impoverished and under a taboo, unless they can be reduced to names, deconstructed, and saved for our modernity by being rewritten.

One must add (only in passing, for it cannot be developed here) that the concept of freedom evident in Barthes's handling of *personnage* and *figure* is such as to privilege the reader over the fictional character. One feels that characters become no more than the small change (as in French *monnaie*) of the text, at the complete disposal of the conventions that govern therein, and even more totally subject to the liberty of the reader. He or she manipulates both text and characters, exploiting the maximal plural of meanings with an arbitrary power that is limited only by the requirement of being collectively significant within the group the reader belongs to. The exemplary power of a hero or heroine struggling for freedom or helping to define it more fully and positively would have no particular exchange value in this scheme. Barthes rejects the kind of behavior that has often been alleged in the case of great characters in fiction, that they took hold of the story and of their author and led to an achievement he never planned or that they cast a spell over the reader that helped to shape his or her life. Barthes would convict such characters of insubordination, as illegitimate aesthetic creatures in rebellion against the arbitrary freedom of the reader.

In *Sarrasine*, Balzac's narrator (since Barthes very much considers the "I"-narrator to be a personage) is an intelligible object with a biography and a meaning in time. But he may oscillate and appear also as figure, without regard to time or personality, depending upon the role (e.g., master or slave to the Marquise) assigned to him by the symbolic code (largely Freudian-Lacanian) in the framing portions of the story.

The fact that personage as well as figure is a liberating aspect of character in fiction emerges more clearly later, when Barthes explains the role we play as readers or critics with regard to the personages of a story and at the same time suggests why he has not provided us with a code of narration.[10] The passage, though rather sportive, raises a very important set of issues connected with characters, authorial discourse, implied author, and reader. Barthes begins by saying that a realistic view of the personage demands motivation, while a realistic view of the consumer-reader's demands leads the author to withhold motives until the unraveling of the story calls for them. He goes on, in an analysis influenced by Derrida:

> Both circuits are necessarily undecidable. Good narrative writing *is* this undecidability. From a critical point of view, therefore, it is as false to suppress the personage as to make him rise from the page in order to make him a psychological personage (endowed with possible motivations): the personage and the discourse are one another's accomplices; the discourse calls forth in the personage its own accomplice: a form of theurgic detachment by which, mythically, God is given a subject, man a companion, etc., whose relative independence, once they have been created, permits *play*. So with the discourse: if it produces personages, it is not to make them play among themselves before us, but [for the discourse] to play along with them, gaining from complicity with them assurance of the uninterrupted exchange of codes: personages are types of discourse and inversely the discourse is a personage like the others.[11]

Since Barthes minimizes the importance of the first suspenseful reading, his kind of reader is not interested in gradually learning the true motives of anyone but rather in uniting himself with the forces and constraints of the story so as

[10] As Jonathan Culler quite reasonably asks in *Structuralist Poetics* (Ithaca: Cornell University Press, 1975), p. 203.

[11] *S/Z*, LXXVI, 178f. Here Barthes seems to adopt a biblical figure much in favor with writers in the ontotheological tradition he rejects. See, e.g., 2

to be able to generate in passing a schema that corresponds to the state of flux of the work being read. Its meaningfulness is entirely due to the undecidable play among circuits that themselves are not fixed but tuneable, independent and free of all external determination, including the determination to be themselves in any natural, substantial, or final mode of being. Here Barthes stresses his idea of freedom (so different from Schiller's), and in its light remorselessly denies us whatever solace might come from the sense that in a world where being is so problematic works of art can at least have a quasi-being, the substantiality and finality of an artistic object capable of being cocreated by a reader or a viewer. It is this *indécidable*, therefore, that would seem to preclude the effective coding of writable narrative.

As for the author in all of this, his greatest praise is to be

---

Samuel 6:21; and especially Proverbs 8:30–31 (though the word the Vulgate gives as *ludere*, "play," is now differently translated). The passage is worth quoting in the original to show how Barthes, though under the direct influence of Derrida, manages to save the function of character in fiction:

Sarrasine est enivré parce que le discours ne doit pas finir; le discours pourra continuer, puisque Sarrasine, enivré, parle sans ecouter. Les deux circuits de nécessité sont indécidables. La bonne écriture narrative est cette indécidabilité même. D'un point de vue critique, il est donc aussi faux de supprimer le personnage que de le faire sortir du papier pour en faire un personnage psychologique (doté de mobiles possibles): le personnage et le discours sont complices l'un de l'autre; le discours suscite dans le personnage son propre complice: forme de détachement théurgique par lequel, mythiquement, Dieu s'est donné un sujet, l'homme une compagne, etc., dont la relative indépendance, une fois qu'ils ont été créés, permet de *jouer*. Tel le discours: s'il produit des personnages, ce n'est pas pour les faire jouer entre eux devant nous, c'est pour jouer avec eux, obtenir d'eux une complicité qui assure l'échange ininterrompu des codes: les personnages sont des types de discours et a l'inverse le discours est un personnage comme les autres.   (p. 184)

Here Barthes's stress upon undecidableness agrees with Derrida's contention that good interpretative analysis (Freud's, for example) can be prolonged indefinitely, and hence is finally undecidable. Barthes has also adopted Derrida's concept of "complicity," rather than structuralist "opposition"; see Gayatri Chakravorty Spivak's introduction to *Of Grammatology* (Baltimore: The Johns Hopkins University Press, 1976), pp. lxxvi–lxxvii.

so lost in the process that his voice or his persona or implied presence becomes quite irrecoverable anywhere in the work, in part or as a whole.

Barthes's model now assumes a clear form. It begins with information (in the sense of the adjectival *informis*, i.e., "un-meaning"), and postulates an information-processing circuitry whose function is to generate intelligibility through delaying, marking, and schematizing units of information. It is easy to think of the writing or the reading process in these terms because we are so habituated to the notion of space as a vast electronic field wherein an innumerable host of circuits and combinations of circuits (including ourselves as human complexes of nerve circuitry), each and all both complete and incomplete, coruscate in some fashion whose final structure (since we do not know of it) does not exist. In no way, however, can this world-picture be equated with a theory of mimetic writing; at the most, writing produces a highly suggestive isotopy, no more.

The great save-all that hovers over the deconstructing activity of Barthes is the notion that all meaning exists in languages of various kinds (phonemic, mathematical, logical, biological, electronic) and that all language is differentially generated from relationships among what we recognize as mental images or models. If we can free ourselves from the established relationships to real referents, we can make a better life and a better world. There is much to be said for this attitude, but it puts one at a great disadvantage in discussing art. In plastic art the physical painting or statue has a unique importance. In writing there is a level of sound that no matter how mental it may become must be voiced in an unwritten, unwritable way. Art, in fact, has provided, and still provides, instances of freedom embodied in and conditioned by the physically permanent. Can it do otherwise?

IN ATTEMPTING to summarize Barthe's contribution in *S/Z*, a comparison to Bergson's *Le Rire* is helpful. Both books develop around central images, sometimes ostensible (as in Barthes's comparison of the space of reading to that of cubist painting) and sometimes covert. Bergson's most important central image is of the human world as a sphere whose surface layer is a hard, dead *pellicule* of social routine. Genuine art—tragedy, serious drama—splits right down through the exterior surface to the central depths and allows us some sense of the vibrant intensity of vital forces at the core of the world process. Comedy, or rather vaudeville, is a slight growth that finds tiny surface cracks to shelter in; in fact it is the servant of the social routine. By exposing inflexible, unadaptable behavior to ridicule, it makes members of society more malleable and responsive to social demands and the conditions of existence in crowded cities. Barthes's central image we have already seen as an enormous unshaped network of circuitry that generates signs when activated, thus providing a vast flow of information. One could be free to program this information in many ways, but unfortunately we are preprogrammed by Western culture so as to make us habitually mistake its mere ideology for a set of natural limitations on the signifying process.

The big difference between these two central images is that Bergson's was as much an ironic figure of speech as a reality judgment, and especially that it did not commit him to a massive onslaught on the whole of Western culture. One of the most striking features of our culture (at least of a sector within its bourgeois component) is a willingness to be self-critical and intellectually self-destructive. Artaud's indictment of Western culture preceded Derrida's and Barthes's by thirty years, and in the previous fifty years between Artaud and Nietzsche much had been said and much had been done, especially by artists revolting against their own bourgeois origins, to prepare the way for an apocalyptic transformation. At the end of a long career marked by close thinking and sustained argument, Bergson made a metaphoric distinction between open and closed societies in the form of an axiology of greater and less value. Barthes, on the other hand, began by adopting Saussure's "phonological revolution" as the basis of a two-part antithesis. He first set the sign against the referent and wiped out the referent in the name of freedom and "the text." Then he set the post-revolutionary or modern against the prerevolutionary or classic, and wiped out the latter, this time in the name of freedom and "the plural." The justification for this second move was homology, the reciprocal of antithesis. Barthes felt he had found an isotopy for linguistics in his own semiological procedures. He had captured the two essential principles: the diacritical nature of meaning and the synchrony/diachrony distinction.

Far from wishing to dismiss Barthes's original argument I would like to place it in a historical perspective that is sufficiently vast to meet his own demand for the use of history.[12] I mean the movement away from classicism into romanticism and realism that began over two hundred years ago. The leading motive of the whole development has been, and still is, freedom: freedom through the whole range of possible meanings of the word. For Barthes, freedom now is keeping language open to the maximum possible plural of meanings.

S/Z begins with a statement on evaluation in which the "poor freedom" of the class of reading one does as a consumer—the readable—is rejected in favor of the richer freedom of becoming a producer, an active writer-reader engaged with the writable. The idle, intransitive consumer-reader is dismissed as "serious"—the word is used by Barthes in its Nietzschean sense, Zarathustra's "when I saw my devil I found him serious, thorough, profound, and solemn: it was the spirit of gravity—through him all things fall." (Elsewhere in the same section, headed "On Reading and Writing," Zarathustra protests: "Another century of readers—and the spirit itself will stink.")[13] In his zest for the plural, Barthes links value to cocreative praxis, i.e., "what

[12] *Essais Critiques* (Paris: Seuil, 1964), pp. 261f.; *Critical Essays,* translated by Richard Howard (Evanston, Ill.: Northwestern University Press, 1972), pp. 264f.

[13] *Thus Spoke Zarathustra,* part 1, "On Reading and Writing," pp. 152f. in *The Portable Nietzsche.*

can be written (rewritten) today," for "the goal of literary labor (of literature as labor) is to make the reader no longer a consumer, but a producer of the text."[14] Both readers and writers should be workers rather than the pensioners of a funded museum-culture or the clients of a proprietor-author. This vaguely Marxist language squares perfectly well, however, with familiar romantic and modernist ideals of active memory and creative imagination and of interplay between one's experience in art and one's experience of life.

Freedom for Barthes means not simply that the principle of mimesis has been abandoned or that the concept of nature has dissolved; rather, the idea of reference to what is known to be real has been superseded by the notion of a freely constituted (i.e., human-made) reality. Nature is not held to be a substantial entity anterior to the literary or scientific operation but a constituted system that has come into being in the process of human manipulation. So Barthes's words "the goal of literary labor (of literature as labor)" distinguish between literature as an essence or an institution and literature interpreted as coming to be in the process of being produced either by a writer or by an active reader who uses his rereadings only to deconstruct his first "natural" reading and to transform the "readable" text into a "writable" one that he is producing or rewriting.

What might seem distressingly arbitrary here is that Barthes distinguishes the writable strictly on the basis of what he himself and his associates would care to write or rewrite. Yet Barthes is no selfish elitist; in fleeing the land of bondage, he will lead the people along with him, and he will also save for their use whatever spoils can be carried out of captivity. He recognizes a residuary value in the classic works—not a rich or generous but a "parsimonious plural." In his labor on Balzac's *Sarrasine* he employs a remarkable variety of procedures, many of them rich in promise for the

---

[14] *S/Z*, I, 4; French, p. 10. The French terms are *scriptible* and *lisible*; the "readable" relation is that of the *propriétaire* (author) of a text and his *client* (reader).

practical criticism of all of us. The whole study is highly writable in that one is puzzled and challenged by its omissions and exclusions even more perhaps than by its surprising disclosures. To begin with, the choice of a Balzac text signals an engagement with the dominant mode of romantic realism just at the crux where it was constituting itself in opposition to romantic idealism. Moreover, the story chosen is no ordinary piece of realism but a philosophical tale dealing (like *Le Peau de chagrin, Le Chef-d'oeuvre inconnu,* and *La Récherche de l'absolue*) with what George Saintsbury called "the nemesis of fulfilled desire" (anticipating by half a century Barthes's "repletion").[15]

More interesting still, *Sarrasine* incorporates its own protest against an anterior classic art: the idealized, idyllic vision that in the 1820s looked away from things as they are toward things as they should be. Balzac's story frames a manifesto of realist art. His narrator cannot help presenting the world as it really is, despite the strongest temptation to adorn his tale. For Balzac in 1830 was taking his stand with Victor Hugo, who had just written in the preface to *Cromwell:*

> the modern muse will see things in a higher and broader light. It will realize that everything in creation is not humanely *beautiful,* that the ugly exists beside the beautiful, the unshapely beside the graceful, the grotesque on the reverse of the sublime, evil with good, darkness with light. It will ask itself if the narrow and relative sense of the artist should prevail over the infinite, absolute sense of the Creator; if it is for man to correct God; if a mutilated nature will be the more beautiful for the mutilation; if art has the right to duplicate, so to speak, man, life, creation; if things will progress better when their muscle and their vigor have been taken from them. . . .[16]

---

[15] *Encyclopaedia Britannica,* 11th edition, s.v. Balzac, Honoré de. The spelling of the title, interestingly, is "Sarrazine," with the errant zed that attracted Barthes to the story in the first place.

[16] Translated by Barrett H. Clark, *European Theories of the Drama* (Cincinnati: Stewart and Kidd, 1918), p. 368.

Anyone who has recently read *Sarrasine* will recognize in this quotation the "armature," as Barthes would say, for the opening paragraph of Balzac's tale, as well as for the whole *Comédie Humaine*. Indeed, Barthes too exploits some of these ideas, for example the important notion of antithesis and transgression. Others he employs by the Nietzschean tactic of asserting the reciprocal—for instance, he associates God the Creator with the ancient classic, whereas Hugo associates him with the revolutionary Christian romantic; but the principle is really the same: freedom. Freedom must be left open for infinite plurality. Hugo saw openness as all-inclusiveness; Barthes sees it as infinite noninclusiveness. It is plain that Barthes in confronting a text of 1830 in 1970 is re-enacting the enterprise of Balzac and Hugo. The third romantic wave extends the curve of the second by first inverting it.

In this broad historical context, one may state a comic meaning of the Balzac story, for Barthes makes *S/Z* state its tragic reciprocal. Their terms may be different, but the concepts in both cases are those that Schiller had already developed in the first wave of revolutionary romanticism: nature, the naive, nostalgia, excess, idealism, realism. *Sarrasine* itself is a frame story. It consists of a recorded series of quasi-historical events (a casual attempt at seduction) enveloping a narrated fable. The recorder tells of escorting an attractive twenty-two-year-old Marquise to a ball at a wealthy bourgeois house where she is momentarily alarmed and disgusted by the apparition of a grotesque old man, and then greatly attracted by a picture of a nude Adonis. The recorder tries to profit by the intimacy he and the Marquise share in these experiences; he offers to tell the story behind both the old man and the Adonis at the hinted price of a night of love. The reluctant Marquise grants a rendezvous. But when the recorder as narrator presents a quite realistic account of La Zambinella, the once famous castrato who is really the old man and was once the imaginary model for the Adonis, the Marquise not surprisingly finds the tale true but countererotic. She accepts the narrative, but dismisses the narrator.

Balzac's frame story is objectifiable as a comically rueful defense of his own art: his narrator is offering honest wares and will not, like a prostitute, dress them up with false accommodations; hence he fails to seduce his audience. His anaphrodisiac fable is the account of a historical murder at Rome in 1758 of a young French sculptor, Sarrasine, for his pursuit of a beautiful male soprano kept by Cardinal Cicognara. Though as a talented sculptor and a thoroughly schooled pupil of Bouchardon he should have known better, Sarrasine insisted upon seeing the beautiful effeminate lad as an ideal woman to such an excess that he attempted to rape "her." The statue he made of "her" (from his overheated imagination, not from the life) was copied in 1791 in a painting where the castrato Zambinella was pictured male, as Adonis; with this Adonis the Marquise so ridiculously fell in love, right after being disgusted by its ninety-year-old original. The moral of the whole narrative is clear: to seduce an aristocratic audience, sensual-minded like the Marquise, the narrator needed to idealize, not to render life as it really is. He needed to be a Boucher or a Bouchardon, not a Balzac.

Barthes pays no attention to this meaning (or, rather, comic objectivity); presumably it is part of the bygoneness he is wiping out. Instead, he proves that *Sarrasine* is not altogether dead by writing something new not about it but within its interstices. He opens up 561 of these in the text (reproduced *in toto*), creating space to be filled with a comment of his own on each *lexie*. He also intersperses 93 brief expositions, full of ideas and catchy (but very valuable) nomenclature. These short essays constitute a thesaurus of critical concepts and procedures, developed from and feeding back into the new wave of French fiction and its *Tel Quel* commentators, but also developing the theory of seminotics in general. By far the most striking innovation is the set of five codes by which Barthes "stars" the individual *lexies* according to the kind of information they contain.

The hermeneutic (HER) and proairetic (ACT) codes are "vectorized" and classic; they function to give diachronic direction to narrative and to bring an old-fashioned linear

story from beginning through middle to end. The hermeneutic code is a means for the setting up and disclosure of
enigmas, thus achieving suspense. The action code shows
the development of nameable sequences of events, familiar
from ordinary life or from reading. The other three codes,
cultural (REF), meaning-images (SEM), and symbols (SYM), are
not linear but "tabular" and hence modern, for they are not
in servitude to truth and an enforced closure. They are free
to signify among themselves, or with the HER or ACT codes,
in the process of transcoding or "braiding" of the text, which
is what Barthes means by writing. For example, the SYM code
(which Barthes draws largely from the psychoanalysis of
Jacques Lacan) can be linked with the HER code of *Sarrasine*
to weave a modern theme: the "enigma" of Balzac's story is
the delayed discovery of a merely literal, anecdotal castration; but Barthes shows that fetishistic femininity is everywhere dominant ("pandemic") throughout the story, and in
his *S/Z* he transcodes it into an emptiness that is shared out
among Sarrasine, the statue he sculpts, and several paintings
and photos that replicate the statue and each other. This
pandemic castration is related by Barthes and his colleagues
to art and the artist by what seems to me a process of pure
mystification, in sharp contrast to the elegance of its objecti-
fication in the Balzac story but in ironic fulfillment of Hugo's
characterization of the idealism he and Balzac opposed.[17]

Besides these five ways of codifying content, Barthes also
makes use of a transformational *rhetoric* by associating conventional figures of speech with richly suggestive terms and
symbols descriptive of what occurs in the writing process.
His antithesis, for example, opposes two plentitudes in a
kind of agon in which crossing the barrier is a source of
"horror," but at the same time a necessary "transgression"
without which the story can not begin. These neologisms
may seem melodramatic, but as one learns that they do
mean something and that Barthes uses them consistently

---

[17] Fredric Jameson, "The Ideology of the Text," *Salmagundi*, 10 (1975),
239-240, deals with Barthes's idealism.

one is more willing to accept them. Sometimes a familiar rhetorical term is thrown overboard: synecdoche, presenting a part for the whole, is said to offer "a truth" as signifying "the Truth" and hence it can have no function in modern writing. But catachresis is more important than before— more important even than metonymy, because it relates two terms of comparison to emptiness rather than to each other. It is much better than metaphor, which (like synecdoche) illegitimately implies a cosmic togetherness instead of a merely differential and local relation.

Linguistics affords Barthes many concepts and terms. It must be said, however, that he is far more indebted to linguistics for a few fundamentally important dogmatic propositions than he is for workaday nomenclature. Derrida's insistence upon rejecting the signifier/signified opposition of Saussure in favor of a "complicity" relation is, however, exceptionally important to Barthes, who associates servitude with the fixed structures of signifieds, and freedom with the infinite multiplicity of signifiers.[18]

Yet Barthes is systematic rather than free-wheeling through much of S/Z. Though he favors reversible, untrammeled circulation of signs, of sexes, and of fortunes as the outcome of his reading of *Sarrasine*, he allows only three approaches to this symbolic field: the rhetorical route, the route of castration, and the economic route. In other ways too Barthes is arbitrary rather than anarchic. His modern rewriting insists on the catastrophic collapse of the reality that Balzac's art of the novel so skillfully built up, and that collapse is simply what Barthes's dogma requires. As a man of today, he disbelieves in the novel and the art of the classic novelist as much as he disbelieves in bourgeois culture. He believes in writing not as a métier distinct from music or painting but rather as a productive activity in one or more of the many kinds of language, verbal and nonverbal. As for

---

[18] Barthes was aware quite early of the more purely formalistic restatement of Saussure's signifier/signified opposition by Hjelmslev, which did away with the need for any notion of referent or reference.

Balzac, he is only worth study to the extent that he loses himself in the text, as Flaubert did in *Bouvard and Pécuchet*. That the book is the expression of the writer, who is its father and proprietor, is just what Barthes is in fact "vomiting" in *S/Z*.

As with books and authors, so with sentences and words; *langue* goes out the window. In place of the slavish lexicon, we have thematics, open to an endless compilation of rubrics. There is no *mot juste*, quite the opposite, an infinite prolongation of the signifying process. Sentencing, denotation, is neither a constative nor an illocutionary act; it is not a judicial or a structuring procedure, only a paste to hold the codes in place provisionally.

Literature itself should be a cacophony, an art of noise. Without noise, it would be instituted as mere idyllic communication. And writing is not communication. There is no one-to-one circuit (as in Saussure's picture of speaker and listener) but only the voice of the reader-of-the-text ("the text as reader," as Barthes might add in a typical parenthesis aimed at wiping out the genitive). For the delaying discourse that processes noise is the only "hero" of the story; it alone speaks. There are, of course, no narrators or characters in the classic sense. Writing exists not to be read but to be (re)produced.

In the "readable," on the other hand, "everything holds together," and the codes are linked as if "naturally" by age-old elegant syntax. Instead of becoming, i.e., structuration, there is being, the already structured; that is, we find stale ideology rather than fresh signifying. So, in the place of field or situation in the modern sense of a space where codes exchange signification, the readable gives us a framed picture created programmatically in three steps: first, announcement, in the story, and then in the storyteller's discourse, as a category of reality offered for analysis; second, presentation of an image in one perspective; and third, a filling up of coded REF materials also seen from one point of view, with the perspectival vanishing-point oriented by the various REF subcodes belonging to the culture. Such, for example, is

Balzac's orgy in *Sarrasine*. His real is an already written "real," and the once lauded art of the realistic novelist is only the trick of producing reality effects with an illusion of gratuitousness that makes them seem natural.

The inadequacy of Barthes's handling of Balzac's comic structure comes out most strongly in his discussion of one of these so-called reality effects. As usual, the picture in the original is framed and put in perspective. In the opening ballroom scene, Balzac emphatically foregrounds the mistress of the house, Mme. de Lanty, by directly pitting the *dégagé* Marquise against her. Mme. de Lanty and her children, Marianina and Fillippo, all inherit the old castrato's former beauty. (As an expression of Balzac's view of the issue of duplication by art and by nature, he makes the girl Marianina, not the boy, inherit Zambinella's soprano voice; moreover, she has a completely natural instrument unmarred by any of the excesses or deficiencies of the great professionals of the day.) Yet since M. de Lanty is an altogether obscure personality, the central enigma for the Paris-on-the-make of 1830 is where their money came from. The answer we learn is, from the beauty, talent, prostitution, artistic exploitation, and finally from the huge independent earnings of La Zambinella, now a grotesque old automaton, but once an international opera star. A *ragazzo* of Naples, castrated and trained by Prince Chigi and kept by a cardinal of the Papal curia, Zambinella after the revolution achieved in bourgeois society a life of dignity; now, in old age, he is cherished by his loving family. For the gifts of value they receive from him, they give gifts of love and care in return. Hence the mystery, impenetrable to the fashionable Parisians. That the de Lanty family should owe their wealth to success in art and should be genuinely grateful for it to the artist is as incomprehensible to Paris society as the poems of Byron or the novels of Ann Radcliffe. Nevertheless, the story of old Zambinella proves what Balzac well knew: that the artist had to pay too great a price in order to win a place in that society.

Barthes ignores this cluster of themes entirely, though one supposes he is aware of them. The exhaustiveness of his commentary, however, forces him to deal with some of Balzac's touches of intimate family life, including Marianina's *addio* to the old star. This action, Barthes says, is nonoperable as the discourse describes it: "She added to the final syllable a marvellously well-executed trill, but in a soft voice, as if to give poetic expression to the emotions of her heart," and then, "Suddenly struck by some memory, the old man stood . . . we heard the heavy sigh that came from his chest: he took the most beautiful of the rings which adorned his skeletal fingers, and placed it in Marianina's bosom. The young madcap broke into laughter, took the ring, and slipped it onto her finger over her glove." Barthes's comment is stupefying: "The laugh, the glove, are effects for the sake of reality, notations whose very insignificance authenticates, signs, signifies 'reality.' "[19] First, the goodbye is perfectly operable. The grandniece, not an operatic actress but a well-brought-up young amateur, plays a little game involving her old granduncle, alluding vocally to a measure in some role familiar to them both (there were plenty of *addios* and *adieux* for the soprano before 1830). Her compliment succeeds; and the niece, instead of hiding the sign of her famous relative's gratitude, chooses to wear his ring openly and playfully. It is a payment in exchange, but even more it is a free gift, like the gift her own harmonious combination of nature and art enables her to offer in free play. In wiping out this true meaning of Marianina's laugh, Barthes himself is responsible for the unsignifying reality effect he blames Balzac for.

Much more inexcusably, however, Barthes misses the perfectly comic fact that the grotesque old castrato's voice is the objectivity that has been reborn in the charming young girl; my guess is that he was systematically conditioned against it. At any rate, Barthes rather ponderously refers to Balzac's story more than once as tragic, although it is noth-

[19] *S/Z*, XXXV, 80f.; French, p. 87. The translator misreads *folle* in the original as *fille*. Barthes ignores the striking nuance in *folle*, and also fails to notice the implication of the phrase "the most beautiful" (rather than "the most costly," for example).

ing of the sort. Even the inserted history of events in 1758 is not tragic but at most grotesque.

If there is anything to deplore in Barthes it is those occasions when he takes his more sweeping and melodramatic ideas too seriously. On doctrinaire principle he entirely misses the comic grotesque in Balzac's story and misrepresents it as tragic. His continual references to the "terrifying essence of passivity" and the like constitute a fake miasma, especially when he intends to impute it to all classic literature. His whole terror-passivity-castration-replication-emptiness-vomiting maneuver is a doctrinaire fiction based on a Nietzschean-Pascalian image (from *Revelation*, actually: the Spirit of God vomiting the lukewarm). It requires violence to the Balzac text in many ways; the byplay between Marianina and old Zambinella is only one of its pleasures that Barthes's reading denies us. Barthes seems at times to wave the castrator's knife before every reader with a stock of historical imagination, like a new Jove menacing Saturn. But rather than succumb to the spirit of gravity, let the historical critic take M. Barthes as he comes: in the third wave of romanticism, after Schiller and Blake, Hugo and Balzac, along with W. C. Williams, Antonin Artaud, and Charles Olsen. For this understanding is what Barthes has directly made possible by the writing of *S/Z*.

Enough remains unchanged between Balzac (1830) and Barthes (1970) to argue for a continuation of the romantic dialectic wherein Barthes appears as the idealist and Balzac as the realist faithful to the harmonious union of nature and the ideal. Both are still in accord with the two types Schiller described at the beginning of the period. The seeming innovations upon which Barthes founds his claims for modernity appear in Balzac too, under different names but with at least equal clarity, as I have been suggesting. The notion of transgression that Barthes develops with such emphasis is not only implicit in *Sarrasine*; it had just been explained and justified at length by Hugo under the rubric of the grotesque and credited with the same initiatory power in art. Castration, asserted at such length by Barthes along with notions drawn from Lacan's psychoanalysis, remains a tendentious and perhaps doctrinaire improvisation upon the Balzacian theme of the nemesis of fulfilled desire. That the writer must empty himself to satisfy his reader is just as contestable as Freud's imputation of a necessary neurosis to the artist; both are versions of the romantic *poète maudit.* Barthes's readable is Hugo's composition by the rules; his writable is the incomprehensible-to-the-bourgeois, like what Balzac's story tells of their response to Byron. Barthes's nausea at replication is not much different from Hugo's "What! copy copies? God forbid!" And both Barthes and Hugo have a liberating theory, one the reciprocal of the other. Barthes's idealism, a false creation of the Nietzschean will, aligns itself with Sarrasine's arrogant disregard for nature in the story. Barthes's reduction of Balzac's story from comic realism (copresence of the grotesque and the ideal) to doctrinaire gravity shows the price he is paying: anxiety to disown the bourgeois is as debilitating as the need to please them.

Barthes did not open a new epoch. Yet what he accomplished is very important. He reinterpreted the romantic impulse toward a fresh outlook on the relations between the human and the natural, which have been problematic for two centuries. Inspired by a second generation of romantic figures (Hegel, Marx, Nietzsche, Freud, Saussure), he found new, practical strategems for their ideas in the thought of his own generation. One of these tactics is the postulate of a Fall separating the classic from our modernity (Schiller used it first, then Hugo). However this idea may be justified in theology or in Saussure's linguistics as a means of establishing synchrony, in human experience there has been so such apocalypse. New events occur, new phases begin, new states of affairs are perceived, converted into others, and pass away; but there is always a bearer or carrier of continued human existence of which these are the modulations.

It is an open question in philosophy whether real enduring things exist otherwise than as combinations of events or systems of processes. But it may at least be argued that, in the highly eventful period between Hugo's Preface to *Crom-*

well and Barthes's *S/Z*, Balzac's tale of *Sarrasine* has endured not as a real but as an artistic object. It lacks the nostalgic pathos of Keats's "Grecian Urn," but it still keeps a brash, comic point: that the muscle and vigor of art belongs in the free service of nature and the ideal. That this point endures with Balzac's story and is not bound up and fallen with an anterior state of it appears from what Jameson calls the "realistic kernel" of Barthes's *S/Z* itself, that "the infatuated artist in reality sees his own image in the castrate . . . so that the gesture of symbolic castration or sexual renunciation is here given to be the very source of artistic productivity."[20]

SNOW WHITE Á LA BARTHES

Before I wind up this study in a chapter of conclusions, I hope the reader will welcome one full-scale inquiry into a contemporary work. Its justification in part is that the text, Donald Barthelme's *Snow White*, has fallen between the cracks of an otherwise much-admired *oeuvre*. Mainly, though, I hope this critique will serve to demonstrate that the essentially comic quality as I have been viewing it in this book is still to be found in contemporary writing. At the risk of prolonging my chapter on Roland Barthes, I take the liberty of employing some of the strategies of this fine critic and writer in order to direct attention to some perhaps neglected pleasures of a recent American text.

Donald Barthelme's *Snow White* ought to qualify as a "text of our modernity," most of all because it is a plural structure of language, without referents and without a center. Its author has not sought through irony or any of the other imperialist methods to achieve an enviable superiority over the reader or over the personages in the text. The productive activity of the reader is indispensable at every level of folding and braiding the work. There are no real givens,

---

[20] *The Prison-House of Language* (Princeton: Princeton University Press, 1972), p. 148.

and nothing is to be taken for granted. There is no nature—
any such assumed states are undercut and dispersed as soon
as they are suggested. The process of dissemination is so
uncentered as to avoid with admirable success even the suggestion of a merely reciprocal or reactive construction.
There is no resultant antimyth—unless, of course, the creative reader should wish to construct one entirely of his own,
beginning perhaps with the seme of Snow White's ebony-
black hair.

Familiar schemes of action in traditional fiction will all be
found to disintegrate functionlessly in Barthelme's tale. Elements of the Grimms' story of Snow White are present: the
helpful dwarfs of the forest, the wicked witch with her mirror, the prince whose role is to come someday; but their relationships are so altered as to deprive them of any meaning
that is still homologous with the original or ur-myth. There
is a proairetism of "the poisoning," wherein the wicked
witch Jane (so identified in a quiz incorporated in the text)
offers Snow White a doctored Gibson cocktail, but it is con-
sumed by Paul, the nonequivalent of the Prince, and he dies
in nonhomologous agony. Snow White has been found in
the forest ("the rescue from the wilderness") *before* the story
begins, and this retrospective naming of an action is never
constituted in the text. The dwarfs—or, I should say, the
seven men; they are never called dwarfs—regret its occur-
rence, perhaps, and call it in question. The most important
proairetism, Snow White's "hair initiative," does not belong
to the Snow White myth at all but to the weakly related Ra-
punzel family of folk tales. Another important plot-line with
several recognizable actions is that in which Bill figures: the
fall from power, the indictment, the trial, and the execution
of a former leader. Here, however, the cited crimes are lacking in interest or significance, consisting merely of the
"hurlment" of two six-packs of Miller High Life beer
through the windshield of a Volkswagen. The more serious
crime of "vaticide" is of scarcely greater significance, unless
one believes that Chinese-flavored baby food is an especially meaningful product. In a somewhat similar but alto-

gether peripheral sequence, a grievance is brought against the band leader Fred within the Musicians' Union; we do not have any further information as to its outcome. Yet to the reader who loves words reflection on "hurlment" (cf. *Geworfenheit*), "vaticide," and "grievance" are an adequate comic supplement for lack of meaning.

Other actions with zero significance in unfolding a plot line are codable symbolically rather than hermeneutically; that is, they do not fit into the developing stages of any enigma, but are rather places of entry into psychic space uncontaminated (as Barthes requires) by deep or privileged meanings. The most important, beyond question, is the activity that constitutes the point of transgression in the relationship between Snow White and the seven men, the ritually performed and socially institutionalized "shower experience." The shower experience is central in the only way Barthes allows: it is an experience of absence, in this case the absence of sex.

The operation braided into the text under the name Bill, who is repeatedly seen to function as the leader among the seven men, effects the transgression that initiates the nonenigma in that he refuses to transgress; he refuses the ritual of the shower experience precisely at that point of the touch and the making-nude where for the other men and for Snow White transgression effects a meaningful exchange by means of a disclosure and a gesture. This gesture itself is made plural through its own system. Barthes might call it in cybernetic language a "byte" or "bit" of the shower-experience system. It emerges in the remarkable line-up of beauty spots with which Snow White is marked—only six, one notes, indicating that the shower experience includes, along with Snow White, only six of the men, and therefore excludes Bill. Bill, for his part, is unwilling to be touched himself at the outset of the story and in addition is shown to be tired of Snow White and hence unwilling to touch her.

The work of the reader is here ready to his hand; he may choose to make much or little of all this. None of the relations is privileged: those that might have been considered so

have all either been cancelled in some fashion or else a relation with an equal and opposite counterprivilege has been
stated, resulting in a complicity of signifiers and lack of the
imperialism that is the precipitator of bourgeois meaning.
The point is made: *Snow White* is a writable not a readable
book; it is genuinely a work of our modernity.

TWO PERCEPTIVE CRITICS have engaged with *Snow White* in the
course of essays concerned with Barthelme's work at large.
Thomas R. Edwards contrasts Barthelme's success in matters
of purely literary concern with his misfires involving social
and political consciousness: "The terms of Barthelme's art
don't easily accommodate the most difficult terms of life,
and a distant and grave sense of absurdity, not feeling close-
up, is what he has to give us."[21] Alan Wilde disagrees to an
extent; he argues that Barthelme's distance should be seen as
a contemporary phenomenon in a movement now two hundred years old from romantic irony to the current writer's
"longing . . . to make contact with the world outside his limited and limiting ego." Wilde ends by attributing to Barthelme, especially in his most recent work, "an ethic of subjectivity and risk," a "persisting sadness," and "a normative
presence forging, tentatively, a morality and an irony for
postmodern (or, possibly, post-postmodern?) man."[22] It will
be noted that neither Edwards nor Wilde adopt Barthes's
notion of a cataclysmic Fall dividing such a work as *Snow
White* from the fictions of Forster, Dickens, or even Fielding.
Edwards dismisses *Snow White* as Barthelme's "thinnest"
work, "a tedious countercultural soap opera," evidently because he believes that in it the author shows at excessive
length his inability to work close to feeling. Wilde in fact
makes little use of the book, for *Snow White* does indeed lack
irony and sadness as well as "a distant and grave sense of
absurdity." I should like to suggest, however, that the book

[21] Thomas R. Edwards, "Barthelme the Scrivener," *New York Review of
Books*, December 1, 1975, pp. 54–55.

[22] Alan Wilde, "Barthelme Unfair to Kierkegaard: Some Notes on the
Post-Modern Literary Imagination," *boundary 2*, 5 (1976), 45–70.

offers a kind of comic writing to which distance, gravity, and modernist irony are irrelevant.

We may begin with what Edwards says about Barthelme's audience: "If he was writing studies in a dying culture, they were also—like *The New Yorker*, where most of his work appeared—meant to seem amusing and unthreatening to the creatures of that culture, living or at least imagining cosmopolitan lives while keeping up with the charming vulgarity outside." Edwards claims (mistakenly, in my opinion) to see here the influence of S. J. Perelman, the *New Yorker* regular, and also a prevalence of in-jokes, and gives his summary judgment of Barthelme in these words: "The touch is delicate, the play of association uncannily supple, but the governing mood remains unshakably chic." The last qualification, however, is belied by its own context, for Edwards' essay conveys a high sense of the values of the stories. The damning word "chic" seems to mean that Barthelme cannot help identifying himself with his *New Yorker* audience and with "the static, ahistorical world that the culture of affluence represents as life."

With this remark Mr. Edwards sends us back to Barthes for the concept of life or nature as something culturally determined that is quite sunk beneath the notice of a genuine writer today, especially with regard to affluent bourgeois culture. One of the most important aspects of the writable text, perhaps its most telling mark, is that it does away with all precoded natural assumptions. Venturesome though it be, I should like to suggest that even in *Snow White* Barthelme's writing is a "text of our Modernity" because he continually shakes and makes questionable our sense of the culture-world as our participation in the affluent life of latter twentieth-century America has given it to us. Further, through a brief analysis of *Snow White* I wish to open the rather obvious case that the main literary quality of his work is neither its irony nor its chic but its comic force. The comic, though consistently implied by critics as a feature of Barthelme's style and vision, is seldom examined therein with attention, nor is it articulated with other qualities of his work so as to arrive at just perspective.

Speaking generally, one may say that a literary quality will be found to come into being in large measure as the result of a literary technique or combination of techniques, provided one keeps in mind that there is much more to it than that. For the critic, discussion of technique rightly serves as an expedient for leading the reader's attention to a quality of the writing that would otherwise go unnoticed or (what for criticism is the same thing) undiscussed. Barthelme's fictional technique has been analyzed in what purports to be an exhaustive manner by Roger Shattuck, who identifies its four components as follows:

1. Montage. "Fragments from everywhere—to replace the old unities."
2. Pastiche. Pastiche, "tickling the entire body of art, will replace the representation of reality."
3. Spontaneous generation. It "generates words out of images and other words as if they were guinea pigs, and acknowledges that the result places us squarely 'In the Labyrinth.' "
4. Supersaturation. "A universe so riddled with subplots and underground connections and echo-chamber effects that no clear story line survives the process of ramification and infinite regress."[23]

These techniques are presented as what is "going on in the literary space around us," but in the manner of a self-fulfilling prophet Mr. Shattuck goes on to claim that all four devices were already in use in Sterne's *Tristram Shandy*. The claim is probably correct; but in that case one should reverse one's field, for obviously there are also important differences between Barthelme's writing and what is to be found already written in *Tristram Shandy*.

I would suggest that Barthelme's most important technique is the very prevalent comic strategem of the "reified metaphor," a device of discourse that begins in a mere sign or figure of speech used as a comparison or allusion and

[23] Roger Shattuck, *New York Times Book Review*, November 9, 1975, pp. 1–2, 50.

then turns into an index or posited state of affairs, what we have been calling an objectivity. A good example is the "symbol" atop the mountain, in Barthelme's story "The Glass Mountain,"[24] which turns out to be a beautiful princess. She is presented in the story as someone real whom you can point to. This in fact is what disgusts and disillusions the hero, who instantly throws her to those wolves, his obscene companions. The technique is meant to be included, perhaps, under Shattuck's third device of generating "words out of other words or images," but this formula gets the process backwards and completely misses its importance. The comic requires just those qualities that supposedly are dismissed by Shattuck's four devices.

The comic needs unities; it needs fictional reality in the sense of presented objectivities that take shape in the reader's imagination. These are the constructs in which the stronger literary and fictional qualities may inhere—most of all, the comic quality. Bergson called attention to the ludicrous potential of turning the figurative expression into a literal one (centuries after the courtesy books of the Renaissance had done the same thing), but I doubt whether he or anyone quite foresaw the extent to which Barthelme would succeed in turning a more or less familiar already coded and dead metaphor into a vivid piece of (fictional) reality, meaningful in various ways but most often comic.

There is an example on every page of *Snow White.* I shall cite one that is extreme but representative and highly functional in the story. Clem, one of the Seven Men, is visiting Chicago:

> "So this is the Free World! I would so like to make 'love' in a bed, just once. Making it in the shower is fine, on ordinary days, but on one's vacation there should be something a little different, it seems to me. A bed would be a sensational novelty. I suppose I must seek out a bordel. I assume they can be found in the Yellow Pages. It is not Snow White that I would be

[24] In *City Life* (New York: Bantam, 1971), pp. 63–72.

being unfaithful to, but the shower. Only a collection of
white procelain and shiny metal, at bottom."[25]

Of this response by the American male to a new big city
much might be said by way of political, sociological, psychological, and moral explanation—except that it would be
perfectly ridiculous to explain anything. Fictionally, what we
have is a functional extension of the "shower experience" as
the comic surrogate for sex, resulting from the literalism of
Clem's images. Alongside his indexes there float abstract
terms, "love" and "unfaithful"—terms that writers "of our
modernity" find it difficult to incorporate into their texts
without some form of distancing or undercutting. Barthelme
too, of course, has reversed the plus and minus signs in his
equation of values; but the number of reversals is so indeter-
minate (undecidable, Barthes would say) that we can hardly
tell whether traditional morality gets a minus or a plus. As
one reader, it seems to me that traditional sex scores higher
than whatever it is that Snow White and the men do in their
shower room, according to the ratio and proportion suggested here, that a bed is better than a shower; but the whole
process only amusingly threatens to become a serious moral
inquiry—only the most humorless and literal-minded
reader would allow the threat to be followed out to a logical
conclusion in an actual train of thought or imagination. Nevertheless, Snow White herself pushes the threat of moral
earnestness to an extreme a few pages later, when Clem
joins her in her shower booth:

> "And who is it with me, here in the shower? It is Clem.
> The approach is Clem's, and the technique, or lack of it,
> is Clem, Clem, Clem. . . . Clem you are downright anti-
> erotic, in those blue jeans and chaps! Artificial insemi-
> nation would be more interesting. And why are there
> no in-flight movies in shower stalls, as there are in
> commercial aircraft? Why can't I watch Ignace Pa-
> derewski in *Moonlight Sonata*, through a fine mist? That

[25] Donald Barthelme, *Snow White* (New York: Bantam, 1968), p. 23.

was a picture. And he was president of Poland, too. That must have been interesting. Everything in life is interesting except Clem's idea of sexual congress, his Western confusion between the concept, 'pleasure,' and the concept, 'increasing the size of the herd.' But the water on my back is interesting. It is more than interesting. Marvelous is the word for it."[26]

There is certainly a plurality here. I would only point to the opacity (the fictive success) of Snow White's enjoyment of the water (see all of page 34), and the "facticity" of another element in the fantastic montage, that Poland is a nation recently threatened with genocide as well as loss of nationhood. Is Barthelme kidding Poland? Paderewski? Is he merely kidding around? If so, at the very least he has managed to use the phrase "in-flight movies" in genuinely literary discourse, probably for the first time in the history of our language, perhaps for the last. I should say he has done much more: in the field of sex, where every kind of comic license has always been allowed so long as there was an established link-up with fertility, Barthelme has introduced a threat of intellectual gravity coupled with prosaic sobriety, and so constituted an original kind of wit. When, as in this case, we have more than just wit, when we have a fictional objectivity incorporating and illustrating and yet resisting the threat of gravity, we have a genuinely comic creation.

As I have been arguing throughout this book, the comic is a quality of the whole. It emerges finally from levels of sound, meaning, and schemata, observably from all three levels at once, but never without being manifested and apparent in a fourth level of structure that encompasses and emerges from the other three together: the world of the literary work of art. The world of *Snow White* is vastly different from that of *The Magic Mountain*, just as it is different from the world of *Tristram Shandy*, but in its admittedly smaller way that world does exist—it has been successfully constituted as an intentional object by its author, with qualities (in

---

[26] Ibid., p. 34.

chief, the comic) that identify it as a valuable work of art.

Everyone has recognized Barthelme's genius for multiple allusion—connotation, Barthes calls this device, approvingly. Take one sentence from the passage just quoted, "Everything in life is interesting except Clem's idea of sexual congress, his Western confusion between the concept, 'pleasure,' and the concept, 'increasing the size of the herd.' " For prose style, there is the neat rhythm of the sentence and the repeats of hard c (echoing the beginning of the passage), especially the way the first syllable of the inspired word *"congress"* is reinforced by *"con*fusion . . . *con*cept . . . *con*cept" in what follows. The impact of "chaps" strikes visually and aurally through everything else. The rhythm of the sentence supports, on the second level, one of the leading ideas of the story, summing up the distasteful Clem as representative of repugnant sexual contact. The final word "herd" makes this point with a witty fulfillment-contrast to "congress." On the third, schematic, level, a highly characteristic scheme is emergent in the sevenness of the Seven Men. Snow White can hardly perceive them individually, only plurally. Even their leader Bill is only a function of the other six. Snow White cannot therefore be called promiscuous; to be some kind of service facility is her function. The relation of the Seven Men to her sexually is limited to the shower. What remains as the larger finally emerging context of the story's world shows Snow White as nothing more than "horsewife," that is, a hard-working slavey who cooks, washes up, and cleans house for the Seven Men while entertaining thoughts of a prince who will come someday to enrich this life of hers.

For any literary objectivity to manifest itself as such in fiction, there also must be an ethos, that is a mode of behavior convertible into terms of human values, usually what we have called a natural concrete ethic. In *Snow White* (and I am not sure this has been remarked enough) the ethos is that disclosed by Women's Liberation and its attendant consciousness-raising. It seems to me that Barthelme ought to be on the women's side, for the more artful the comic is, in the West at least (not Clem's West, but Barthes's), the more

it has always been on the women's side, beginning with
Aristophanes' *Lysistrata*. I cannot be sure, for it is undecidable; yet in *Snow White* even Jane, the wicked witch, is not
quite so unsympathetic as Hogo (ex-Roy) Pontiac de Bergerac, of whom she is the "sleepie." But no privileged behavior is set up. Everything Barthes (or Robbe-Grillet or Ortega y Gasset) has to say about the elimination of character
and motive from modern fiction is amply fulfilled in *Snow
White*. None of the proper names is a personality in the classic sense rejected by Barthes in *S/Z*. *Bill is simply a function*,
not a subjectivity. He serves as the combination of *pharmakos*
and leader. Dan functions as the spokesman for a fun version of existentialist anxiety, then becomes the successor to
Bill as leader. The others thereby become, more than anything else, nonleaders (i.e., followers). We learn that the
seven of them are the equivalent of two men of former
times; so, reifying the epic hyperbole of Homer and Virgil,
Barthelme tells us that they average two-sevenths the size of
regular men—but he never once stereotypes them as dwarfs.
Clem is vaguely a Texan cowboy, Kevin lacks self-confi-
dence, Hubert is unusually oafish, and Edward and Henry
are even more obscure than the rest: that is all we know, and
all we want to know. The nonhero Paul is braided into the
text as a fixated convert, still a Saul really, or an Augustine
who never stops saying "not yet." The text judges him according to the natural concrete ethic of today, Freud's. He
rejects the appeal of Snow White's black hair as it hangs out
of the window, for it suggests parental responsibilities
("teeth . . . paino lessons"). But he is caught regressively by
the sight of her bare breasts, even though his quest has led
him to a monastery. No one is more scandalized by this than
the villainous Hogo Pontiac de Bergerac; the upshot (un-
planned) is Paul's agonized death by poison.

    To anyone who feels that a prototype or analogue for all
this is not possible, I would suggest a work that has exerted a
considerable underground influence, whether on Barthelme
or not I have no wish to speculate here. It is Kenneth Patchen's *Journal of Albion Moonlight*.[27] This book, written and

[27] New York: New Directions, 1961.

first published in 1940 by Patchen himself, contains a plurality of ideas and fictional devices sufficient for *Snow White* and a dozen other avant-garde novels. The trial and execution of Bill, the Gothic Hogo de Bergerac, the shadowy companion figures of the Seven Men, the running suggestions of political and social malaise, the peculiar melange of literally real and grotesquely out-of-this-world events are all there in Patchen's novel. Perhaps most important is the replacement of historical narrative, extensively if not totally, by simultaneity. Patchen was probably inspired by Blaise Cendrars' *Prose de transsibérien*, published in 1913 as a *livre simultanée*. In *Snow White*, Barthelme also synchronizes several proairetic sequences, as Barthes would call them: the "hair initiative" of Snow White and its rejection; Paul's and Hogo's voyeurism and rivalry; Jane's vendetta against Snow White; the downfall of Bill. Like Patchen's, however, these sequences have a very weak narrative force and are allowed to sprawl across each other's paths rather metonymically.

Paul actually sees and rejects Snow White's "hair initiative" before it comes to a manifestation in the text (on pages 89–102, probably the best in the book). At the time we learn of it he is in his "baff"—here in the literalness of changing two letters Barthelme indexes the infantile significance of the water/shower/sex scheme or theme. Does he also index irresponsibility? Maybe he does, but who cares? We already knew about that. We already know a lot, in fact. What Barthelme does is to set some of what we already know in our culture-world in a kind of literal concrete opposition to its normal computer-banked abstraction and dormancy. He gives everyday culture the impact of a stylistic and fictional objectivities and brings it to lively imaginary activity in our minds. The possibility of comparison to the poet Patchen, along with all the recognitions that come to us as we apply Barthes's labels, suggests that there is more than cleverness in Barthelme. In addition to producing genuine contemporary comic fiction, he has a gift of comic allusiveness that in its rich ambiguity approaches the poetic.

~10~

CONCLUSIONS AND
CONTINUING ISSUES

THIS BOOK is meant to serve literary criticism by offering a discovery technique for the comic along with examples of its operation and theoretical and historical arguments for its validity. I have treated the comic as a quality that is derivable from certain works of literary art in which readers can succeed in objectifying imaginative structures that freely maintain themselves despite threats of alteration, threats that somehow seem to arise out of or to be invited by the comic objectivity itself. This seeming formula is no more than a brief description, aimed at identifying what a reader intuits along with his feeling of gratification at something comical in a literary text. The need for such an identifying procedure became clear twenty years ago. When black humor, absurd theater, and sick comedy were the fashion, it began to be painfully evident that the available superiority and incongruity theories authorized many sins against the comic and were actually being exploited by some writers to generate a great deal of woeful stuff. "Funny as a crutch" might sum up one's response to much of it, then and now. Yet it would have been, and still is, ridiculous to attempt to prove that something is not funny. A critic can only offer as dissuasion the fact that a valid technique of discovery is defeated by the work in question.

A valid discovery technique was developed by Aristotle for the tragic structure of Athenian drama. It still works, even though it has ceased to apply to new plays. That it does not apply is evidence for a negative condition: namely, that tragic dramas of the Athenian kind are no longer being produced. Aristotle's description, however, was aimed at a particular art form with a simple origin and a rapid historical development into an elaborate structure of qualitative (synchronous) and quantitative (diachronous) parts. His definition of the essential tragic structure was used as a model for new tragic writing, but always in rather different art forms, throughout the European revival of the theater. It continues to help us to define the complex quality we call the tragic and what has been called the "tragic sense of values." Though it had its historical source in one Greek city and its structural conceptualization in a single document, the *Poetics,* "tragic" is now a term that is understood and applied all over the world. And if the word loses much of its meaning in common use, the essential experience can be retrieved by reading the tragedies of Aeschylus, Sophocles, and Euripides, no matter what one's culture may be. One can then reject the use of "tragic" when it would be merely synonymous with "shocking" or "sad" or "irremediable." In this process literature (helped by criticism) has functioned not only to define human feelings more accurately, but even to extend feeling itself to new areas of recognition.

Just as Athenian tragedy brought its new kind of feeling to a long series of alien cultures, the great works of comic writing have extended the range of our feelings. If one cannot describe comic structure in anything like Aristotle's detailed account of tragedy, it is because the comic is a much more simple and inclusive experience than the tragic. It is less precisely determined; indeed, it is free by its nature. It cannot be identified, as the tragic can almost be, with but one kind of protagonist, one order of plot, one milieu, and one level of language. Comedy was imported into Greece and developed there into two distinct major forms, Aristophanes' and Menander's, the second a far more universal form even than Greek tragedy, the first seemingly irreproducible but perhaps greater in its way than any comic art form that has since come into being.

A conceptual grasp of comedy and the comic was very slow in coming not only because the comic quality was less closely bound to a single art form than the tragic but also because the actual perception of what was comic underwent development. Comic ethos, the recognition of what constituted comic behavior, has been presented in this book as a passage from various modes of exploiting the superior/inferior relation to a far more open scheme of free exchange among equals. Moreover, the term "equal" has been found not to mean either "much the same as" or "amorphous"; there is a profusion of sharply profiled individuality of structure in the comic ethos. I have argued that the comic quality is to be found most of all in characters, or more accurately perhaps in that process called "the discussion" wherein characters can best come into their own and show themselves in works of literary art.

For one to be able to identify the comic quality, at the very least one must be able to objectify a process with a direction (not a mere flux) and a structure that involves participating parties (hence identities) and that poses a genuine, even likely, possibility of change to one or more of the identities or to the process itself. Hence we are talking about an open process, not a closed one. We can feel the right comic gratification while this threat of change is successfully overcome, and as long as the parties have continued to be themselves in essential ways despite their openness and even propensity to alteration.

For this idea of the comic, a phenomenological approach affords the necessary grounding, especially in Husserl's vindication of the notion of content. If one does not restrict oneself to the formalist view that literariness is exclusively a matter of language, one may talk of fictive objectivities that can be distinguished in a text by many different readers with a common focus on the text as a work of literary art. In turn, the work may legitimately be said to have its origin in the intention of its author, whose outlook the readers are already able to share in some degree as sharers in human experience (including experience in the use of language); and that literary scholars can help them to understand that intention and outlook more fully. For the critic, the notion of a fictive structure not exclusively linguistic is particularly helpful when dealing with translated works—a vital consideration in view of the universal character of the comic quality found in such works as *Gargantua and Pantagruel, Don Quixote, Gulliver's Travels,* and *Tom Jones,* which have inspired authors in many different languages.

My argument, it seems to me, has derived another important advantage from phenomenological notions of intention and content, in its recognition that any act of objectivation can succeed in bringing into focus only a particular aspect of a work of art. The reader cannot in any one act confront the whole content of a literary work of art as an objectivity. In fact, the author could not intend the work through a single act either, whether in composing it or in planning it as it is to become for the reader. For one thing, language intervenes and can even take the initiative to a greater or lesser degree. Sometimes already published writing will take on a new aspect because it is found to contain something to which we are alerted by the appearance of a new work, perhaps many years later. Innovation, when viewed thus, becomes a two-way process and includes a component of genuine renewal in the life of older works of art, one that cannot be written off as recuperation. In this book I have tried to show how literary criticism can play a part in this process of renewal by describing kinds of content and bringing into focus objectivities belonging to older works that have not been recognized before.

With this view of the literary work of art as founding in its own life an ever-renewed succession of objectifying acts, both aesthetic and critical, it has been possible in the preceding chapters to uncover comic objectivities, even in quite well-known texts, that have gone for years without general critical recognition. This uncovering of new content should not, to my way of thinking, be confused with interpretation in the usual sense of the word. (In one very special sense, associated with Heidegger, "interpretation as" appears to be an initiatory phase of perception itself without which we could not be aware of anything—for all perception is said to be perception of something *as* something.) Normally the interpretation of a canonic work of literary art is a means of relating the work to some general notion of ourselves or our society for further mutual understanding and evaluation. A reconstruction (that is, a new organization by the critic of the objectivities found in a work of art) will not concern itself with this employment of the work as literature but will remain content with seeking a new or better sense of its structuring, for its own sake and for the sake of the art.

For a concluding illustration, let us set the procedure in motion one more time. As we know, during the nineties Henry James became quite dissatisfied with critical inattention to the general drift of his work, its "figure in the carpet," or what we may call its intention. Perhaps he was additionally vexed because he knew his own fictional method contributed to the critical failure, for he was already in the habit of playing tricks on his readers. Not the usual tricks of concealment, delay, and suspense, but the far more intriguing deception made feasible (even legitimate) by the interposition of a character, the "central consciousness," whose perspective is made responsible for almost the entire complex of objectivities actually brought to readable focus in the text. The trick is to determine this consciousness and its perspective in such a way as to allow certain potential aesthetic qualities to emerge in a cocreative reading, perhaps in spite of the central character. In *The Pupil,* one of James's best and most characteristic novellas, the manifest perspective is supplied through Pemberton. As the tutor he is an active participant in the story, but his pupil Morgan Moreen and the Moreen family are much more important figures. The critic needs to read the story several times to disentangle Morgan and Mrs. Moreen with bare conceptual adequacy from the obtuse perceptions of Pemberton and the hints of the narrator, an oracular informant who sometimes misleads in the act of telling important truths. Hence Morgan Moreen has been seen by the most eminent critics as a tragic figure. I propose that Morgan is a comic figure, and I believe that a convincing argument can be offered along lines laid down in this book.

Our original feeling of sympathy with Pemberton is quickly extended to Morgan: from a cynical child, disrespectful of his elders, he is converted to a pitiable, deprived one who needs to be taught how to play and who must be protected from those vulgar, snobbish gypsies, his family. Misunderstood thus, the story reads entertainingly to the end—all in Pemberton's perspective. One is disgusted with Mrs. Moreen, her airs and her soiled gloves, and with Mr. Moreen, tagged redundantly with being a mere "man of the world." One is happy in a way with the death of Morgan, for it frees him from his family, who would only continue to yank him, like a puppet at the end of a string, from one European capital to another, to more and more public degradation. It takes perhaps four more readings to turn this perspective right side up, with the help of an intention just visible in the whole series of hints from outside the Pemberton consciousness. If we apply these hints to the actual events of the story and to what is actually said by the characters therein, we first realize that Pemberton learns much more from Morgan than he could possibly teach. At last we discover that Morgan has nothing to learn from Pemberton in the art of play. He uses Pemberton in a great boy's game that he invents, a game of escape, a scheme that Henry James uses as a central image to structure the whole culminating movement of his story.

The game-image is introduced at the turning-point of one of several fine discussions between tutor and pupil; it is the turning-point of the story. Morgan has just told Pemberton the cautionary tale of his beloved nurse Zénobie, whom the family cheated, dismissed, and then lied about. That this story itself is partly a lie is one of our later recognitions. Then Morgan speaks out:

"We must be frank, at the last; we *must* come to an understanding," said Morgan, with the importance of the small boy who lets himself think he is arranging great affairs—almost playing at shipwreck or at Indians.

"I know all about everything," he added.   (Section VI)
The Moreens, like the Swiss Family Robinsons, are indeed to be shipwrecked, but it is Morgan's firm intent to escape not only from the wreck but from the family too. At their first meeting he had fixed upon Pemberton as his rescuer, and ever since he has played upon Pemberton's own rather snobbish distaste for the Moreen way of life (Bohemians wanting to be Philistines), and especially upon Pemberton's timidity and anxiety about money. Morgan counts upon the shipwreck; he becomes confident his weak heart will not prevent him from escaping, in the Pemberton "lifeboat," to an Oxford degree and a solid reputation won in America (these are future moves in his plan of attack). Essentially what alienates Morgan from his family is their humbleness, their timidity, their failure to be gallant: "Morgan had a romantic imagination, fed by poetry and history, and he would have liked those who 'bore his name' (as he used to say to Pemberton with the humour that made his sensitiveness manly), to have a proper spirit" (Section VII). We have already learned from the high point of a beautiful discussion in Section V and probably in the first reading that Morgan himself is afraid of nothing at all, not even the loss of the unpaid Pemberton, though he has "thought of it a long time." He encourages Pemberton to confront his parents, and if he confirms the tutor's rather flabby resolve by finally bursting into tears, they are tears of honorable shame ("manly sensitiveness") at the meanness of his father and mother. At some point (the third reading?) one sees that Morgan is masterfully manipulating Pemberton; he wants "the poor young man" to accumulate some money, and rather than wait for the family shipwreck he wants to bring it about. This time and twice more he succeeds in egging Pemberton into making a demand for money.

The storm brewing in Morgan's game plan is dramatized as an event in the story "one sad November day, while the wind roared round the old palace and the rain lashed the lagoon" in Venice where the Moreens are staying (Section

VII). Pemberton, not being aware of the plan, has at the bottom of his heart a mean idea, "the recognition of [Morgan's] probably being strong enough to live and not strong enough to thrive," even though his "natural, boyish rosiness" makes "the beating of the tempest" seem to him "only the voice of life and the challenge of fate." On this sad day when Mrs. Moreen is so desperate as to try to borrow sixty francs from Pemberton, Morgan most cheerfully helps his tutor to depart—after he has promised, however, to earn a lot of money quickly for them both to live on. The lifeboat is being commissioned.

The Pupil is a story that develops its momentum rather slowly, but its denouement is catastrophic. Pemberton, recalled by Mrs. Moreen, finds the family evidently "going to pieces"; this is where he pictures Mrs. Moreen "pitching Morgan into some sort of lifeboat." He realizes he has come to be one of the family: "He felt quite enough bound up with them to figure, to his alarm, as a floating spar in case of a wreck" (Section VIII). Now Morgan "often" talks of their "escape," "as if they were making up a 'boy's book' together." Pemberton, however, finds that "his youth was going and that he was getting nothing back for it." To him the affection of a surviving but not thriving Morgan Moreen is not an acceptable reward. "So," we are told, "Pemberton waited in a queer confusion of yearning and alarm for the catastrophe which was held to hang over the house of Moreen."

That the text is playing with terminology (including Aristotle's terms for the tragic) becomes apparent in the next paragraph with an extraordinary pun on the Moreens' concurrent loss of Amy and "amiability" and with Pemberton's insight "that if Mrs. Moreen was trying to get people to take her children she might be regarded as closing the hatches for the storm. But Morgan would be the last she would part with." In the following paragraph the brunt of the storm has come, the Moreens' rooms are "a scene of proprietary mutiny," Paula and Amy are under closed hatches, Ulick has "jumped overboard," and Mrs. Moreen is indeed pitching

Morgan to Pemberton in his lifeboat. As the thought of being taken away to live with Pemberton "for ever and ever," Morgan has "a moment of boyish joy, scarcely mitigated by the reflection that, with this unexpected consecration of his hope—too sudden and too violent, the thing was a good deal less like a boy's book—the 'escape' was left on their hands." This moment is "immediately followed" by Morgan's death; his heart fails before he can be aware of Pemberton's mean-spirited response to his final appeal.

Evidently more than one story is to be found in *The Pupil* (at least three, and we well might think of the successive layers of disclosure in James's presentation as an additional kind of plot). The first is a sort of factual account, like the one James himself heard from a physician in Italy, of a vagabond family of Americans, like James's own uprooted family but interesting in a more Bohemian way. Give them a *very* interesting child, make him the mainspring of the story's machinery, lend him the appeal of a bad heart and an early death, and one has the ingredients of a good story for the *Atlantic*. Additionally, use the newly developed technique of the central consciousness and make the reflector a not-too-unusual Yank—A.B. (Yale), M.A. (Oxon.) ("his English years had been intensely usual")—who has paid "his tiny patrimony" for that Jamesian pearl of great price, a "full wave of experience." This Pemberton story is of one frightened by poverty, conventional in responding to life's gifts of experience, badly self-deceived in thinking first that he knows a snob when he sees one and secondly that he is not a snob himself.

The third story is the "boy's book" that Morgan writes, and lives, with the quite servile collaboration of Pemberton. It is based on a reversal of roles, with Morgan tutoring his tutor to know and enjoy everything that life in European cities has to offer (in the bosom of a family that knows its Europe from the inside) and in return exacting from him the payment of being freed from his family and given a start in a reputable form of career—in America, probably. This scheme emerges into clarity from the most obscure bit of dialogue in *The Pupil* at the point when Morgan tells the tutor, "You've got to go," for he himself is nearly grown up. Pemberton replies,

> "There are such a lot of jolly things we can do together yet. I want to turn you out—I want you to do me credit."
>
> Morgan continued to look at him. "To give you credit—do you mean?" (Section VI)

When Morgan presses the ostensible tutor to demand payment, it is Morgan's own services that are to be remunerated; the money Morgan has earned is to be used for his liberation and setting up rather than for rewarding Pemberton's meager efforts. The longer the older man continues his tutelage, the deeper he goes into debt to his teacher-pupil.

Morgan's scenario works, so far as he can know, and he takes his leave of life in a last moment of joy ("boyish joy") at its success. Were he able to live out the career he has so vaguely in mind, however, one's sense of Morgan as a free spirit would be sadly marred. His chosen role model for a reputable adult life is his maternal grandfather, who had " 'property' and something to do with the Bible Society" (Section VII). Morgan's death cannot be tragic, therefore, if only because he is too much a child (as the text insists, again and again) to recognize what a fall would be involved should he become that kind of person. Even more to the point, Morgan's death spares him the recognition of Pemberton's meanness. This anagnorisis might indeed have thrust Morgan across the threshold between childhood and maturity; but it does not come, and Morgan (i.e., the objectivity of Morgan we have now formed) is not altered but triumphant as his life completes its course.

The story is worth dealing with at this length not because of its recognized merit but because so often the present recognition is moralistic and uncritical, dragged down by an interpretation inspired by that "spirit of gravity" that Nietzsche said "makes all things fall." The critics find a villain in the Moreens' vulgarity and snobbery and make Morgan its victim. But this is only an interpretation of the Pemberton story, the wrong story, the story Henry James battled against by showing us again and again that the pearl of experience, like gold, is where we find it, even if it be among the Moreens. A more adequate performance of *The Pupil* will focus on an objectivity that makes Morgan a comic hero rather than a victim. For the theory developed in this book the figure then becomes paradigmatic. Morgan is an outstanding individual, self-consistent and self-determining (not to say narcissistic), who seeks and gains freedom and lives in a personal atmosphere of freedom. His "figure" is threatened, however, by a yearning (quite natural in a romantic child) for "reputation," both of the chivalrous kind that is won in a duel and the rather contradictory variety that is conferred by secure wealth and status (since he is ashamed of his family for being insecure and unsettled). Above all Morgan is a child, with the enthusiasm, warmth, and heedless game-playing imagination of a boy. One might say that the worst threat is that he should grow up, especially to an adulthood of security and status. Like Falstaff, Morgan is threatened by the kind of status he seeks. His genuine nature repeatedly struggles against it, for he is more an adventurer than any of his family (witness his overseeing of Pemberton's appeal to the American consul for passage money, much in the spirit of a confidence man). Tom Sawyer (especially in *Huckleberry Finn*) might well occur to one's mind at this point as another fabricator of "boy's book" plots that commandeer adults for rather servile instrumental roles.

Morgan's story belongs to the modern stage of comic ethos where the reversal from superior to inferior has occurred and its comic quality is built up, above all, in discussions. These profit greatly be being seen as a process, itself defining the figures of pupil and tutor and at the same time presenting the familiar Jamesian milieu in a fresh, amusing light. The process is immediately enjoyable in itself, but it is made comic by our sense of the risks Morgan takes with his own peculiar existence. The supine ordinariness of Pemberton is itself a threat, because it seems to attract Morgan. It responds, however, to Morgan's "humour," and the consensus of their discussions is that the Moreens "were a hundred times cleverer than most of the dreary grandees . . . they rushed about Europe to catch up with." Morgan's humor permits him to see the value of his family, but it does not undeceive him about his urge to revert back to their austerely reputable American ancestry. This self-deception is what makes Morgan not ridiculous but immature in the Jamesian sense that he fails to perceive that the value of experience disappears in conventional satisfactions. Such immaturity is harmless in one who is still a child, and comic in Morgan, but it means that he must not be allowed to grow up, or he will cease to be comic.

This insight provides us with a lead for a final set of conclusions regarding the nature of the comic in relation to irony, insight, and humor. What has been brought to light in the chapters on Bergson, Freud, and Nietzsche only serves, in my view, to support what Kierkegaard had to say about humor: that it is not merely a form of undeceiving perception, as irony is, but includes a measure of undeceiving self-perception as well. Morgan Moreen can properly be called humorous because he not only saw the ridiculousness and the irony of his family's situation but (in an obscure manner) was also conscious of being himself a member of that family and its genuine product, a hundred times *too* clever, hence ridiculous for abusing them so. As a child, he cannot be expected to make the full movement of humor to the forgiving acceptance of foolishness in the whole human family of which we are all members.

The comic recognition, however, involves more than a character's humorous perspective of self-awareness: we readers must recognize Morgan's own identity as after all a Moreen, and an Ultramoreen, "that millionth" boy, possessed of "a kind of homebred sensibility which might have been bad for himself but was charming for others, and a whole range of refinement and perception—little musical vibrations as taking as picked-up airs—begotten by wandering about Europe at the tail of his migratory tribe" (Section II). The comic quality is found in such striking individuals and in entities, in selves.

If the comic is to survive, and its nature is to survive, it will outlast, in literary art at least, the present wave of attacks upon the subject and the individual personality. The most severe test of all would come if freedom should one day cease to be the most valued of human desires and goals; if, for example, a commonality of status, risk, and reward should become the most valued object of human activity. Till then, the procedure of discovery offered in this book should continue to find a rich comic yield, sometimes in the strangest places.

SELECTED BIBLIOGRAPHY

THE FOLLOWING LIST of readings is not offered as complete. I have included all titles to which I have made more than passing reference, and one or two that I admire but have not been able to use in this study. Where I have dealt textually with a work in translation, the original is cited. Fuller bibliographies may be found in the cited works by Corrigan, Goldstein and McGhee, Mauron, and Sypher. An extensive recent compilation is the one by R. B. Gill, "Some Psychological and Sociological Works Relevant to Satire," *Scholia Satyrica*, III (1977), 3–14; most of the papers deal with humor.

Aristotle. *The Ethics of Aristotle: The Nicomachean Ethics.* Translated by J.A.K. Thomson. Baltimore: Penguin Books, 1955.

————. *Poetics.* Translated by S. H. Butcher. In his *Aristotle's Theory of Poetry and Fine Art.* London: Macmillan, 1902.

————. *Rhetoric.* Translated by W. Rhys Roberts. In *The Basic Works of Aristotle*, edited by Richard McKeon. New York: Random House, 1941.

Aristophanes. *Clouds.* Edited by K. J. Dover. New York: Oxford University Press, 1968.

Barber, Cesar L. *Shakespeare's Festive Comedy.* Princeton: Princeton University Press, 1972.

Barthelme, Donald. *Snow White.* New York: Bantam, 1968.

Barthes, Roland. *Critical Essays.* Translated by Richard Howard. Evanston, Ill.: Northwestern University Press, 1972. *Essais critiques.* Paris: Seuil, 1964.

————. *S/Z.* Translated by Richard Miller. New York: Hill and Wang, 1974 (the translation should be used with caution). *S/Z.* Paris: Seuil, 1970.

Beckett, Samuel. *Waiting For Godot*. New York: Grove Press, 1954.

Bergson, Henri. *Laughter*. Translated by Fred Rothwell. In *Comedy*, edited by Wylie Sypher. Garden City, N.Y.: Doubleday, 1956. *Le Rire*. Geneva: Skira, 1945.

––––––. *The Two Sources of Morality and Religion*. Translated by R. Ashley Audra and Cloudsley Brereton. Garden City, N.Y.: Doubleday, 1954.

Bradley, A. C. "The Rejection of Falstaff" (1902). In his *Oxford Lectures on Poetry*. London: Macmillan, 1959.

Céline, Louis-Ferdinand. *Journey to the End of the Night*. Translated by John H.P. Marks. New York: New Directions, 1960.

Cervantes, Miguel de. *Don Quixote*. In *The Portable Cervantes*, translated by Samuel Putnam. New York: Viking Press, 1951.

Cicero, Marcus Tullius. *De Oratore* (etc.). See Lauter, Paul.

Clark, Barrett H. *European Theories of the Drama*. Cincinnati: Stewart and Kidd, 1918. (Includes translated excerpts from theorists, sometimes more full than those in Lauter or Dukore.)

Coleridge, Samuel Taylor. *Lectures on Shakespeare, Etc.* Everyman edition. New York: Dutton, n. d. (See especially pages 241–262 on *Don Quixote* and humor.)

––––––. *Literary Remains*. Edited by Henry Nelson Coleridge. London: Pickering, 1839.

Congreve, William. Letter to John Dennis "Concerning Humour in Comedy." In Lauter, Clark, Dukore. (I have modernized the spelling in my citations.)

Cornford, F. M. *The Origin of Attic Comedy*. Garden City, N.Y.: Doubleday, 1961.

Corrigan, Robert W., editor. *Comedy: Meaning and Form*. San Francisco: Chandler, 1965. (A good sampling of more recent writing.)

Della Casa, Giovanni. *Galateo, or The Book of Manners*. Translated by R. S. Pine-Coffin. Baltimore: Penguin Books, 1958.

Derrida, Jacques. *Of Grammatology*. Translated by Gayatri

Chakravorty Spivak. Baltimore: The Johns Hopkins University Press, 1975.

————. *Speech and Phenomena*. Translated by David B. Allison. Evanston, Ill.: Northwestern University Press, 1973.

Donatus. "Preface" to *Commentary* on Terence. In Lauter.

Dryden, John. *Of Dramatic Poesy and Other Critical Essays.* Edited by George Watson. Two volumes. Everyman edition. New York: Dutton, 1962.

Dukore, Bernard. *Dramatic Theory and Criticism.* New York: Holt, Rinehart and Winston, 1974. (Includes pertinent selections from Aristotle, Cicero, Donatus, Guarini, Schiller, Hugo, Shaw.)

Edwards, Thomas R. See *New York Review of Books,* Dec. 11, 1975, pp. 54–55 (on Barthelme).

Freud, Sigmund. *The Interpretation of Dreams.* Translated by James Strachey. New York: Avon Books, 1972. (Reprint of vols. IV and V of the standard edition.)

————. *Jokes and Their Relation to the Unconscious.* Translated by James Strachey. New York: Norton, 1963. (Text of the standard edition.) London: Hogarth, 1953——.

————. "On Humor." In *Works.* Standard edition XXI, 161–166.

Frye, Northrop. *Anatomy of Criticism.* Princeton: Princeton University Press, 1957.

Gide, André. See John Keith Atkinson, "Les Caves du Vatican and Bergson," *Publications of the Modern Language Association of America,* 84 (1969), 328–335.

Goldstein, Jeffrey H., and McGhee, Paul E. *The Psychology of Humor.* New York: Academic Press, 1972. (Annotated list of papers on humor 1900–1971.)

Grant, Mary A. *The Ancient Rhetorical Theories of the Laughable.* Madison: University of Wisconsin Press, 1924. (Much general information; good on Cicero.)

Guarini, Giambattista. *Compendium of Tragicomic Poetry* (1601). Translated by Jay Gilbert in his excellent *From Plato to Dryden.* Detroit: Wayne State University Press, 1962.

Gurewitch, Morton. *Comedy: The Irrational Vision.* Ithaca: Cornell University Press, 1975.

Hazlitt, William. *Lectures on the English Comic Writers.* Everyman edition. New York: Dutton, 1951. (See Lectures I, "On Wit and Humour," II, "On Shakespeare and Ben Johnson," and VIII, "On the Comic Writers of the Last Century.")

————. *The Round Table.* Everyman edition. New York: Dutton, 1957. (For "Of Modern Comedy.")

Hegel, Georg Friedrich Wilhelm. (See excerpts in Lauter from *Lectures on Aesthetics;* also extensive references to the Hegel corpus in the article by Anne Paolucci cited below.)

————. *Hegel: On the Arts: Selections from G.W.F. Hegel's Aesthetics or the Philosophy of Fine Art.* Abridged and Translated by Henry Paolucci. New York: Ungar, 1979.

Heidegger, Martin. "The Origin of the Work of Art." In *Poetry, Language, Thought,* translated by Albert Hofstadter. New York: Harper and Row, 1975.

————. *What Is Called Thinking?* Translated by J. Glenn Gray. New York: Harper & Row, 1972.

————. "Who is Nietzsche's Zarathustra?" In *The New Nietzsche,* edited by David Allison. New York: Dell, 1977.

Heilman, Robert Bechtold. *The Ways of the World: Comedy and Society.* Seattle: University of Washington Press, 1979.

Herrick, Marvin T. *Comic Theory in the Sixteenth Century.* Urbana: University of Illinois Press, 1964.

Hume, Robert D. *The Development of English Drama in the Late Seventeenth Century.* Oxford: The Clarendon Press, 1976.

————. "Some Problems in the Theory of Comedy." *Journal of Aesthetics and Art Criticism,* 31 (1972), 87–100.

————. "Theory of Comedy in the Restoration." *Modern Philology,* 70 (1973), 302–318.

Husserl, Edmund. *Crisis of European Sciences and Transcendental Phenomenology.* Translated by David Carr. Evanston, Ill.: Northwestern University Press, 1970.

————. *Ideas: General Introduction to Pure Phenomenology.*

Translated by W. R. Boyce Gibson. New York: Collier Books, 1962.

——. *Logical Investigations.* Translated by J. N. Findlay. Two Volumes. New York: Humanities Press, 1970.

Ingarden, Roman. *The Cognition of the Literary Work of Art.* Translated by Ruth Ann Crowley and Kenneth R. Olson. Evanston, Ill.: Northwestern University Press, 1973.

——. *The Literary Work of Art.* Translated by George G. Grabowicz. Evanston, Ill.: Northwestern University Press, 1973.

——. "Phenomenological Aesthetics: An Attempt at Defining Its Range." *Journal of Aesthetics and Art Criticism,* 33 (1975), 257–269.

Jameson, Frederic. *The Prison-House of Language.* Princeton: Princeton University Press, 1972.

Kafka, Franz. *Amerika.* Translated by Willa and Edwin Muir. New York: Schocken, 1962.

Kant, Immanuel. *Critique of Judgment.* Translated by James Creed Meredith. Oxford: Clarendon Press, 1952.

Kaufmann, Walter, editor. *The Portable Nietzsche.* New York: Viking, 1954. Includes Kaufmann's translation of *Thus Spoke Zarathustra, Twilight of the Idols,* and "Homer's Contest."

——. *Tragedy and Philosophy.* Garden City, N.Y.: Doubleday, 1969.

Kierkegaard, Søren. *The Concept of Irony.* Translated by Lee M. Capel. Bloomington: Indiana University Press, 1968.

——. *Either/Or.* Translated by David F. Swenson and Lillian Marvin Swenson. Two volumes. Garden City, N.Y.: Doubleday, 1959.

Lauter, Paul. *Theories of Comedy.* Garden City, N.Y.: Doubleday, 1964. (An unusually fine collection of the most important texts; includes cited texts from Cicero, Congreve, Donatus, and Hazlitt.)

Man, Paul de. *Blindness and Insight.* New Haven: Yale University Press, 1971.

Mann, Thomas, *Buddenbrooks*. Translated by H. T. Lowe-Potter. New York: Vintage, 1961.

———. *Last Essays*. Translated by Richard Winston et al. New York: Knopf, 1958. (Includes "On Schiller.")

Mauron, Charles. *Psychocritique du genre comique*. Paris: José Corti, 1964.

Meredith, George. "An Essay on Comedy." In *Comedy*, edited by Wylie Sypher.

Merleau-Ponty, Maurice. "Indirect Language and the Voices of Silence." In *Signs*, translated by Richard C. McCleary. Evanston, Ill.: Northwestern University Press, 1964. See pages 38–83.

———. "On the Phenomenology of Language." In *The Essential Writings of Merleau-Ponty*. Edited by Alden L. Fisher. New York: Harcourt, Brace and World, 1969.

Miller, R. D. *Schiller and the Ideal of Freedom*. Oxford: The Clarendon Press, 1970.

Morgann, Maurice. *Shakespearean Criticism*. Edited by Daniel A. Fineman. Oxford: The Clarendon Press, 1972. (Includes *An Essay on the Dramatic Character of Sir John Falstaff*.)

Nietzsche, Friedrich. *The Birth of Tragedy and The Genealogy of Morals*. Translated by Francis Golffing. Garden City, N.Y.: Doubleday, 1956.

———. *Beyond Good and Evil*. Translated by Helen Zimmern. In *The European Philosophers From Descartes to Nietzsche*, edited by Monroe C. Beardsley. New York: Modern Library, 1960.

———. *The Case of Wagner*. Translated by Walter Kaufmann. New York: Vintage, 1967. (The volume begins with Kaufmann's translation of *The Birth of Tragedy*.)

———. *The Portable Nietzsche*. See Kaufmann, Walter.

———. *The Will To Power*. Translated by Walter Kaufmann and R. J. Hollingdale. London: Weidenfield and Nicolson, 1968.

Paolucci, Anne. "Hegel's Theory of Comedy." In *Comedy: New Perspectives*, edited by Maurice Charney. New York: New York Literary Forum, 1978. See pages 89–108.

Patchen, Kenneth. *The Journal of Albion Moonlight.* New York: New Directions, 1961.

Plato. *The Dialogues of Plato.* Translated by Benjamin Jowett. Two volumes. New York: Random House, 1937.

Pynchon, Thomas. *V.* New York: Bantam, 1964.

————. *The Crying of Lot 49.* New York: Bantam, 1967.

————. *Gravity's Rainbow.* New York: Viking Press, 1973.

Renoir, Jean. Interview in *The New Yorker,* August 23, 1969, pp. 34ff.

Ricoeur, Paul. *Freud and Philosophy.* Translated by Denis Savage. New Haven: Yale University Press, 1970.

Roth, Philip. Interview in *New York Times Book Review,* February 23, 1969, pp. 2, 23–25.

Saintsbury, George. "Balzac, Honoré de." In *Encyclopeadia Britannica.* Eleventh edition. S.v.

Sartre, Jean-Paul. *What Is Literature?* Translated by Bernard Frechtman. New York: Harper and Row, 1965.

Saussure, Ferdinand de. *Course in General Linguistics.* Translated by Wade Baskin. New York: McGraw-Hill, 1966.

Schiller, Friedrich. *Letters on the Aesthetic Education of Man.* Translated by Reginald Snell. New Haven: Yale University Press, 1954.

————. *Naive and Sentimental Poetry.* Translated by Julius A. Elias. New York: Frederick Ungar, 1966. (In addition, Dukore gives several of Schiller's important essays.)

Scholes, Robert. *The Fabulators.* New York: Oxford University Press, 1967.

Shattuck, Roger. *New York Times Book Review,* November 9, 1975 (review of Barthelme).

Spivak, Gayatri Chakravorty. "Introduction" to *Of Grammatology* by Jacques Derrida. Baltimore: The Johns Hopkins University Press, 1975.

Sypher, Wylie. "The Meanings of Comedy." In *Comedy.* Garden City, N.Y.: Doubleday, 1956. Also includes Bergson's *Laughter* and Meredith's "Essay on Comedy."

Theophrastus. *Characters.* Edited by R. G. Ussher. London: Macmillan, 1960. (Greek text and commentary.)

Todorov, Tzvetan. *The Fantastic: A Structural Approach to a Literary Genre.* Ithaca: Cornell University Press, 1975.

————. *The Poetics of Prose.* Translated by Richard Howard. Ithaca: Cornell University Press, 1977.

Vonnegut, Kurt Jr. *Cat's Cradle.* New York: Dell, 1970.

Waugh, Evelyn, *A Handful of Dust.* New York: Dell, 1959. (With *Decline and Fall*).

Wilde, Alan. "Barthelme Unfair to Kierkegaard: Some Notes on the Post-modern Literary Imagination." *boundary 2,* 5 (1976), 45–70.

Wilson, J. Dover. *The Fortunes of Falstaff.* Cambridge: Cambridge University Press, 1964.

INDEX OF NAMES AND TITLES

WORKS AND CHARACTERS are cited alphabetically, followed by authors' names; further references may be found in the Selected Bibliography as well as in the text. Authors' names are indexed where general reference has been made to their work.

SUBJECT INDEX

Library of Congress Cataloging in Publication Data

McFadden, George, 1916–
  Discovering the comic.

  Bibliography: p.
  Includes index.
  1. Comic, The.   I. Title.
BH301.C7M38   809'.917   81-15825
ISBN 0-691-06496-2   AACR2